PHILLY DOGS have more fun

The Best Places to Go and Things to Do with Your Dog in the Greater Philadelphia Area

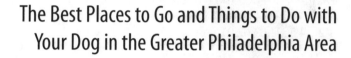

Carol S. Armen

Camino Books, Inc.
Philadelphia

Manufactured in the United States of America

1 2 3 4 5 04 03 02 01

Library of Congress Cataloging-in-Publication Data

Armen, Carol S.
    Philly dogs have more fun : the best places to go and things to do
with your dog in the greater Philadelphia area / Carol S. Armen.
        p. cm.
    ISBN 0-940159-58-9 (trade paper : alk. paper)
    1. Travel with dogs—Pennsylvania—Philadelphia Region—
Guidebooks. 2. Philadelphia Region (Pa.)—Guidebooks. I. Title.

SF427.4574.P4 A76 2000
636.7′009748′11—dc21

00-044491

Cover and interior design: Jerilyn Kauffman

This book is available at a special discount on bulk purchases for
promotional, business, and educational use. For information write to:

Publisher
Camino Books, Inc.
P.O. Box 59026
Philadelphia, PA 19102

www.caminobooks.com

This book is dedicated to dogs, of course—all dogs, but especially:

To my own wonderful dogs, Meg, Georgie, and Beau.

To the dogs on my street: the ones who sadly had to leave us and whose voices are still missed every day, Angus Hillman, and Sir Winston of Narberth; and the ones whose voices still ring out to give the neighborhood joy, Chloe and Wagner, and Maggie.

And to the honorary members of the canine circle around me: Rufus Parnelli, Jr., Amaze Me Mindy, Jasmine, and Lexington.

This book is also dedicated to Jim Stevenson, my husband. His patience was tried on many an occasion during the creation of this book, but he did his best to help in a practical way when he could, and frequently rose above his irritation with the process to offer moral, emotional, and even spiritual support — all that a wife could ask. Thank you, sweetheart. I love you.

❖ ACKNOWLEDGMENTS

Assistance in the preparation of this book came from many different directions. Most of it came from people too numerous to name, and much of it from people whom I could not name even if there were sufficient space, because their generous help came to me unsigned through cyberspace. So, thank you very much to everyone who answered my e-mails, letters, calls, and other pesterings: though I do not name you, my gratitude is heartfelt, and this book would have been impossible without each of you. Whether the answer to the basic question of dog-friendliness was "yes" or "no," you offered help beyond the call of duty, and it was much appreciated.

Thank you to each and every one of my friends, relatives, and acquaintances (including my boss!) who had to listen to me talk (or whine) about the book, offered suggestions, and even helped me out with research. Special thanks to Susan and Jeff for looking into parks for me—I can't tell you how much I appreciated your help, especially since the research couldn't possibly have been of interest to you in light of your non-dog-ownership! And special thanks to Julie and Bob, for touring the Thomas Leiper House on my behalf, and to Julie for introducing me to the wonderful world of horse events, thus helping me to get a break every now and then in the guise of research, and also for allowing Rufus to model.

Finally, thank you to publisher Edward Jutkowitz, and his assistant Michelle Scolnick, of Camino Books, for their guidance, patience, help, and work in the production of this book.

Can I say it enough? Probably not. To everyone, thank you, thank you, thank you.

❖ CONTENTS

❧ INTRODUCTION

When I started doing the research for this book, I wondered if there would be enough dog-friendly sites and activities in the Greater Philadelphia area out of which to make a book. I even planned on filling the extra space with all kinds of little practical advice blurbs I have no special qualifications to write except for what I've learned from my own dogs.

Well, let me tell you: there are infinite opportunities for you and your dog to enjoy each other's company in and around Philadelphia. More opportunities than anyone could compile in one book, in fact. And new sites and events are added every day. So don't think of this book as all-inclusive. Think of it as a snapshot and a selection of sure bets as of the time of the book's writing, and take it from there: if you see something in a news-paper or see a flier somewhere for something interesting, call the listed number and see if your dog can come. And actually, since things do change, it doesn't hurt before you invite your dog to come along to the places and events listed in this book to call and make sure dogs are still welcome.

For the purposes of this book, I have defined the Greater Philadelphia area as including Philadelphia County (of course), and also most of Bucks County, Montgomery County, Delaware County, Chester County, and selected sites in New Jersey, including much of Camden County and much of Burlington County. The defining criterion was basically whether you could get there in under an hour, and preferably closer to a half-hour. And some places are included because they are near other places.

About Me

I love Philadelphia. I lived in Center City for eight years, and it was wonderful. I can only imagine how wonderful it is now, since the "renaissance," with so many choices, so many things to do and places to go and eat and shop. But many, many of the gems that make Philadelphia shine have been there all along: public art, more American history packed into one place than any other place I can imagine, and terrific parks.

I got engaged to my husband in Philadelphia and in between our engage-ment and our wedding, we adopted our first dog. Meg is a 15-pound smooth-hair fox terrier mix. She's undersized for a fox terrier, and she looks a lot like a toy, so her genetics are up for questioning. But she was a great apartment dog (now she's a great house dog). If she couldn't wait for us to take her outside, she would do her business on newspapers, which we could easily clean up.

We moved to our house in Narberth in 1995, and put up a fence, so Meg could take advantage of our back yard in a safe manner. And since we were now prepared, in 1997, we got the dog of my dreams. Definitely not an apartment dog, Georgie is a 120-pound Newfoundland, and she is my canine love. She's big, she slobbers, but I think every single thing about her is perfect. She has gone many places with me, including Maine.

Once, while we were hiking as a family (my husband, me, and the two dogs) in Maine, we took a wrong (and much steeper) trail and ended up in a sort of precarious situation. Go up, or turn back? Either way would be hard. We decided to go up.

I went first, Meg the Mountain Goat following. Then it was Georgie's turn. She was scared, and unsure how to get up. She chose a harder way than Meg and I had, and at one point she was literally scrabbling for a hold with her front paws . . . then she hauled herself up, bounded up to where I was sitting with a look of absolute joy on her face, and lay right down beside me to rest in safety. (My husband got up just fine, if you want to know. He's a mountain goat himself.)

I will never put Georgie in a situation like that again, but I also will never forget those moments of anxiety, relief, and love. She was afraid, but she had the heart to try, and during those moments I felt an incredible bond with her. We have great moments on a regular basis, but those are the moments that turn one into a true dog lover. I was reminded of that time recently, when we were walking on an icy path in Vermont while on vacation: I slipped and fell—and Georgie came running back with that wonderful look on her face that said "Are you all right, Mom? Can I help you?"

You can't have those kinds of moments if your dog stays at home while you go out. It's only out in the world, operating as a team, that you build that kind of bond. So take your dog out and give yourself the opportunity to see what tremendous love your dog has for you. (And for those of you who might be worried at this point by my obvious adoration of Georgie, don't be—Meg gets lots of love and attention, too. She's just a different dog.)

And there are *such* dog-friendly opportunities to enjoy out there in the world, all within an hour's drive! After doing the research for this book, I feel very lucky to live in an area so rich with historically interesting sites, beautiful scenery, fantastic parks, wonderful community festivals and events, and so much more. It is amazing how much there is in the Greater Philadelphia area. And so much of it is dog-friendly.

What's in Here?

For both residents and visitors to the Greater Philadelphia area, this book is a resource full of places where you and your dog can walk, run, play, learn, see, shop, stay, and even eat together. Whether you've been in the area for a day or lived here all your life, you'll find things in here you never knew about and certainly didn't know you could do with your dog!

As you peruse the many options, consider what kind of place or event is involved, and *know your dog*. Will there be crowds? Will there be loud noises? Is it hot? Is it cold? Will there be children? How does your dog handle these situations? Hopefully you will have exposed your dog to many different situations to make sure he or she is well socialized and adjusted to the modern world, but there still might be some things your dog just won't enjoy. The goal is for both of you to have a good time, so if you think one option is iffy, pick another one.

Use common sense. For example, my dog Georgie doesn't particularly like going into stores. Like I said, she's a Newfoundland, and a very long-bodied girl besides—about 48 inches from nose to butt, and if her tail is up (though it wouldn't be in a store), you can add about 24 inches more. She is fully aware of her size, and when she feels she is in a smallish space, she will actually back up like a truck (all she's missing is the beeping sound) in order to leave the space, rather than turn around. Taking her into a store full of stuff wouldn't be fun for either of us. On the other hand, I've seen more agile Labrador retrievers meandering quite happily through stores of various kinds. It depends on the dog. Know your dog. I can't say it enough.

A few general notes. The reason dogs cannot enter eating establishments is the health code imposed by municipalities almost everywhere but France. However, many places with outdoor, sidewalk seating can and will allow your dog to sit by your table while you enjoy coffee, a drink, or a meal. Some of these places may let you *come in* with your dog to pick up takeout; if I know of some, I ain't telling. If *you* know of some, keep it quiet, okay? We don't want to get these wonderful, dog-friendly places in trouble. And no matter where you go, there's always *somewhere* you can enjoy a bite to eat or a beverage with your dog. If all else fails, look for the local Rita's Water Ice or Dairy Queen: they often have outdoor benches or tables.

This book lists some stores into which you can take your dog, other than pet stores, but only those that were easy to find out about without canvassing every store in the Greater Philadelphia area. I'm sure there are many more that may let you bring your dog in: these are just the ones I know for sure. So if you are walking around window-shopping with your dog, and you see a place you'd like to investigate—ask if your dog can come in. I'm not a big believer in leaving dogs tied up outside if you can help it. I'm also not a big believer in leaving dogs in cars if you can help it (and never, *ever* in the summertime, windows cracked or not).

I wrote this book with responsible dog owners in mind. Dog owners who clean up after their dogs, and keep their dogs on-leash in public places (with the exception of enclosed spaces where off-leash activity is permitted, or when their well-trained dogs are competing in some kind of match). The image we all cherish of the obedient dog trotting happily behind us, off-leash, is from a time when this country was mostly rural. There are many more distractions and dangers now. You owe it to your dog, as well as to other people and animals, to keep your dog on-leash.

To illustrate my point, let me tell you a brief story. My husband and I were driving down Main Street in Manayunk one afternoon when a small, white dog very nearly ran out in front of our car. The dog's owner was several feet ahead on the sidewalk, holding the leash in his hand. The small, white dog almost ran into the street because a large, beige dog was walking *on*-leash with his or her owner down the sidewalk toward the small, white dog, and the smaller dog apparently wasn't accustomed to bigger dogs. Not only did the white dog's owner allow his unprepared dog to be endangered, he missed a training opportunity: this is what we do when a big dog approaches—we calmly walk on by.

So please be responsible. And if you take me up on my offers to get you and your dog out of your own neighborhood and into someone else's, make sure you're prepared. Take water for your dog in a container he or she can drink from (our dogs drink out of sport bottles—though with the Newfy's jowls a lot of the water ends up on the ground), and plastic bags for cleaning up. Take a pet first aid kit as well. And in case your instincts aren't as good as your dog's and you're heading for an area you aren't familiar with—take a map!

So, what can you do with your dog? Well, think about what your dog likes to do. If your dog is similar to my dogs, he or she likes to go out, sniff around, see what's going on in the world, explore. I have yet to meet a dog that is a true homebody. Take your dog places! It will enrich both your lives.

Philadelphia County

The boundaries of Philadelphia County are exactly the same as those of the City of Philadelphia, and the land within those boundaries is jam-packed with places to go and things to do with your dog. The Philadelphia Department of Recreation oversees 55 active parks, and the Fairmount Park Commission oversees a whole bunch more throughout the city. There are historic areas in abundance in Philadelphia, of course, and terrific urban walks to enjoy with your canine companion. There are street festivals, charity runs, and places to eat, drink, and sleep. One of the greatest things about Philadelphia is that it is such a *walkable* city, and practically everywhere you go there is something interesting that both you and your dog will enjoy. So get out there and start exploring!

One general comment: keep in mind that things change in Philadelphia very quickly. While I researched this book, restaurants opened, and restaurants closed. Other changes happen daily. Where I know some changes are in the works, I've included them. But there's no way to know what will have changed between the time I'm writing this and the time you are reading it. When in doubt, call the place you're thinking of going before you go.

❧ WEST OF THE WISSAHICKON

Manayunk

Dogs love Manayunk almost as much as people do. It's a great place to hang out. Set between the Wissahickon Creek and the Schuylkill River, there is access to recreation on both sides: on the towpath beside what remains of the Schuylkill Canal, and in the trail areas of the Wissahickon Gorge. Beyond that, there are great window-shopping (and sometimes indoor shopping), eating, drinking, and street festival opportunities, all in a very dog-friendly environment.

Manayunk's Main Street is a National Historic District, and it is lined with over 65 shops with items ranging from clothing to jewelry to antiques to bikes. There is a plethora of bars, restaurants, and coffee shops where you can get takeout food from sandwiches to ice cream. There are also many places with outdoor seating, and many of them may allow your dog to sit outside with you. The places I know for sure are:

▸ **Bucks County Coffee Company, 4311 Main Street, 215-487-3927.** While you sit outside enjoying the atmosphere of Main Street and a cup of gourmet java, and maybe an item from the café menu, your dog can have some water from the two large dog bowls Bucks County Coffee keeps chained out front. (Heck, your dog can get a drink of water there even if you're just passing by.)

▸ **Chloe's Water Ice & Ice Cream, 4162 Main Street, 215-482-5600.** Chloe's offers a unique selection of ices made from real fruit, as well as soft ice cream, frozen yogurt, and soft pretzels. They're open only during the warmer months, but there's an adjacent area of shaded tables and benches, available year-round, where you can sit with your dog. My dogs especially enjoyed a small cup of strawberry ice there (yes, I made them share).

▸ **Le Bus Main Street, 4266 Main Street, 215-487-2663.** Le Bus has outdoor seating from March/April (as soon as the weather is warm enough) to the end of September or "when [it gets] too cold to sit outside without a personal heater" (which generally is closer to November or sometime in December). They will provide your dog with either water or ice on request, and you can enjoy generous portions of midrange-priced homemade foods (they offer a kids' menu, too), weekend brunch, fabulous Le Bus breads, or a selection from their full bar.

▸ **Main-LY Desserts, 4247 Main Street, 215-487-1325.** They have outdoor seating from April to October, and will give your dog water or ice on request. As for you—the name says it all, don't you think? Well, you're thinking wrong. Main-LY Desserts offers brunch, lunch, and dinner menus as well as baked goods.

I've seen many a dog entering a shop in Manayunk, although officially, only a couple of stores seem to have an actual policy in this regard. You can definitely take your dog into:

▸ **Smith & Hawken, 2 Rector Street (toward the towpath from Main), 215-509-6082.** You and your dog are welcome to browse together through the store's selection of upscale and environmentally safe garden tools and supplies, candles, seeds and bulbs, decorative items, and more. Smith & Hawken has a national policy of allowing dogs on-leash in their stores (at least the freestanding ones: I don't think I would try taking a dog to the Smith & Hawken in the King of Prussia Mall).

And your dog will absolutely insist on stopping by:

▸ **The Happy Hound, 4460 Main Street, 215-487-2117.** I'll let owner Debbie Brown speak for herself: "The store is dedicated to dogs! We are a dog biscuit bakery and retail pet supply store. All treats are baked on the premises and we also have unique treats and gift items. Our homemade treats have no added sugar, salt, or preservatives. We give out treats for dogs as well as kids for the Halloween trick-or-treating event. We will be doing Christmas stockings for dogs and cats this year and we also do birthday cakes for dogs. We will be doing more events in the future." As if all that weren't enough, you can "return anything that [your] dog doesn't like and we offer a 100% guarantee on all of our Iams and Eukanuba dog food." No wonder your dog wants to go in!

If you've finished dining and shopping, take your dog for a walk along the towpath and visit **Canal View Park, Gay and Main Streets.** The towpath, which parallels the canal, is a segment of the 22-mile **Schuylkill River Trail.** For more information on the Schuylkill River Trail, contact the Pennsylvania Department of Conservation and Natural Resources (DCNR) at 888-PA-PARKS, or visit their Web site at www.dcnr.state.pa.us and follow the links.

Manayunk is enjoyable on any day, but there are quite a few annual events you and your dog may want to make sure you don't miss, and according to the Manayunk Development Corporation, your dog on-leash is welcome at all of them:

▶ **Manayunk in Bloom (March/April, Easter weekend).** The Main Street shops have special floral window displays, and you may see the Easter Bunny wandering around, handing out candy. (Remember not to give chocolate to your dog!)

▶ **Canal Day (May).** Canal Day celebrates the opening of the Schuylkill Navigation System in 1824 (without which there might well have been no Manayunk). There are Victorian costumes, a parade, plenty of live entertainment, and sidewalk vendors.

▶ **Manayunk Cycling Celebration (June).** This festival takes place in conjunction with the annual First Union U.S. Pro Cycling Championship (see below). It includes family entertainment, a bicycle stunt show, and a chance to watch amateur cyclists attempt Manayunk's infamous "Wall" at Main and Levering Streets.

▶ **First Union U.S. Pro Cycling Championship (June).** The cyclists pass through Manayunk several times during the day, and the toughest part of the course is Manayunk's steep "Wall." This event draws cycling teams from around the world, and you'll see many practicing in the days prior to the race.

▶ **Manayunk Arts Festival (June).** Browse the booths of over 250 artists from all regions of the U.S. while live jazz fills the air and Manayunk restaurants offer selections of great food curbside. The festival is held on the last weekend in June to help kick off Philadelphia's annual "Welcome America!" Fourth of July extravaganza.

▶ **Indian Summer Festival (September).** This is a celebration of summer's end. (Well, with the heat and humidity of Philly's summers, some of us *do* celebrate the end! Georgie stops lying around wishing for snow and gets frisky again.) Besides showcasing Main Street's restaurants, the festival includes seven hours of entertainment on three stages.

▶ **Trick or Treat Street (October).** Feel free to dress up your dog (and yourself) and go out to watch while shops give out treats all along Main Street.

▶ **Discover the Magic of Manayunk This Holiday Season (Thanksgiving weekend through December 25).** Another opportunity to dress up your dog (with a different costume, one would hope) and come out to enjoy the festivities. And in mid-December, come to Canal View Park for Manayunk's Chanukah celebration.

▶ **Hartstrings Jingle Bell Run/Walk for Arthritis (Mid-December).** This 5K walk, 5K run, or half-mile fun run down Main Street benefits the Eastern Pennsylvania chapter of the Arthritis Foundation. Looks like another opportunity to get out your dog's Santa hat and have a great time!

▶ **Festival of Trees (December).** Held in the parking lot of WGTW-TV in Manayunk, 3900 Main Street. Call 215-930-0482 for details.

For more information on Manayunk's restaurants, shops, and events, call the Manayunk Development Corporation at 215-482-9565, or visit their Web site at www.manayunk.com. You can also have them send you a guide, or pick one up at the Visitors Center in Center City at 16th Street and JFK Boulevard.

Roxborough

Manayunk's neighbor is a nice little area. There is access to the trails of the Wissahickon Gorge at the end of streets like Gorgas Lane. There are also a couple of events you and your dog might want to attend:

▶ **Festival of the Arts (May).** Held in **Gorgas Park, 6400 Ridge Avenue at Hermitage Street.** A free weekend event during which you and your dog can enjoy fine arts and crafts, music, performances, and food.

▶ **Independence Day Parade (July).** Take your dog to get into the patriotic spirit.

Andorra

Near Roxborough is Andorra. Among other attributes, Andorra is home to Courtesy Stable, 901 Cathedral Road, where the **Philadelphia County 4-H** holds events that might interest you and your dog-owning kids. In 1999, Philadelphia's 4-H started a canine club that meets at the stable and focuses on basic obedience and some agility. Philadelphia's 4-H is also trying to set up an annual pet contest at the stable. The contest will include categories such as Pet with the Most Spots, Pet with the Longest Ears, Pet with the Longest Tail, Pet That Looks Most Like Owner, and more. Vendors will be present, as will pet-related groups distributing useful information.

For more information on the Philadelphia County 4-H's dog-related events, contact the Penn State Extension (through which Pennsylvania's 4-H program is run), 4601 Market Street, 2nd Floor, Philadelphia, PA 19139, 215-471-2228.

❖ EAST OF THE WISSAHICKON

Chestnut Hill

Chestnut Hill is a beautiful part of Philadelphia, and one you and your dog can definitely enjoy together. The residential areas with their grand old

homes, the shopping district, and the area parks all offer dog-friendly opportunities.

If you're looking for shopping options, head to the Chestnut Hill shopping district along Germantown Avenue. There are over 100 shops offering
upscale goods of all kinds: antiques, books, gifts, apparel, home furnishings,
jewelry. The window-shopping in Chestnut Hill is amazing, and there are
benches everywhere when you and your dog want to rest: look for them
along Germantown Avenue, in front of the Borders bookstore, and at the
Top of the Hill Plaza.

You and your dog can pick up a newspaper or magazine at the Chestnut
Hill News Stand, 8606 Germantown Avenue. If your dog gets thirsty, Baker
Street, 8009 Germantown Avenue, has bowls of water outside their
premises. There are plenty of places to pick up takeout food from bakery
items to pizza to sandwiches. Or the two of you can go to:

▶ **Borders Café, 8701 Germantown Avenue, 215-248-1213.** You can pick up salads, sandwiches, pastries, and more inside, as well as coffee or another beverage, and sit outside with
your dog while you enjoy them.
▶ **Cafette, 8136 Ardleigh Street (just off Germantown Avenue), 215-242-4220.** You and
your dog can sit outside together here, as long as the weather is good, and enjoy vegetarian
dishes and homestyle American food. They will supply water for your dog on request.
▶ **Garden Gate Café, 8139 Germantown Avenue, 215-247-8487.** You can sit outside with your
dog here year-round, and sip coffee (or hot chocolate in winter) and enjoy "light snacks to hearty
fare." They will provide water and treats for your dog. This is a very nice, dog-friendly place.
▶ **xando, 8605 Germantown Avenue, 215-753-1707.** Xando offers food, coffee during the
day, and bar beverages at night. They have outdoor seating from April to November, and
your dog can sit there with you.

There may be other places with outdoor seating in Chestnut Hill that will let
your dog sit with you while you dine. I know for sure that your dog is *not*
allowed to sit with you at the Chestnut Grill and Sidewalk Café.

Some of the stores in Chestnut Hill will probably allow you to bring your
dog inside with you, if you ask. And you can definitely bring your dog on-
leash to:

▶ **Laurel Hill Gardens, 8125 Germantown Avenue, 215-247-9490.** They will let you
browse their fine outdoor nursery stock with your dog on-leash.
▶ **Yard Co., 8430 Germantown Avenue, 215-247-3390.** This unique shop carries a variety
of garden-related items, gifts, natural toiletries, and a lot more. Of special note for you and
your dog are the separate section of pet-related gifts and items and the water bowl Yard Co.
keeps outside for passing canines.

According to some sources, the Chestnut Hill shopping district officially
extends from 8700 to 7900 Germantown Avenue. Cresheim Valley Drive,
which cuts across Germantown Avenue following the line of the Cresheim
Creek, seems to be a more natural border. In any event, if you walk down the
avenue a bit, and you and your dog are still hungry, you can eat together at:

▶ **Night Kitchen, 7725 Germantown Avenue, 215-248-9235.** Night Kitchen is a bakery and café, with outdoor seating from May to November, as the weather permits. They will provide water for your dog on request, and they offer vegetarian doggy treats for sale. You can get breakfast and lunch, fresh bread, coffee, cakes and cookies, and other delicious baked items here for yourself.

Nearby, though it might technically be in Mt. Airy, is:

▶ **Cresheim Cottage Café, 7402 Germantown Avenue, 215-248-4365.** There is patio seating overlooking a lovely garden where you can sit outside from April to October and enjoy "seasonal American cuisine in a comfortable historic setting," as they say. They will provide bowls of water for your dog and are happy to meet any other requests they can accommodate. They would like you to know that "many of our servers and our general manager have dogs at home." The café serves lunch, dinner, and Sunday brunch, and has a full selection of beers, wine, and mixed drinks.

There are plenty of reasons to go to Chestnut Hill any time of year. But there are also some special events you and your dog may not want to miss:

▶ **Chestnut Hill Garden Festival (April/May).** Take your dog to enjoy the activities, music, dancing, and food, as well as judged floral and other horticultural displays in the windows of the Chestnut Hill shops. For information, call 215-248-8600.
▶ **Fourth Friday Night Adventures (September, October, and November).** The shops stay open every fourth Friday between 6:00 p.m. and 9:00 p.m., and there is live entertainment and a generally festive atmosphere.
▶ **Fall for the Arts (October).** Admission is charged for this, but lots of dogs attend—I'm told that the Chestnut Hill Business Association is considering letting people in for free and charging for dogs! At any rate, you can bring your dog on-leash to enjoy the live entertainment, strolling performers, and demonstrations, and browse the offerings of 170 artists. There's also a scarecrow contest, a petting zoo, and more.
▶ **Wooden Train Halloween Parade (October).** Kids in costume are such fun to watch. Dress up your dog and go.
▶ **Holiday Festival of Lights & Fourth Friday Celebration (November).** Held on Thanksgiving.
▶ **Sunday Shopping and All That Jazz (November and December).** Held on the Sunday after Thanksgiving and the two Sundays after that. Stroll the streets and enjoy the live music. Watch **Sleigh Rides with Santa.**
▶ **Stag & Doe Nights (December).** Held on Wednesday evenings through December 23. Street musicians and carolers stroll along Germantown Avenue, and other holiday events are featured.

For more information on Chestnut Hill, stop by the Chestnut Hill Visitors Center, 8426 Germantown Avenue, 215-247-6696, or visit the Chestnut Hill Business Association's Web site at www.chestnuthillpa.com.

Okay, your dog has had enough of this touring and loitering about. Come on, Mom . . . come on, Dad, there are great doggish parks around, I can *feel* it, I can *smell* it! (Yes, your dog really does think that *doggish* is a word.) Your dog is right about those parks. Try these:

▶ **Pastorius Park.** Located between Roanoke and Millman Streets, from Abington Avenue to just short of Sunrise Lane, Pastorius Park is lovely and full of amenities for both dogs and humans, and both of you will love it. There are almost always other dogs there for your dog to meet, and there's a good mix of shade and large, open spaces where you and your dog can romp and run. Legally, your dog should do this on-leash. However, many people let their dogs off for brief play sessions with other dogs, and there is enough space in the park for that to be relatively safe. The park contains a shallow, man-made pond that is generally used as a doggy swimming hole: again, people let their dogs off-leash to do this (since it's pretty darn hard to swim on a leash). There are plenty of benches here, along with restrooms, and there is water available. It's a great park. And you and your dog might want to come back for free **"Concerts in the Park"** on summer Wednesdays. Bring a picnic and enjoy the music.

▶ **Dodge Preserve.** Located along Valley Green Road, Dodge Preserve is a Natural Lands Trust property, and its 6-acre wooded area contains a half-mile trail that you and your dog on-leash are welcome to walk. Along the way, you'll see upland and riparian woodland, and can look for wildlife and listen for songbirds. In addition, there are ruins—the foundations of former estate buildings. Georgie and I find ruins in the woods very picturesque. Picnicking, bicycling, and swimming are prohibited in Natural Lands Trust preserves.

The Wissahickon

Chestnut Hill is embraced by this portion of Fairmount Park. If you follow Valley Green Road into the park, you will cross the Wissahickon Creek and arrive at Forbidden Drive. At the heart of the Wissahickon Valley, this portion is one of the most dramatically beautiful areas of Fairmount Park, containing a fairly deep ravine enclosing the creek. The entire lower Wissahickon is a National Natural Landmark.

There are lots of opportunities here for both passive and active recreation for you and your dog. You can sit and watch the ducks in the Wissahickon Creek in front of the Valley Green Inn. Past the inn, Forbidden Drive rises above the water, and trails lead down to the creek to allow access for fishing, hanging around, or cooling your feet or paws. There are a couple of "beaches" where dogs and their owners tend to congregate to let their dogs swim and play in the water. As in Pastorius Park, dogs in Fairmount Park are supposed to be on-leash at all times, but some dogs just have to swim and it's hard to do that with a leash. One place you might see dogs swimming is the beach under the bridge that leads from Forbidden Drive to Kitchen Road. It's flat there, and there are fewer rocks, so dogs have easy access to the water.

Forbidden Drive itself is paved but closed to motor vehicle traffic (which, incidentally, is why it is called Forbidden Drive—I'm not kidding, that really is how it got its name). Joggers, walkers, cyclists, and equestrians abound, especially on weekends. It's a good place for your dog to learn to pass other dogs, and even the great big dogs called "horses," without getting excited. Just about a mile from the Valley Green Inn is Livezey Rock, where you can watch rock climbers moving up its 35-foot-high and rather sheer face. The rock is 60 feet long, providing room for lots of climbers.

If Forbidden Drive is too tame for you and your dog, try some of the Wissahickon Valley trails. Maps are available from the Friends of the Wissahickon and can be purchased at the Valley Green Inn, as well as at some Borders bookstores. Mountain bikers and equestrians may be on some of the trails (the green-blazed trail is a multi-use trail): mountain bikers are required to have a permit, which limits the number of such users, and they are supposed to go no more than 7 miles per hour and yield to all other trail users. However, it is safer for you and your dog to assume they might go a bit faster, mountain biking being what it is.

There are also marked trails where mountain bikers aren't permitted (look for the blue-blazed trail). Because of heavy trail use, your dog must be kept on-leash, but both of you can get a great hiking workout on the trails, and it is virtually impossible to get lost. And despite heavy trail use you can still see abundant wildlife: my dogs and I have seen some beautiful deer as we've hiked.

Once you and your dog have played and exercised to your hearts' content, you can go to:

▶ **The Valley Green Inn, 215-247-1730.** Built in 1850–51, the inn is open seven days a week, year-round, for lunch, dinner, and Sunday brunch. You may in the past have seen some dogs on the Valley Green Inn's porch while their owners were eating. Dogs are not actually permitted there for health code reasons. The inn's policy is to allow you to tie your dog to the front of the porch, where your friend can see you and rest while you eat. If your dog can sit quietly and wait for you, go ahead and enjoy one of the inn's wonderful meals on the porch. But if you think your dog might not be comfortable with this setup, don't despair: the inn is expanding its existing walk-up snack bar, making more selections available, and changing the seating area on the north side from park benches to tables with umbrellas. Once the project is completed, your dog will be welcome to sit with you in this outside area. In addition to hot dogs, popcorn, ice cream, chips, and assorted nonalcoholic beverages, the expanded snack bar will offer hamburgers, cheesesteaks, chicken Caesar salads, and more. I've been told that the inn also will be putting out bowls of water for the convenience of its canine customers, and it is "considering [offering] some gourmet dog bones and the like" at the snack bar. For more information on the Valley Green Inn, visit www.valleygreeninn.com.

Looking for more exercise after your meal? There's another area to explore in this part of Fairmount Park:

▶ **Andorra Natural Area.** At the northern end of the Wissahickon Valley, this is a mountain bike–free zone. It includes 210 acres of woodland, old forest, and meadow, with 5 miles of trails. Part of Andorra's land used to be Richard Wistar's 19th-century estate, and you can see a European beech allée, along with a huge, multitrunked beech tree left over from the estate.

Another part of Andorra was a nursery for 80-some years, so Japanese scholar trees and bigleaf magnolias can be spotted amid the native trees. The Andorra Tree House Visitor Center is at the top of Northwestern Avenue, and used to be the nursery's chief propagator's house: it was built around an old sycamore tree, hence its name. On the porch of the center you will find displays about the Andorra Natural Area and free information, including trail maps. Below the center are an old dam and pond that were once a reservoir. Next to the tree house are portable toilets.

There are lots of walks and races along Forbidden Drive that you and your dog might want to come out to watch: look for them in the local newspapers. One event you and your dog will definitely want to see is:

▶ **The Wissahickon Day Parade (April).** This is an annual spring procession of horse-drawn carriages and horseback riders. A wonderful thing to watch. For more information, call the Riders of the Wissahickon, 215-482-9303.

(Mt. Airy/Germantown)

It's not very clear where Mt. Airy ends and Germantown begins, and I'm not sure if Mt. Airy is claiming part of Germantown or Germantown is claiming part of Mt. Airy. I think Johnson Street is supposed to be the official border. In any event, as you head south on Germantown Avenue from Chestnut Hill, you will find plenty of takeout food, but not a lot of places to sit and eat it with your dog. On the other hand, there *is*:

▶ **Carpenter Woods, Wissahickon and Mt. Pleasant Avenues, West Mt. Airy.** This is a great park and quite doggish, as your dog would say. There are shaded and open areas, and paths you can follow through the woods. Dogs tend to congregate in the meadow: informal dog playgroups form, and dogs are often temporarily let off-leash, although *legally* . . . you get the point. There are benches here for you to rest on.

There's a plethora of history in Mt. Airy/Germantown, and you and your dog might want to take a walking tour, or go to see these sites individually:

▶ **Cliveden, 6401 Germantown Avenue.** The grounds of Cliveden are open Monday through Friday from 10:00 a.m. to 4:00 p.m. and on weekends from noon to 4:00 p.m. There is no charge to tour the grounds with your dog. Cliveden was home to descendants of Pennsylvania Supreme Court Chief Justice Benjamin Chew, and has remained substantially unchanged since its construction from 1763 to 1767. For more information, call 215-848-1777. And you may want to come back for:
   The Battle of Germantown Reenactment (October). You may enjoy this with your dog, *if* your dog can handle the sound of guns firing.
▶ **Deshler-Morris House, 5442 Germantown Avenue.** The hours here vary by season, but it is a National Parks Site, so dogs on-leash are permitted on the grounds. The house was constructed in 1772–73 as the summer home of David Deshler, a Philadelphia merchant. It served as the headquarters for British general Sir William Howe during the Battle of Germantown in October 1777. It was also the official residence of President Washington in 1793, during one of Philadelphia's infamous yellow fever epidemics.
▶ **Grumblethorpe, 5267 Germantown Avenue.** Built in 1744 as a summer house, Grumblethorpe is on the National Register and is owned by the Philadelphia Society for the

Preservation of Landmarks. Inhabited by the Wister family until 1910, it includes John Wister's house and piazza, gardens, outbuildings, and tenant houses. Dogs on-leash are permitted on the grounds. Open from mid-March to Christmas, Tuesday, Thursday, and Sunday, 1:00 to 3:00 p.m. Admission may be charged. For more information, call 215-925-2251.

▶ **Loudon Mansion, Germantown Avenue between Apsley Street and Abbottsford Avenue.** Loudon Mansion dates from 1801 and is Greek Revival in style. Its grounds are now Loudon Park, overseen by the Fairmount Park Commission. There are 7 acres of open space here for you and your dog to explore.

▶ **Rittenhouse Town, 206 Lincoln Drive.** You and your dog on-leash can tour together the grounds of Historic Rittenhouse Town, an 18th-century industrial village that was the site of the first paper mill in the U.S. and is now a National Historic Landmark. The mill provided paper for newspapers and pamphlets and for cartridges and gun wadding during the Revolutionary War. There are picnic areas, so bring a picnic lunch and make it a pleasant half-day. It is open most weekends from 10:00 a.m. to 4:00 p.m. Admission is charged. Come back in December when Rittenhouse Town is decorated for the season by the Roxborough Garden Club. There are also other events to come back for:

Paper Mill Run at Rittenhouse Town (September). An annual 5K run through the Wissahickon Gorge.

Colonial Trades Fair at Historic Rittenhouse Town (September). Papermaking demonstrations, colonial crafts, militia drills, and more. Admission is charged.

For more information on historic sites in the Mt. Airy/Germantown area, as well as literature for a self-guided walking tour of the Germantown area, stop by the Germantown Historical Society & Visitors Center, 5501 Germantown Avenue, or call 215-844-0514.

There's another place you and your dog will enjoy in the Mt. Airy/Germantown area:

▶ **Awbury Arboretum, 1 Awbury Road.** Established in 1916, the arboretum grounds originally were an estate purchased in 1852 by Quaker businessman and philanthropist Henry Cope as a summer retreat; it became a year-round residence. The house, now the arboretum's headquarters, was built in 1860. Awbury is one of the last 19th-century estates that retains its house and original landscaped grounds intact. The arboretum is open daily from dawn to dusk, and is absolutely free. You can walk, jog, and bike at Awbury, and you can pick up a self-guided tour brochure at the house, which is open Monday through Friday, 9:00 a.m. to 5:00 p.m. Though it should go without saying, especially in this sort of a special place: please clean up after your dog.

What else can you and your dog do in the Mt. Airy/Germantown area? You can go to events! The following are all very dog-friendly:

▶ **Germantown MusicFest (April/May).** This free, open-air concert is held at Germantown High School, Germantown Avenue and High Street. You and your dog will have a great time.

▶ **Mt. Airy Day Community Fair (May).** This is an annual celebration of the Mt. Airy community, East and West, in all its diversity. The fair is held on the grounds of Cliveden and Upsala, in the 6400 block of Germantown Avenue. Your dog on-leash is welcome.

- **Awbury Arboretum Plant Sale (May).** Held as part of the events of Mt. Airy Day. Annuals, perennials, herbs, and vegetables will be for sale.
- **We Bloom Where We Are Planted Festival (June).** Sponsored by the East Mt. Airy Neighbors, this is part of Philadelphia's "Welcome America!" Fourth of July event. You and your dog can enjoy a parade along Chew Avenue, sports events, and food and sales booths.

᛫ SELECTED POINTS NORTH

Northern Liberties

Once upon a time, William Penn set aside almost 10,000 acres of land north of the city proper (and lands to the west as well) as "Liberty Lands"—each purchaser of land in the city proper received some of the northern (or western) lands for free. Two centuries later, the Northern Liberties area, bounded by Spring Garden Street on the south and Girard Avenue on the north, was filled with industrial sites. However, more recently, the residents of Northern Liberties have been quietly turning the area into a community.

One highlight of Northern Liberties you can view with your dog is:

- **Edgar Allan Poe National Historic Site, 532 North 7th Street.** Poe lived in this house with his mother-in-law and tragically consumptive wife in the early 1840s. Because it is a National Park Site, you can take your dog into the courtyard and contemplate the house where legend says Poe wrote "The Raven."

Between 3rd and American Streets (the pedestrian access is from American Street) is a tremendous neighborhood triumph:

- **Liberty Lands.** This ex-tannery, ex-Superfund site has been turned into a wonderful neighborhood greenspace, and it is still evolving. There are community gardens and a central commons. And with tremendous wisdom, area residents also created **Dog Park,** at Orianna and Poplar Streets. (It's a little hard to find: the sign says "Orianna Hill Park." Because of the one-way streets, we ended up going north on 3rd Street, west on George Street, south on 4th Street, then east on Brown Street and finally north on Orianna to make sure we didn't miss the park.) Dog Park is fenced, so it is safe for your dog to run and play with his or her friends off-leash.

Some great annual events happen in Northern Liberties:

- **"Lawn Chair Drive-In," the Northern Liberties Neighborhood Association Film Series (Summer Wednesdays).** The series is free, and your dog can watch with you. For more information, call 215-627-7766.
- **Northern Lights Festival (June).** This annual house-decorating competition involving creative light displays makes a summertime wonderland of Northern Liberties homes and businesses. Walk or drive through the neighborhood to enjoy it.
- **The Welcome America Neighborhood Arts Festival (June).** Held on the kickoff weekend for the citywide "Welcome America!" Fourth of July celebration, at the Liberty Lands. Besides the arts festival, there is live music, a parade, and more.

▶ **St. Michael's Russian Orthodox Church Outdoor Festival, 4th Street and Fairmount Avenue (September).** You can bring your dog on-leash to browse the traditional crafts, and enjoy folk music and food. The festival is free. For more information, call 215-627-6148.

▶ **Houndoween (October).** A Halloween party, including a costume competition, for Northern Liberties dogs—of which there seem to be quite a few! Held in Dog Park. Dress in a costume that complements your dog's and maybe you'll win a prize.

For more information on community events, call the Northern Liberties Neighbors Association at 215-627-6562, or visit their Web site at www .nlna.org.

Temple University

Temple University is an open, 87-acre urban campus with interesting architecture, works of art, and a unique, wonderfully diverse atmosphere to enjoy. Vendor trucks will provide you with plenty of food and beverage options as you and your dog explore the campus. Founded in 1884, the main campus is located mostly between Oxford and Diamond Streets, and between 11th and 16th Streets. The university is hoping to create a pedestrian mall between Cecil B. Moore Avenue and Norris Street on 13th Street, where students from the newly relocated Tyler School of Art may exhibit sculpture and other works. In the meantime, there are two other pedestrian malls: Park Mall and Berks Mall.

Other outdoor spaces for you and your dog to enjoy include:

▶ **Founders Garden.** Located across from Berks Mall, Temple founder Russell Conwell and his wife are buried here, and there is a bronze bust of Dr. Conwell to admire.

▶ **Alumni Circle.** At the intersection of Berks Mall and Park Mall, Alumni Circle has places to sit.

You and your dog can come back to the area for:

▶ **The Annual Cecil B. Moore Avenue Jazz/Blues Fest (September).** Between Broad and 18th Streets, you and your dog can enjoy some amazing jazz and blues. For more information, call 215-763-8804.

⚫ BENJAMIN FRANKLIN PARKWAY

The Benjamin Franklin Parkway is a marvelous, monumental-scale vista, modeled on the Champs Élysées of Paris. It starts at the intersection of 16th and Arch Streets and cuts diagonally across the northwest quadrant of Center City, culminating in the gorgeous Philadelphia Museum of Art.

If you stand on the steps of the art museum and look back down the Parkway, you and your dog can see an unusually fine view of City Hall. There are controversial plans to change the Parkway between Logan Circle and the art museum to make the area more pedestrian-friendly. Pedestrian-friendly would be good, but some believe that the plans that have been presented may go too far and spoil the Parkway's Champs Élysées effect.

In any event, you and your dog can take a walk up (or down) the Parkway and have a great time. In warm weather, you can look at the international flags lining the Parkway: almost every nation on earth is represented here, and there are labels on the poles so you know which flag you are looking at.

While you and your dog are exploring the Parkway, there are places where the two of you can stop to rest and take some sustenance:

▶ **Mace's Crossing, 1714 Cherry Street, 215-564-5203.** Mace's Crossing has outdoor seating from May to September, and you can sit here with your dog as long as other customers don't object. They will provide your dog with water or ice on request.

▶ **Peacock on the Parkway, 1700 Benjamin Franklin Parkway, 215-569-8888.** The Peacock serves an "upscale but affordable" lunch geared for business people in a hurry, as well as a more leisurely dinner. They offer Northern Mediterranean cuisine with an emphasis on seafood. You can sit outside with your dog, as soon as it is warm enough to do so ("even if with coats!") until the weather cools down (end of October), and also during Indian summer (December). Your dog will be given a bowl of water and "lots of love and attention!"

You and your small dog can stay overnight just north of the Parkway at:

▶ **Best Western Center City Hotel, 501 North 22nd Street, 215-568-8300.** A conveniently located hostelry with 183 rooms. They will charge your small dog $10 per night.

During the summer, there are frequent events on the Parkway, including lots of running events you and your dog can watch and cheer on. If you want to know when races will take place, check the local newspapers, or Web sites that list races, big and small, such as www.kicksports.com. Other dog-friendly events on the Parkway include:

▶ **Nightout and Fireworks Spectacular (End of June).** This is the kickoff for Philadelphia's great big "Welcome America!" Fourth of July celebration. There's more involved than just fireworks: it's a night of free entertainment along the Benjamin Franklin Parkway. Bring a blanket and a picnic basket, browse with your dog along the Parkway, and then find a place to sit and enjoy whatever is going on around you. If your dog is fireworks-jaded, you can stay to watch the glorious display set off behind the art museum. But if your dog doesn't care for fireworks because they are loud and scary, leave before the show starts.

▶ **Sweet Sounds of Liberty Concert and Fireworks Spectacular (July).** This is the second fireworks event held during "Welcome America!" Again, use your judgment and your knowledge of your dog to decide whether to stay for the fireworks.

▶ **Festival de las Americas (August).** This is the largest Hispanic festival in the city. You and your dog can enjoy lots of music, crafts, and food. For more information, call 215-457-2100.

▶ **Juggling Festival (October).** Held at the Friends Select School, 17th Street and the Parkway. The Philadelphia Jugglers' Club puts on workshops, games, and a public show. Free for you and your dog.

▶ **Rothman Institute 8K Race (November)**

▶ **Thanksgiving Day Parade (November).** You and your dog can see floats, marching bands, and giant helium balloons. And, of course, Santa and his elves make an appearance.

Fairmount (Art Museum Area)

North of the Benjamin Franklin Parkway is a neighborhood commonly known as the Art Museum area. This is a fun area to walk around, and in the morning it looks like a dog-walker's paradise: I've never seen so many people walking dogs at one time. There's a lot to see here: Spring Garden Street was an early city suburb, and there are very pretty houses along it. At 1700 Spring Garden Street, in the third U.S. Mint Building, is the Community College of Philadelphia. At the corner of 17th and Brandywine Streets, there are community gardens to admire. And there is Eastern State Penitentiary, between 20th and 22nd Streets on Spring Garden Street, built in the 1820s and a National Historic Site.

You and your dog can take a break from walking around the Art Museum area at:

▶ **Fairmount Bagel Institute, 2501 Olive Street, 215-235-2245.** The Fairmount Bagel Institute serves breakfast and lunch, and they have outdoor seating all year, weather permitting, where your dog can sit with you while you enjoy a bagel or a sandwich. They'll provide water for your dog on request, or, if you'd like, a bagel! They are open seven days a week.

There are a few events in the Fairmount/Art Museum area that you and your dog might enjoy attending:

▶ **Great Eastern State Breakout (June).** This is a 5K race through the area that benefits Eastern State Penitentiary Park.
▶ **Bastille Day Street Party (July).** You and your dog can celebrate in a French-themed block party, with music and food. You are encouraged to come dressed appropriately (and for those whose dogs like to dress up, I can hear your pup barking "Liberté! Egalité! Fraternité!" which means he or she wants to be a French dog for the day). There is a reenactment of French revolutionaries storming the Bastille and capturing Marie Antoinette (who throws Tastykakes and Twinkies from the Eastern State Penitentiary towers while crying, "Let them eat cake!"). Be aware that there is some firing of guns and a roaring crowd of revolutionaries, so if your dog isn't impervious to such sights and sounds, you might want to leave before the storming begins.
▶ **29th Street Festival (August).** Strawberry Mansion–area street fair featuring live music, speakers, games, and the 29th Street Performing Arts Dancers. Call 215-223-5221 for more information.
▶ **Pep the Dog Weekend (September).** Another event put on by Eastern State Penitentiary. Pep was a black Lab who served a life sentence in the prison, beginning in 1924. You can't actually bring your dog to this event, but adults and children seven and over (younger kids cannot tour the site) can save $1 on tour admission by showing a photo of their pet—dog, cat, or anything else.

There's one more event you and your dog might be interested in, but I don't know if it is annual or not: I did not get a response to my inquiries. Nevertheless, this special event has happened in the recent past, and if it happens again, it's too good not to mention:

▶ **Bastille Day at Cuvée Notredame (July 14).** Your dog may be able to enjoy a free gourmet dinner on the restaurant's outdoor deck while you enjoy a French or Belgian dinner (for a price). When this event was held in 1999, prizes were awarded for the best-dressed dog, the dog with the best French accent, and other categories. Call 215-765-2777 as the day approaches to see if this event is happening again.

Of course, one site you and your dog will definitely want to spend time enjoying in the area is:

▶ **The Philadelphia Museum of Art.** Built between 1916 and 1928, the Philadelphia Museum of Art is more than just the steps Sylvester Stallone ran up in *Rocky*. The famous steps are flanked by marvelous fountains, and lead to a huge terrace and the third-largest art museum in the country.

In front of the museum is Eakins Oval. A huge fountain there, *The Washington Monument* by Rudolf Siemering, includes an amazing amount of sculpture, including many people and animals. It's another favorite of my dog Georgie's and mine.

Behind the art museum, in summer, you and your dog can enjoy watching:

▶ **International Folk Dancing.** For more information, call 215-352-4432.

(Lower Fairmount Park)

Just beyond the back of the art museum is a marvelous doggy playground: Lower Fairmount Park. It is one of the oldest parks in the country (established in 1812), and one of the largest municipal parks in the world, with over 8,500 acres. The first stop you and your dog should make here is:

▶ **The Fairmount Water Works.** The waterworks were built between 1812 and 1815 (the center pavilion was added in 1872 for the Centennial Exhibition) and are a National Historic and Engineering Landmark. The open pavilions and overlooks offer terrific views of the Schuylkill River and Falls. As this is being written, the Fairmount Water Works are under restoration. The Engine House has been restored with use as a restaurant in mind, including outdoor seating on the terrace in front. Plans for the rest of the waterworks include a marketplace and a site for festivals and other special events.

As a result of the waterworks restoration, Fairmount Park is getting more parking: about 300 spaces on or near Aquarium Drive, which leads from Kelly Drive to the waterworks. That will make it easier for you and your dog to take regular trips to Fairmount Park. Near the waterworks, your next stop should be:

▶ **The Azalea Garden.** Especially when the azaleas are in bloom, but really any time of year, the Azalea Garden is lovely, and has some neat small sculptures including the popular *Puma* by William Zorach. If you and your dog go on a weekend, it's best to go in the morning, because in the afternoon, wedding parties tend to use the space for photographs.

Between Kelly Drive and the Schuylkill River are trails where you will find other walkers, joggers, cyclists, in-line skaters, picnickers, and even painters trying to capture the Schuylkill and the ultra-picturesque old bridges that span it. This is a great place to take your dog on a sunny weekend afternoon, or a cool fall day, or any other time. Along the way you will see:

▶ **Boathouse Row.** These Victorian boathouses are owned by area rowing associations, and you and your dog should walk along and look at them from this side (you can get the view of the other side along West River Drive across the river). **Lloyd Hall,** first in the row, was added by the city in recent years, and has water available for your dog and restrooms available for you, as well as a café with outdoor seating where you can enjoy a light meal with your dog beside you. (You can also get water for your dog from "Chief," as he's known, who vends pretzels and other items across from Boathouse Row by special dispensation, and puts out a bowl for dogs, under a cooler of water with a spout.) Various events are held at Lloyd Hall, including:

Folk Dancing from Around the World (Summer). For more information, call 215-945-1316.

Rockin' on the River Concert Series (Summer). The concerts are free.

Philadelphia Juggling Club (Summer)

Halloween Folk Dance Party (October)

Take your dog to see the Glen Benning Rock Garden along Kelly Drive, near the natural stone bridge. (Be very careful crossing Kelly Drive!) Then cross back over and get some good, healthy exercise walking or running along the river.

By the way, Boathouse Row is there for a reason: the buildings house the clubs of the Schuylkill Navy (the Fairmount Rowing Association, the Crescent Boat Club, the Bachelors Barge Club, the University Barge Club, the Malta Boat Club, the Vesper Boat Club, the College Boat Club, the Penn Athletic Club Rowing Association, the Undine Barge Club, and the Philadelphia Girls' Rowing Club), and are the local center for rowing as a sport. As a result, there are frequent races on the water that you and your dog can have a great time watching. The Schuylkill Navy, founded in 1858 and the oldest amateur athletic governing body in the country, holds the following major regattas every year, as well as many smaller races: the **Stotesbury Cup Regatta (May)**, **Middle States Regatta (May)**, **Schuylkill Navy Regatta (June)**, **Independence Day Regatta (July)**, **Philadelphia Youth Regatta (July)**, **Bayada Regatta (September)**, **Navy Day Regatta (October)**, and **Philadelphia Frostbite Regatta (November)**.

The Schuylkill Navy also holds a cross-country run on Thanksgiving Day, commonly known as the **Turkey Trot**, in which the clubs compete on land, running 5 5/8 miles through the Fairmount Park area. For more information on this event and the regattas, visit the Schuylkill Navy's Web site at www.boathouserow.org/navy.html.

Besides the Schuylkill Navy regattas, the largest collegiate regatta in the country is held on the Schuylkill River during the second week of May:

▶ **The Dad Vail Regatta.** This is a major city event. Hundreds of colleges and thousands of athletes participate. It is great fun to watch, which is why it draws such a crowd. Make sure your dog can handle all the activity.

East Fairmount Park contains a number of historic houses overlooking the Schuylkill River. You'll need to drive to where they are, but once there, put your dog on-leash and admire the architecture. Afterward, you can romp around together in lots and lots of open space.

If Fairmount Park just doesn't provide enough exercise for you and your dog (hard to imagine!), you can follow the **Schuylkill River Trail** right out of Philadelphia County into Montgomery County. The trail is the spine of the Schuylkill River Heritage Corridor, a five-county area designated as a State Heritage Park. The trail follows the Fairmount Park trails to the Manayunk Canal Towpath and then heads out through Conshohocken, Bridgeport, and Norristown, to end at Valley Forge National Historical Park. Along the way, there is access to business and cultural districts, restrooms, drinking water, picnic tables, and 911 phones. Dogs are permitted on the trail on leashes not exceeding 6 feet, but they must be attended to at all times, and, of course, you have to clean up after your dog. Walkers, runners, and cyclists use the trail; if you and your dog move slowly, keep to the right and be prepared to be passed from behind. For more information on the Schuylkill River Trail, contact the Pennsylvania DCNR at 888-PA-PARKS or visit www.dcnr.state.pa.us.

😺 CENTER CITY

Center City has one feature that comes in very useful on long walks around town with your dog: street vendors. You can get every type of food there is, as well as juices, water, and more, from these vendors. And Center City is a wonderful place to take long walks with your dog.

East of Broad Street

There are a lot of interesting sites for you and your dog to explore east of Broad Street. For example:

- **Reading Terminal Headhouse, Market Street between 11th and 12th Streets.** The headhouse, now the entrance for the Pennsylvania Convention Center, is gorgeous. The Reading Terminal Market, behind the headhouse, is off-limits to your dog, but there's an event you and your dog might want to check out:

    Sidewalk Sizzle and Ice Cream Freeze (July). The Reading Terminal Market goes outside at 12th and Arch Streets on a Saturday. Sidewalk sales, free entertainment, and more. For information, call 215-922-2317.

- **Jewelers' Row.** It really is two intersecting rows: 8th Street between Chestnut and Walnut Streets, and Sansom Street between 7th and 9th Streets. This is the oldest diamond district in the country, established in 1851. You and your dog can do some fabulous window-shopping here.

- **Antique Row.** Runs along Pine Street, from 9th Street to 17th Street. There are over 40 shops here, providing more great window-shopping, and I'm told some of the shops might let you bring your dog inside. You can always ask.

▶ **Chinatown.** Chinatown is a compact neighborhood of restaurants and markets between 9th and 12th Streets, and between Vine and Arch Streets. There's some scattered good window-shopping here, including stores featuring Oriental screens, Buddhas, fabrics, porcelain tigers, and dragons.

Philadelphia is a city full of community events, and the area east of Broad is no exception. You and your dog can try a few of these:

▶ **Pridefest America (May).** Includes an outdoor block party/music festival with arts and crafts, food, and more, at 12th and Locust Streets. For more information, call 800-990-FEST, or visit www.pridefest.org.

▶ **Pride Day (June).** Begins with a memorial service at Spruce and Juniper Streets, followed by a parade.

▶ **OutFest (October).** You and your dog can enjoy this free block party held in the name of Pride, centered near 12th and Locust Streets. Hailed as the largest national coming-out event in the world, there's a flea market, live entertainment, rides, games, and food. For more information, call 215-875-9288.

▶ **Mural Arts Month (October).** The Philadelphia Department of Recreation's Mural Arts Program is the leading such program in the country, having sponsored the painting of more than 1,800 indoor and outdoor murals since 1984. Mural Arts Month kicks off with a new mural dedication and a free street party, with live music and refreshments. There are other events as well. For more information, call 215-568-5245.

▶ **Philadelphia Dog Show (November).** You can't bring your dog with you, but inside you can certainly see more dogs than you've ever seen at one time in your life (unless you've been to the Westminster Kennel Club's show). This is the premier event of the Kennel Club of Philadelphia, and it is quite a show. (Hey, the American Kennel Club was founded in Philadelphia, so why wouldn't it be?) Saturday is a traditional benched show. Dogs have to stay until the show is over, occupying stalls on raised platforms when not in the ring. Owners and handlers may be on hand to tell you about their breed of dog and its characteristics. There are only six benched shows in the U.S., the most famous of which is the Westminster Kennel Club's. Along with the conformation competition, the Philadelphia Dog Show includes agility, flyball, and other demonstrations, along with lots of vendors: 30 to 40 dog-related jewelers, artists, clothiers, antique dealers, and specialty food and dog supply sellers. Pick up some free samples of dog kibble at the dog food stands as a consolation gift for your left-at-home dog. You can also pick up information from breed rescue groups, humane societies, therapy-dog organizations, Penn's veterinary school, and the Harcum College vet tech program. Admission is charged.

There are plenty of places east of Broad where you and your dog can get something to eat together. Try these:

▶ **Millennium Coffee, 212 South 12th Street, 215-731-9798.** Coffee, tea, espresso, and juice beverages are available here, as well as sandwiches, soups, chili, and desserts. Outdoor seating is available year-round, weather permitting. They will provide a bowl of water or ice for your dog, on request. Anything else dog owners should know? "Lots o' dogs. Your pup can make new friends and play catch in the alley," they say.

▶ **Two Sisters Ala Mode, 1141–43 Pine Street, 215-574-4277.** You can get homemade soups and chili, charbroiled sandwiches, wraps, omelets, and more here, but the biggest emphasis is on desserts and ice cream. Outdoor seating is available from April to October. They will give your dog water or ice if you ask for it, but even better than that, during the summer months they sell "Frosty Paws," a non-dairy frozen treat for dogs.

▶ **Stellar Coffee, 1101 Spruce Street, 215-625-7923.** Coffee, of course, and the usual coffee-shop snacks. They allow people to sit at their sidewalk tables with dogs, and will provide water for the dogs.

You and your dog can stay overnight east of Broad at:

▶ **Clarion Suites, 1010 Race Street, 215-922-1730.** Features 96 rooms in the restored 1890 Bentwood Rocker factory. Listed on the National Register of Historic Places. Small pets (30 pounds or less) are allowed with a $100 deposit.

▶ **Philadelphia Marriott, 1201 Market Street, 215-625-2900.** Boasts 1,198 rooms. Small pets only, with a $100 deposit required.

▶ **Ten-Eleven Clinton, 1011 Clinton Street, 215-923-8144.** You can e-mail them at 1011@concentric.net, or visit their Web site at www.TenEleven.com. Seven rooms in an 1836 Federal-style townhouse with a private courtyard. Dogs might be permitted on a case-by-case basis: ask when you call to make a reservation. Note that there is a two-night minimum stay at this bed and breakfast.

(City Hall/Broad Street)

City Hall

City Hall, dominating Penn Square at Broad and Market Streets, was built between 1871 and 1901. It is the largest city hall in the country, and the most elaborate as well. Its tower rises 548 feet, and the bronze statue of William Penn by Alexander Milne Calder (1894) on top is 37 feet tall and the largest piece of sculpture on a building in the world. City Hall's monumental arched portals and pavilions ornamented by Calder lead from all directions to a central courtyard. As you and your dog explore City Hall, look for sculpture in surprising places. Don't forget to check out the buildings and plazas surrounding City Hall.

Avenue of the Arts

It's also called Broad Street, but because of the concentration of arts venues along Philadelphia's central north–south corridor, from Dauphin Street in North Philadelphia to Washington Avenue in South Philly, it has been "renamed" the Avenue of the Arts. Redevelopment projects have happened and continue to happen and are planned to happen to tie the whole thing together. The centerpiece, in my opinion, is:

▶ **The Academy of Music, corner of Broad and Locust Streets.** Built between 1855 and 1857, the red-brick Academy of Music has gaslights along its exterior walls that are lit to this day. Along the sidewalk here, and along other blocks of the Avenue of the Arts, is Philadelphia's Walk of Fame: embedded plaques honoring Philadelphia-connected artists who have contributed to the arts in a major way, such as Frankie Avalon, Chubby Checker, Hall & Oates, Patti LaBelle, and Bessie Smith. During the summer there are daytime and evening performances by **Avenue Artists.**

You should also stop at the **Arch Street United Methodist Church, 55 North Broad Street.** The building is Gothic Revival, and was built in 1870. The church is known for, among other things, its annual "Blessing of the Animals."

The Avenue of the Arts and the City Hall area are the sites of many events you and your dog will enjoy:

▶ **Mummers Parade (January 1).** See the comics, fancies, and brigades for which Philadelphia is famous.

▶ **Blue Cross Broad Street Run (May)**

▶ **Marian Anderson Award Procession and Ceremony and Regional Arts & Culture Festival (June/July).** Marian Anderson was an internationally known concert singer and the first African American to star at the Metropolitan Opera. For information, call 215-683-2083 or -2081.

▶ **Welcome America! (July).** Philadelphia's tremendous birthday bash. The skyscrapers are lit red, white, and blue, and there are parades, fireworks, and music in various outdoor venues. The offerings differ from year to year, so watch the newspapers for the schedule.

▶ **Bastille Day Dog Walk (July).** An annual walk benefiting the Lupus Foundation of Pennsylvania and Delaware. This is a great cause, and a great walk around Center City. There are stops along the way for water and a rest. For more information, call 610-828-2550.

▶ **Puerto Rican Day Parade (September).** This is Center City Philadelphia's showcase of Puerto Rican and Latino culture.

▶ **Columbus Day Parade and Italian Festival (October).** A parade, live music, traditional South Philly food, and family entertainment.

▶ **United Way Day, City Hall Courtyard (October).** United Way of Southeastern Pennsylvania, the Mummers, and WOGL helped kick off the 1999–2000 campaign in a block party celebration at noon. For more information, call 215-665-2517.

▶ **Philadelphia Marathon (November).** The 26-mile, 385-yard marathon starts and finishes at the Philadelphia Museum of Art.

▶ **Annual A.B.A.T.E. Toys for Tots Parade (November).** And what is A.B.A.T.E.? The Alliance of Bikers Aimed Toward Education. The Delaware Valley chapter forms a parade of about 50,000 motorcycles bearing gifts at Delaware Avenue and Spring Garden Street, and bikes its way west to the Children's Hospital of Philadelphia. It's been happening since 1980, and it is quite a sight, and sound. (Use caution with noise-sensitive dogs.)

▶ **Center City Holiday Festival (December).** The festival starts in the courtyard of City Hall, decorated appropriately with lights, garlands, and the city's Christmas tree. Santa Claus, riding an antique fire engine, leads a parade along Market Street. Along the way, there is live entertainment on the sidewalks.

▶ **Make It a Sunday (December).** This event is sponsored by the Center City District. Marching bands, stilt-walkers, holiday elves, brass ensembles, and Victorian carolers perform.

▶ **Avenue of the Arts Tree Lighting (December).** Held at the Academy of Music. Costumed Nutcracker characters, actors, singers, choirs, and others will be on hand to make it quite an event.

You and your small dog can stay overnight together at:

▶ **Park Hyatt Philadelphia at the Bellevue, 1415 Chancellor Court, 215-893-1234.** The Park Hyatt has 170 rooms, and small pets are permitted.

West of Broad Street

Schuylkill River to Fitler Square

There's a place in this area of the city to which you *have* to take your dog:

▶ **Center City Dog Park, 25th Street between Locust and Delancey Streets.** The dog park is part of the Markwood Playground in Schuylkill Park. The park is open all hours, and features an enclosed area ringed by trees, in which your dog can play, wrestle, chase, and romp with other dogs, *off-leash*. There are lots of benches you can sit on while you watch your dog. This is a great park, very well used, with a nice balance of shade and sun.

But there are lots of dog-friendly highlights in Center City west of Broad Street. Take some exploratory excursions into some of the smaller streets in the area with your canine companion: Panama, Smedley, Hicks, Carlisle, Waverly, or Pine. If you'd like a more formal tour, the Foundation for Architecture gives tours of Philly's "Littlest Streets," and as long as no one else is bothered, they will let you bring along your dog on-leash.

Then take your dog to see another highlight of the area:

▶ **Fitler Square, 23rd and Pine Streets.** Edwin H. Fitler was mayor of Philadelphia from 1887 to 1891, and the square was named for him in the year of his death, 1896. The square itself is a nice urban park, surrounded by charming houses and a generally great neighborhood atmosphere. Come back to Fitler Square for events such as:

Annual Fitler Square Spring Fair (May). Antiques, food, flowers, books, and more on sale.

Rittenhouse Square

Rittenhouse Square, bounded by Walnut Street, Rittenhouse Square Street, and 18th Street, is one of the most beautiful and active urban parks I've ever seen. I had the pleasure of living just a couple of blocks from it (as did our older dog, Meg) for four years, and it was wonderful to have it so close by. Meg loved it, especially since many of the area doormen stand outside in nice weather and keep dog treats in their pockets that they distribute freely to passing canines. Walk east along Locust Street from the square and you can admire the Curtis Institute, St. Mark's Church, and other wonderful buildings.

Rittenhouse Square is wonderfully maintained, full of sculpture, with a marvelous fountain, and it is lovely in every season. It is a great place to walk your dog, jog with your dog (around the outside is the best place for that), picnic with your dog, or sit on a bench and people-watch with your dog. In the Rittenhouse Square area are the most prestigious addresses in Philadelphia proper, but on any nice day you will find a very diverse crowd in the square itself. You may see dogs off-leash here, but legally, they are required to be on-leash, and since the square is such an active park, it's probably best to leave your beast on-leash.

In Rittenhouse Square, more and more events are taking place each year that you and your dog can enjoy. The events may differ from year to year, but look for these in the local newspapers:

▶ **Easter Promenade (March/April).** Come out and watch lots of extremely well dressed children from all over the city show off their finery.
▶ **Rittenhouse Square Flower Market (May).** Plants, gardening tools, auction items, and food. For information, call 215-732-5098.
▶ **Rittenhouse Square Concert Series (Summer).** Pack a picnic dinner and a blanket, and enjoy a terrific variety of bands. Teach your dog to dance. The series is free.
▶ **Rittenhouse Square Fine Arts Annual (June).** Take your dog to browse through the aisles of fine art. For more information, call 877-689-4112.
▶ **Ball on the Square (June).** Sponsored by the Friends of Rittenhouse Square. Your dog will love to watch this.
▶ **Twilight Concert & Film Festival (Late June/July).** Part of the annual Marian Anderson Award celebration. Events related to the Marian Anderson Award change from year to year, depending on who is honored. Dogs are permitted at all venues of the Marian Anderson Award celebration at which they normally would be allowed. Check the Philly papers to see what events are scheduled.
▶ **Rittenhouse Square Picnic in the Park (July 4)**
▶ **Rittenhouse Square Tree Lighting (December)**

Near Rittenhouse Square is a commercial district known as Rittenhouse Row. The shops in Rittenhouse Row make for some fabulous window-shopping, and some of them will probably let you bring your dog inside. The businesses of Rittenhouse Row sponsor events, such as:

▶ **The Rittenhouse Row Spring Festival (May).** Enjoy live music, dance, street performers, food, and fashion, from 19th and Walnut Streets to the Avenue of the Arts.
▶ **The Rittenhouse Row Halloween Celebration (October).** There is trick-or-treating along the row and a costume contest at the Warwick Hotel.
▶ **Rittenhouse Row Christmas.** The shops have extended hours from Thanksgiving to New Year's.
▶ **New Year's Celebration (December 31)**

There's one more really great thing about the Rittenhouse Square area. There are places you can get a great meal or a drink, and have your dog sit with you while you watch all the activity around the square. Try one of these:

▶ **Rouge, 201 South 18th Street, 215-732-6622.** Rouge offers casual bistro fare, with daily specials. They have outdoor seating from April to November, and pride themselves on an upbeat environment. They will provide bowls of water and dog treats for your dog.

▶ **Devon Seafood Grill, 225 South 18th Street, 215-546-5940.** This is where you want to go for upscale casual seafood, or aged steaks, or selections from the raw bar, and a complementary selection from the wine list. Outdoor dining is available in spring, summer, and fall. They "have had water bowls for our doggie friends—but they kept getting stolen." So if your pup is thirsty, just ask, and the staff will provide. Anything else dog owners should know? "We are one of three dog-friendly restaurants on the same block on beautiful Rittenhouse Square!"

So, what's the third?

▶ **The Square Bar, 18th and Locust Streets, 215-546-9400.** Interesting, creative Italian cuisine in both "small plate" and entrée portions, by Tony Clark. Facing Rittenhouse Square in a row with Rouge and Devon Seafood Grill.

Also try the **Gallery Café, 233 South 20th Street, 215-567-3808.** They have outdoor tables where you can sit with your dog.

You can stay overnight with your dog in the Rittenhouse Square area at:

▶ **The Rittenhouse Hotel, 210 West Rittenhouse Square, 215-546-9000.** The hotel has 98 rooms and is very upscale. Pets are allowed, without restrictions, and of course the park is right across the street for walking.

▶ **The Warwick Hotel, 1701 Locust Street, 215-735-6000.** The Warwick is lovely, just a block from the square, and your pet can stay there for no extra fee, no restrictions.

For more formal tours of the Rittenhouse Square area, the Foundation for Architecture offers tours of Rittenhouse Square East and Rittenhouse Square West, and your on-leash, well-mannered dog can come along. Or just take your dog for a walk around the nearby streets by yourself: it's easy to find interesting things to look at. Delancey Street in particular has some amazing residences.

Does your dog need to go shopping? Try:

▶ **Rittenhouse Square Pet Supply, 135 South 20th Street, 215-569-2555**

Logan Square to Broad Street

This is the business center of the city, and there are some amazing skyscrapers that have brightened the skyline since 1987:

▶ **One Liberty Place, 17th and Market Streets,** was the first to break a long-standing "gentleman's agreement" that no building would rise higher than the clock tower of City Hall. It was completed in 1987.

▶ **Commerce Square, 20th and Market Streets.** Built in 1987 and 1992, respectively, the twin skyscrapers enclose a gorgeous courtyard and fountain. This is a nice place for you and your dog to rest.

There's also a beautiful fountain and plaza between **One and Two Logan Square**, and another one on the north side of the **Bell Atlantic Tower** (all at 18th and Arch Streets). Visit them with your dog and see which he or she likes better.

While you are checking out plazas, there is one you and your dog will definitely not want to miss:

▶ **John F. Kennedy Plaza, 15th and Arch Streets.** Along with a pretty spectacular fountain that will drizzle water on you if the wind is blowing, no matter how far away from it you walk, is Robert Indiana's famous *LOVE* sculpture, and a fabulous view up to Alexander Milne Calder's statue of William Penn on top of City Hall.

You can stay overnight with your dog in the area at:

▶ **The Four Seasons Hotel, 1 Logan Square, 215-963-1500.** One of Philly's five-star hotels, the Four Seasons will let you bring a small dog—a very small dog—with you to stay. Meg could stay, but Georgie couldn't: only dogs 15 pounds and under are allowed.
▶ **Best Western Inn, 501 North 22nd Street, 215-568-8300.** There are no size restrictions on dogs, but there is a $10 charge per night.
▶ **Crowne Plaza Philadelphia, 18th and Market Streets, 215-561-7500.** The hotel has 445 rooms, and your dog can stay, with no restrictions, for a refundable $125 deposit and a nightly $25 fee.
▶ **Korman Suites Hotel Buttonwood, 2001 Hamilton Street, 215-569-7000.** Korman Suites is an extended-stay hotel, and for stays between one week and one month, there's a $100 nonrefundable fee per pet. Your dog can stay here if he or she weighs 45 pounds or less. For stays longer than one month, there is a maximum annual charge of $400.

Are you and your dog hungry? Stop by:

▶ **Dock Street Brasserie, 18th Street between Arch and Cherry Streets, 215-496-0413.** Dock Street offers an authentic brasserie menu with classic French cuisine, as well as hand-crafted, freshly brewed beer from the on-premises brewery. Lunch, dinner, and Sunday brunch are served. Outdoor seating is available from April to October, weather permitting, and they will provide a bowl of water for your dog on request. During the first week in October, they have an Oktoberfest, with special brews and a menu of German food in addition to their usual offerings. And, of course, they are "one block off the Ben Franklin Parkway which leads to West River and Kelly Drives, great places to walk dogs."

Doggish events in the area:

▶ **Annual Fur Ball (January).** Benefits Morris Animal Refuge. Your dog can't come, but you can, dressed as your favorite animal. Admission is charged. I'm mentioning the ball here because it has been held in the past at the Wyndham Franklin Plaza, but the location varies. Check the local newspapers for the date and place.
▶ **Annual Philadelphia St. Patrick's Day Parade (March)**
▶ **Labor Day Parade and Family Celebration (September).** Union members march, and there are speakers and other entertainment.

Old City

History, history, history. You can't escape it in Old City. That just may be why they call it "Old." The cool part is that you can see most of what Old City has to offer with your dog. Start here:

▶ **Independence National Historical Park.** A National Parks Site, the park is open to dogs on-leash, as long as you clean up after them and do *not* leave them tied up outside while you go into a building. Most of the buildings are worth seeing from the outside even if you can't go in. There are plans to change the blocks between Chestnut Street and Race Street, and between 5th and 6th Streets: for you and your dog, the important part is that there will be more grassy areas with plenty of benches. Other highlights of the park will remain the same, and include:

▶ **Washington Square, 6th to 7th Streets, and Walnut Street to just past Locust Street.** This is a beautiful park, as well as the site of the Tomb of the Unknown Soldier of the American Revolution.

▶ **Independence Square, 6th and Walnut Streets, northeast of Washington Square.** It was here that the Declaration of Independence was first read publicly, on July 8, 1776.

▶ **Franklin Court, between 3rd and 4th Streets, and Chestnut and Market Streets.** There is a "Ghost House" here, designed by Robert Venturi, on the site where Benjamin Franklin's house once stood. The paving stones of the court are inscribed with quotes from letters that passed between Mr. and Mrs. Franklin regarding the design and decoration of the house— Benjamin was in Paris at the time.

Other historical sites in the Old City area that you and your dog might want to take in during your rambles include:

▶ **The Betsy Ross House, 239 Arch Street.** Where Betsy allegedly stitched the first American flag in 1777. The two-story colonial home has been restored. Come back for the **Flag Day Celebration (June),** featuring ceremonies, speakers, and the Marine Marching Band.

▶ **Elfreth's Alley, north of Arch Street, between Front and 2nd Streets.** This is the oldest continually occupied residential street in the country, and is lined with houses built between 1720 and the early 1800s. People really live here, so please be considerate as you admire this marvelous street. You might want to come back for:

    Elfreth's Alley Association's Fete Days (June). Included are colonial crafts, a street fair, and entertainment. Admission is charged. For information, call 215-574-0560.

There are some historically themed events in the area that you and your dog may want to check out:

▶ **Sons of the American Revolution Annual Commemoration of George Washington's Birthday (February).** On the Chestnut Street side of Independence Hall, color guards, fife and drum corps, and others gather for a ceremony and parade.

▶ **Philadelphia Liberty Medal Presentation Ceremony (July 4).** Held in front of Independence Hall. The Liberty Medal honors individuals or organizations that have made a significant contribution to the pursuit of liberty and freedom across the world.

But history isn't all Old City has to offer. There are plenty of other things to see and do. During the 1980s and '90s, galleries and restaurants sprang up all over Old City. One thing you can definitely do with your dog in Old City is grab lunch, dinner, or a drink. Try one of these:

▶ **Continental Restaurant & Martini Bar, 138 Market Street, 215-923-6069.** The Continental is a casual restaurant and martini bar, serving dinner seven nights a week, along with weekend brunch. If you sit outside, your dog can come with you, and outdoor seating is available when the weather permits. They will provide ice and water for your dog on request.

▶ **Fork, 306 Market Street, 215-625-9425.** Fork's menu includes seasonal offerings, and there is a good wine list. They have outdoor seating from April to October, and they will give your dog water on request.

▶ **Lucy's Hat Shop Restaurant and Lounge, 247 Market Street, 215-413-1433.** Lucy's offers Continental food with Mediterranean influences, and they have outdoor seating "all we can." You can sit outside with your dog, and they will provide a bowl of water for your dog on request.

▶ **Marmont, 222 Market Street, 215-923-1100.** Marmont serves Mediterranean dishes. They have outdoor seating from April to November; feel free to sit here with your dog. The Marmont staff will provide your dog with water or ice on request.

▶ **Philadelphia Fish & Co., 207 Chestnut Street, 215-625-8605.** They have outdoor seating from May until it gets too cold out, on a raised deck that is separated from outside foot traffic. They will provide a bowl of water for your dog on request. For you, they offer lunch and dinner.

▶ **xando Coffee & Bar, 325 Chestnut Street, 215-399-0215.** According to xando, this is "everyone's favorite place for coffee and community. Coffee by day, liquor bar by night, we also serve food." Xando has outdoor seating all year, and you can sit here with your dog. They will offer your dog water. The person with whom I communicated said, "I never thought of offering dog treats, but we will definitely start that." Anything else they wanted dog owners to know? "Many of us who work here are dog owners and dog lovers, [and] we …love to watch them with their owners enjoying the outdoor café."

While you're in Old City, there are two stops your dog will definitely want to make:

▶ **City Critters, 224 Market Street, 215-922-5003.** Dogs on-leash are permitted inside. Check the place out. Or rather, let your dog check it out.

▶ **Front & Chestnut Dog Park.** Its name is its address. It isn't completely enclosed, and there are signs posted here that dogs must be kept on-leash. Nevertheless, informal dog play does take place here. Just be sure to block the exits: there are busy city streets nearby.

Other places in Old City you and your dog might want to take a quick tour of include:

▶ **Piers 3 and 5, north of Market Street and Penn's Landing.** There's a walkway here lined with terrific sculptures by Andrew Leicester.

▶ **Welcome Park, 2nd Street between Chestnut and Walnut Streets.** Designed by the architectural firm now called Venturi, Scott Brown & Associates, Welcome Park contains a huge map of William Penn's original plan for the city, a representation of Penn's statue on top of City Hall, and a representation of Penn's house, on the site of which the park sits. There are benches here where you can sit and rest with your dog and enjoy this very cool space.

Of course, there are events in Old City of interest to you and your dog:

▶ **The Historic Neighborhood Consortium Summer Concert Series.** At different times and at different places within walking distance of Independence National Historical Park, singers, musicians, and dancers perform.

▶ **Historic Philadelphia, Inc. (Summer).** This nonprofit organization was started in 1994, and sponsors the Town Criers, wandering acting troupes that put on historical short plays in venues around Old City. There are over 20 actors involved so far, and they do *not* step out of character, no matter what.

▶ **Annual Fringe Festival (September).** Dogs on-leash are permitted at all outdoor venues and in all public rights-of-way during this 10-day, wild and outrageous event celebrating the arts in a cutting-edge way. On a case-by-case basis, some of Old City's art galleries will probably permit your dog on-leash inside. In any case, there are plenty of outdoor venues. You and your dog can experience visual art, dance, drama, movies, music, comedy, poetry, and performance art, sometimes when you least expect it. Admission is charged for some shows, but many of the outdoor performances and art can be seen for free. And don't forget to attend the opening-night block party.

▶ **First Fridays in Old City (September through December).** The over 40 galleries of Old City stay open late and provide cocktails, snacks, and music. Stroll around and see who will let you bring your dog inside.

▶ **Old City Holiday Shopping Gala (December).** Music, refreshments, and more.

Is your dog small? If so, you can both stay overnight in Old City at:

▶ **Best Western Independence Park Inn, 235 Chestnut Street, 215-922-4443.** Rated three diamonds by AAA, with five stories and 36 rooms. They accept small pets for a $10 charge.

(Society Hill)

Society Hill is a beautiful, old residential area, and contains the largest concentration of 18th-century architecture in the U.S. The historic ambience and lovely streets give you the feeling you're really walking through colonial Philadelphia. It's a great place to take your dog for a walk and to explore.

The Washington Square West area has lots of little streets tucked in between the bigger streets that have an amazing array of architecture to offer. Many of the homes in Society Hill are what are called "trinities"—three stories, basically of one room each. Check out Fawn Street, Camac Street, Cypress Street, Panama Street's 1200 block, and Irving Street where Jessup Street intersects.

If you want to take a more formal tour of the Society Hill area, you can sign up for a tour with:

▶ **Centipede Tours—Candlelight Strolls.** From May to mid-October on Fridays and Saturdays, weather permitting, guides in colonial dress will take you through hidden gardens and
courtyards in Society Hill. The guide will tell you all about the customs and lifestyles of
Society Hill's 18th-century residents. Admission is charged, and the tour lasts 90 minutes.
Well-behaved dogs on-leash are permitted to come along.

Or call the Foundation for Architecture, 215-569-3187, which offers tours on
a regular basis. Dogs can come along as long as they are well-behaved and
the tour is outdoors-only.

Besides touring, there are some regular Society Hill events you and your
dog can check out together:

▶ **The Creative Collective Craft & Fine Arts Fair, Historic Headhouse Shambles, 2nd and
Pine Streets (Weekends from May to September).** Under the shelter of the Headhouse
Shambles, Society Hill's "New Market" in 1745, are gathered more than 100 artists from the
region as well as the craftswomen of the Creative Collective. Browse through offerings of
jewelry, glass, ceramics, prints, wood objects, paintings, photography, clothing, and more. For
more information, call 215-790-0782, or visit their Web page at www.libertynet.org (follow
the links to the Creative Collective).

▶ **Guinness Oyster Festival, Headhouse Square (October).** This is a great family event that
includes live music and clowns. In the company of your dog on-leash, you can also enjoy
oysters and other seafood, and pints of Guinness. For more information, call 215-574-9240.

▶ **Halloween Howl, Headhouse Square (October).** A free event for the whole family, with
live music, a magic show, and hayrides.

When you and your dog just want to hang out in Society Hill, there is:

▶ **xando Coffee & Bar, 215 Lombard Street, 215-925-4910.** Outdoor seating is available
from April to November, and they will provide your dog with water on request.

Penn's Landing

Penn's Landing along the Delaware River (logically enough, marking the
spot where William Penn landed in 1682) offers more than a view of the
water. It extends from Lombard Street to Market Street, and in that stretch
there are historic vessels, works of art, places to sit and people-watch, room
to jog, the RiverRink (Philadelphia's own version of Rockefeller Plaza's outdoor ice skating rink), and large public spaces in which there is often something going on, especially in the summer—all with the stunning backdrop of
the Ben Franklin Bridge. Penn's Landing is dog-friendly, on a daily basis as
well as for most of the events held in its public spaces (exceptions, according
to the Penn's Landing Development Corporation, are fireworks events and
the Yo! Philadelphia Festival, because they are simply too crowded).

There are plans in the works to change Penn's Landing as Philadelphians
have known it. There's a hotel under construction, and a planned family
entertainment center between Market and Walnut Streets. Once construction

is finished, it remains to be seen which events will be held in which outdoor spaces and which will be dog-friendly, but no doubt there will still be plenty of old and new opportunities to enjoy Penn's Landing with your dog. Keep an eye on the Penn's Landing Development Corporation's Web site for information on the new development as time goes on: www.pennslanding corp.com.

In winter, you can take your dog to watch the action at the Blue Cross RiverRink, on Columbus Boulevard between Chestnut and Market Streets. Public skating sessions are held at various times during the week and on weekends. You and your dog can enjoy watching the skaters from the Chestnut Street Bridge. There are frequent events at the rink that are also fun to watch, including:

▶ **Ice Sculpting Festival (January).** Call 215-925-RINK for more information.
▶ **Santa Skate (December).** Santa arrives by helicopter and skates with the public.

There are vendors in the vicinity of Penn's Landing if you want to grab an easy bite to eat, or get a soda or juice or a bottle of water to enjoy with your dog. Or bring a picnic! In nice weather, there are few places in the city more pleasant to hang out than on Penn's Landing. In the daytime, you can watch tourists and regular users come and go, as well as boats on the Delaware River in summer. At night, you can watch the lights on the Ben Franklin Bridge dance when the PATCO (Port Authority Transit Company) trains go across. (The direction in which the lights dance tells you which direction the train is going, which is pretty cool.)

Penn's Landing events vary from year to year, but most are annual. For information, call 215-922-2FUN. Regular and special events include:

▶ **Bell Atlantic Jazz Festival (May).** Some events take place indoors, but at least one usually takes place on Penn's Landing (or another outdoor venue). For information on what's happening this year, visit www.jazfest.com.
▶ **Israel Independence Day Celebration (May).** Celebrate the anniversary of the founding of Israel.
▶ **Jam on the River (Late May).** This is a combination of the old Jambalaya Jam and River Blues festivals. Admission is charged.
▶ **Marine Day (May/June).** This is a free event celebrating the local maritime industry.
▶ **Poetry & Music on the Waterfront (Summer).** On Wednesday evenings, you and your dog can enjoy poetry readings and the music of a jazz ensemble.
▶ **WPEN Big Band Series (Summer).** Watch people taking the free swing dance lessons (you can take them too if your dog can dance), and enjoy the terrific live music.
▶ **Children's Special Sundays (Summer).** Magicians, animal and nature shows, crafts, jugglers, and more.
▶ **Italian National Day (June).** Come and celebrate the 1948 establishment of republican democracy in Italy.
▶ **Islamic Heritage Day (June).** Includes a bazaar, arts and crafts, and traditional foods.

▶ **Portuguese Heritage Day (June).** This event includes bands, folk performances, and food.

▶ **Irish Heritage Festival (June).** Enjoy Irish dancing, bagpiping, string bands, and cuisine.

▶ **Family Days/Ice Cream Festival (Early July)**

▶ **Lighted Boat Parade (July).** Take your dog to Penn's Landing to watch the parade sail up and down the Delaware River.

▶ **Singer/Songwriter Weekend (July).** Free concerts presented by Independence Blue Cross and WXPN. For details, call 800-565-WXPN, or visit the WXPN Web site at www.xpn.org.

▶ **Hispanic Fiesta (July).** Free music, food, dance, and crafts from Puerto Rico and parts of Latin America.

▶ **Annual KYW Craft & Fine Arts Festival (July).** Besides the arts and crafts of some 75 artists, there is music—opera, jazz, and classical. (There may be fireworks, so use caution toward dusk if your dog is sensitive.)

▶ **German Festival (August).** Free music, crafts, food, and dance.

▶ **Polish American Weekend (August).** Polka music, dancing, and more.

▶ **Festival of India (August).** Dancing, vendors, and food.

▶ **Caribbean Festival (August).** Enjoy lots of great music and food.

▶ **African American Cultural Extravaganza (August).** Children's performers, live music, dance troupes, a marketplace featuring craft and food vendors, and more.

▶ **Mexican Independence Day (September).** Enjoy the "Cry for Independence" ceremony, live music, food, entertainment, crafts, and more.

▶ **Sippin' by the River (September).** A wine- and beer-tasting festival benefiting the Crohn's and Colitis Foundation of America. You and your dog can enjoy live jazz and sample a variety of food, wines, and beers. Admission is charged.

⁂ SOUTH STREET

South Street is an experience. A weekend night might not (or then again it might) be the best time to have that experience with your dog. But South Street's combination of boutiques, bizarre stores, restaurants, and cafés makes it a really fun place to take a walk, do a little window-shopping, then find a seat at the nearest café and watch other people. People-watching is a major event on South Street.

The South Street area is defined as Front to 10th Streets and Lombard to Bainbridge Streets, although it is creeping west toward Broad Street. Your dog can sit with you at a variety of places: even the giant, muraled **McDonald's** on South Street has tables on the sidewalk. But if you and your dog are looking for a different dining experience, you may want to try:

▶ **Beau Monde, 624 South 6th Street, 215-592-0656.** Beau Monde is an "elegant crêperie." They have outdoor seating from late March to early November, and of course your dog can sit with you. They "have been known to give bowls of H₂O to thirsty dogs. . . . We think of dogs in the café as exactly the European image we'd like to have." (The folks at Beau Monde believe that some of the local galleries and antique stores will allow you to bring your dog inside, though this may depend on the size of your dog! The South Street area is definitely a place where it would be worth asking.)

▶ **Bean Café, 615 South Street, 215-629-2250.** They have a table in front where you and your dog can enjoy delicious coffees and maybe a brownie or other treat.

▶ **Jamaican Jerk Hut, 1436 South Street, 215-545-8644.** The Jamaican Jerk Hut offers Caribbean dishes. They have outdoor seating from April to September where your dog can sit with you.

▶ **MontSerrat American Bistro, 623 South Street, 215-627-4224.** An American/eclectic restaurant. Outdoor seating is available year-round, and they will provide water and doggy treats on request. "Customers have been known to buy their dogs dinner as well. Many dogs walk by [our] café—so [your] dog needs to be doggy friendly." For more information either give them a call or visit www.montserratbistro.com.

▶ **Philadelphia Java Company, 518 South 4th Street, 215-928-1811.** This is a friendly neighborhood coffee shop where you can sit outside with your dog year-round. They will offer your dog water or ice or treats, and they have raised money for Center City's Morris Animal Refuge, so they are good animal folks. The staff would like you to know that if you come with your dog, you will both "simply get the best treatment. Come and join us weekend mornings."

▶ **Rhino Café, 212 South Street, 215-923-2630.** The Rhino specializes in fresh, light salads and sandwiches, as well as coffee drinks and juices. Outdoor seating is available all year. "We provide bowls of water upon request, as well as doggy treats when available. The Rhino is an extremely dog-friendly café." (And, according to my contact at the Rhino, Blockbuster Video across the street may permit dogs inside.)

South Street is a sight to see on any day, but you and your dog may especially want to witness (or even participate in):

▶ **Mardi Gras on South Street (February).** Feel free to dress up in costume, or just watch all the people who have. Things get pretty wild as the evening goes on, so you may want to get your dog safely home before midnight or so.

▶ **Easter on South Street (March/April).** This wonderful parade welcomes both pets and people dressed in Easter finery. So get out your dog's Sunday best and go for a promenade. You (or your dog) might even win a prize. At the very least, you will have a great time.

(🐾 QUEEN VILLAGE)

Queen Village, between South Street and Washington Avenue, from Front Street to about 5th Street, started out as a Dutch and Swedish settlement, then became a workers' neighborhood. Now it's a sort of trendy riverfront district, and a pleasant place to go for a walk with your dog. There are some benches in Queen Village to rest on, and small parks at 3rd and Bainbridge Streets and at Catherine and Queen Streets.

Queen Village also has one very famous historic site you can enjoy with your dog:

▶ **Gloria Dei (Old Swedes') Church, Columbus Boulevard and Christian Street.** This is the second-oldest Swedish church in the country, built around 1700. It still has an active congregation. It is a National Historic Site, and a National Park Site, which means you can take your dog onto the (outdoor) premises.

🐾 BELLA VISTA

Bella Vista is the area to the immediate west of Queen Village, and includes the Italian Market, on 9th Street between Christian and Dickinson Streets. Are you and your dog hungry? Feel like shopping? The Italian Market can accommodate both of those desires. It is a large, old-fashioned street market, offering all kinds of food as well as dry goods. There are shops and boutiques, with vendor tables set out front from Wednesday to Sunday. I don't know how easy it is to take a dog through on a busy day, but it's on a public sidewalk, so you can try if you want to. Stop by:

▶ **D'Angelo Bros., 909 South 9th Street, 215-923-5637.** They've been sausage makers for years, but now they have started a sideline: special meat blends for dogs. Lamb and rice, beef, venison—see what they've got for your dog to try.
▶ **Renzulli's, 922 South 9th Street, 215-629-1704.** They offer hot dogs, ice cream, water ice, and funnel cake, right in the heart of the market, and there are tables in front of their store from April to October, weather permitting, where you can sit with your dog. They will give your dog water on request.

Although Bella Vista is a less trendy neighborhood than Queen Village, it holds a couple of great festivals:

▶ **Welcome to Bella Vista (July).** The Bella Vista Arts Faire and Cookout is part of the city-wide "Welcome America!" celebration.
▶ **Cianfrani Park Fall Festival (September).** Held in **Cianfrani Park, 8th and Fitzwater Streets,** this annual event includes a flea market, raffles for prizes from the Italian Market and South Street businesses, food, live entertainment, and more. Your dog on-leash is free to enjoy it with you.

🐾 POINTS FURTHER SOUTH

South of South Street, there are a few major themes: Passyunk Avenue, Mummers, and sports. Why not start with East Passyunk Avenue, the linear heart of South Philly? There's lots of takeout food available here, and a few places to stop and eat it. If you want to try one of those world-famous Philly cheesesteaks, this is where you get it. You and your dog just have to choose which place: Pat's or Geno's.

▶ **Pat's King of Steaks, 1237 East Passyunk Avenue, 215-468-1546.** Along with cheese-steaks of all varieties, Pat's serves all kinds of other fast food. Outdoor seating (or standing) is available all year, and you can bring your dog. If you ask for water for your dog, "We will fill up a bowl. We are dog-friendly."

▶ **Geno's, 1219 South 9th Street, 215-389-0659**, is diagonally across from Pat's. I must say I don't have the official word on whether Geno's is dog-friendly, but Geno's and Pat's are fierce competitors, rumor has it, so you can always give it a try.

If your dog wants to do some shopping, he or she can do it at:

▶ **Paws & Claws Pet Shoppe, 1834–36 East Passyunk Avenue, 215-463-1999.** You can bring your dog on-leash inside here and the staff will provide treats and a happy greeting. They do their best to make both owners and pups happy. In December they have pictures with Santa for your dog.

You and your dog might want to come back to the area for:

▶ **Holiday Shopping on East Passyunk Avenue (Saturdays in December).** Santa is on hand, and the avenue's 165 unique shops, from clothes to shoes to jewelry to gifts, offer great holiday window-shopping. For more information, call 215-468-7710.

How about some Mummers? You and your dog should stop by:

▶ **The Mummers Museum, 1100 South 2nd Street** (that's "Two Street" to area natives) **at Washington Avenue, 215-336-3050.** The Mummers Museum opened in 1976. No, you can't take your dog inside, but the architecture is pretty interesting. And if it's summer, and Tuesday, stick around for:

   String Band Music Under the Stars (May to September, weather permitting). Takes place behind the Mummers Museum. You and your dog can experience an old-fashioned block party atmosphere, South Philly–style.

Down where sports is the theme, across from the complex where the Flyers, Sixers, Phillies (at the moment, anyway), and Eagles play, you and your dog can get sportive in this fabulous park:

▶ **Franklin Delano Roosevelt Park, Pattison Avenue and South Broad Street.** The 330 acres here hosted the American Sesquicentennial in 1926. As a result, there are some absolutely beautiful structures, and a lovely man-made lake. There's lots of space to walk or run with your dog, and the two of you will have a great time here. Near the park you will also find:

▶ **The American Swedish Historical Museum, 1900 Pattison Avenue, 215-389-1776.** When the museum's gates are open, you can explore the grounds with your dog. The land the museum stands on was given to Swedish settlers in 1653, and the building housing the museum was designed in the Swedish Manor House style. The museum holds some outdoor activities in warm weather, mostly on the museum grounds, but sometimes in the park; either way, your dog on-leash can come with you to enjoy events such as:

   Midsommarfest (June). Enjoy music, food, games, folk dance performances, and the traditional dance around the midsommarpole. Admission is charged.

   Viking Encampment (September). Viking reenactors set up an encampment on the museum's grounds and demonstrate sword battles, cooking, shipbuilding, and more, dispelling myths and providing great fun! The link between Vikings and this continent?

There's evidence that a group of Vikings landed off the coast of Newfoundland, Canada, in about 1000 A.D. (In fact, *their* dogs may have had something to do with the breeding of *my* dog Georgie.) Admission is charged.

Also held in Franklin Delano Roosevelt Park is:

▶ **The ALPO Canine Frisbee Disc Championships (June).** One of eight qualifying events across the country over the summer. There is a limit of 50 dog/owner teams for participation in the event, but no limit on spectators, whether human or canine. These are the Northeast regional finals: the two finalists will go on to compete in Washington, D.C., in September. Admission is free. For additional information, call 888-444-2576, or visit www.friskies.com.

And there's another point south you will definitely want to take your dog to visit:

▶ **Fort Mifflin on the Delaware, Fort Mifflin Road, 215-492-3395.** This fort was used during both the Revolutionary War (for defense) and the Civil War (as a prison). It is open from April 1 to November 30, Wednesday through Sunday, 10:00 a.m. to 4:00 p.m. Admission is charged, but they are very dog-friendly here. You can bring your dog onto the premises, and wander anywhere but inside the buildings; you can join outside tours as well. It's a very interesting site, with parade grounds, walls, bastions, batteries, and a moat.

   Events at Fort Mifflin change from year to year, but here's a sampling of some that have been held in the past:

   Freedom Blast (July).   Part of the "Welcome America!" celebration. Relive Revolutionary War land and sea battles, and enjoy colonial crafts and games, food, and music. (Note: The battles involve some loud noises, so you might want to keep your dog at a distance, or even take him or her home before they begin.)

   Civil War Garrison Days (October).   A living history event that includes women's programs, artillery and weapons demonstrations, and more.

   The Battle for Fort Mifflin (November).   This annual weekend event commemorates the 1777 Battle for Fort Mifflin, of course. Again, there will be firing of guns, so use your knowledge of your dog to decide whether to attend.

You and your dog will absolutely love a trip to:

▶ **The John Heinz National Wildlife Refuge at Tinicum, 86th Street and Lindbergh Boulevard, 215-365-3118.** *Tinicum* is an Algonquin word meaning "islands of the marsh." The John Heinz site is a 1,200-acre U.S. Fish and Wildlife Refuge area and the largest remaining freshwater tidal marsh in Pennsylvania. There are 10 miles of trails, boardwalks, and observation blinds winding through marshes, ponds, and woodlands, and along the Darby Creek. The refuge is open daily from 8:00 a.m. to sunset, and you and your dog on-leash can enjoy it together. There is no admission charge. An especially great time to go is late August to mid-October, when Baltimore orioles and other songbirds are moving south.

Deep south in Philly is where you will find a concentration of dog-friendly hotels, clustered near the Philadelphia International Airport. Although some of the hotels may not be strictly within Philadelphia proper, they include:

▶ **Airport Ramada Inn, 76 Industrial Highway, 610-521-9600.** Small pets can stay for free as long as they are in a crate when in the room. There are grounds where you can walk your small pet.

▶ **Comfort Inn Philadelphia Airport, 53 Industrial Highway, 610-521-9800.** Pets under 25 pounds can stay here for $10 a night. There are grounds for walking your small dog.

▶ **Motel 6, 43 Industrial Highway, 610-521-6650.** There are no restrictions here, and no extra charges. Your dog is welcome.

▶ **Philadelphia Airport Marriott, 8950 Essington Avenue, 215-492-9000.** Boasts 419 rooms and three diamonds from AAA. Pets can stay for a $100 fee. Call for more information.

▶ **Philadelphia Airport Residence Inn, 4630 Island Avenue, 215-492-1611.** Has 102 rooms in two stories, and three diamonds from AAA. Pets can stay: there's a $100 fee but no size restrictions, and they have decent grounds to walk your dog. Call for more information.

▶ **Red Roof Inn, I-95 and PA Route 420, 610-521-5090.** Pets can stay for no extra fee, there are no restrictions, and there are grounds on which to walk your dog.

😺 WEST FAIRMOUNT PARK

West Fairmount Park offers two major areas for doggish activities. Both can give your dog a healthy amount of exercise, and will be a lot of fun for both of you. The first area is West River Drive, which is closed to traffic from April to October on Saturdays and Sundays from 7:00 a.m. to 5:00 p.m. This car-free walking or jogging experience along the west side of the Schuylkill offers wonderful views of Boathouse Row, the waterworks, and Philadelphia's skyline.

The second area in West Fairmount Park that you and your dog will want to check out includes the acres and acres of grassy fields surrounding mansions and leftover 1876 Centennial Exhibition structures. You have to drive to get to them, but once you're there, you can enjoy historic structures, lovely works of art, and wide-open spaces to romp in with your dog. West Fairmount Park has about 1,200 acres in all.

Make sure you don't miss:

▶ **The Horticulture Center, Belmont Avenue and Montgomery Drive.** Ordinarily, dogs on-leash are not allowed at the Horticulture Center. However, in October 1999, they had a **"Bark-a-thon"** to raise funds for the Japanese House's new roof (made of *bark*, of course): the mayor's dog and a whole bunch of other dogs walked a 5K course. The event was so successful, they decided to repeat it to raise maintenance monies. This is your chance to enjoy the Horticulture Center with your dog—it comes only once a year, so take advantage of it! Call 215-878-5097 for the date and details.

There are plenty of events in West Fairmount Park you and your dog can watch or even participate in:

▶ **Annual Inglis 5-Mile Race (April).** The race benefits Inglis House, which provides long-term care for disabled adults. Call 215-581-0703 for details.

▶ **Annual Clean Air Council 5K Run for Clean Air (April).** For more information, visit www.libertynet.org/cleanair.
▶ **ALPO Frisbee Disc Competitions Philadelphia Community Finals (May).** Held in the field in front of Fairmount Park's Memorial Hall. You can enter up to two dogs in the competition, or just go and watch.
▶ **Annual 10K and 2-Mile Run (May).** Sponsored by the Philadelphia Bar Association. For information, call 215-567-2010, or check the association's Web site at www.philabar.org.
▶ **Annual Race for Recovery (June).** Sponsored by the Wellness Community of Philadelphia. Celebrates National Cancer Survivorship Day. For information, call 215-879-7733, or 888-819-3553.
▶ **Annual Rec Day (June).** Held at the Carousel House, North Concord Drive and Belmont Avenue. This free exposition lets disabled persons have some fun and participate in sports. There's also a free picnic and entertainment.
▶ **Work to Ride Celebrity Polo Match (June).** Benefits a nonprofit, community-based program for underprivileged youth centered on horses and riding. Call 215-877-4419 for details.
▶ **You've Gotta Have Guts Race (October).** A 5K run or walk to benefit the Philadelphia/ Delaware Valley chapter of the Crohn's and Colitis Foundation of America. For information, call 215-396-9100.

❖ UNIVERSITY CITY

University City is bounded by the Schuylkill River, Spring Garden Street as far west as 44th Street, south to Market Street, west to 52nd Street, south to the SEPTA High Speed Line at Florence Avenue, and from there southeast to the Schuylkill River again. It's a diverse area full of history, and has a lot to offer dog owners and dogs ready for some walking and sightseeing.

University of Pennsylvania and Environs

The University of Pennsylvania includes 262 acres bounded by Chestnut and Pine Streets, and 32nd and 40th Streets. It is a wonderful place to visit with your dog. There are lots of places to sit and rest, and a lot to see. Your dog will practically sing as you explore: "Oh, walk, and walk, and walk some more! That's what I have these four legs for!"

The core of the University of Pennsylvania campus is a National Historic District, bounded by Hamilton Walk, South Street, 32nd Street, Walnut Street, 36th Street, Spruce Street, and 30th Street. There are things to see everywhere on campus. Look for the following highlights:

▶ **Locust Walk.** One of the famous outdoor corridors on Penn's campus. Along it you can see many interesting buildings and sculptures.
▶ **Blanche Levy Park.** This is in the heart of Penn's campus, and in and around Blanche Levy Park you and your dog should look for some great outdoor sculpture.

- **The Quadrangle, 3700 Spruce Street.** The buildings here were designed by the firm of Cope and Stewardson, built between 1895 and 1954, and completed by the Speakman dormitories between the Triangle and Big Quad.
- **Smith Walk.** Another outdoor corridor, where you and your dog can admire Hayden Hall, 3320 Smith Walk, built in 1896 and part of the University City Historic District; Bennett Hall, 3340 Walnut Street, the first hall built for women on campus (in 1924) and part of the University City Historic District; and *War Memorial Flagpole*, 33rd Street at Smith Walk, with bronze sculpture around the base, and steps that are a nice place to stop and rest.
- **Hamilton Walk.** Yet another historic outdoor corridor along which you and your dog can see the Botanical Gardens, in the midst of several buildings.

Elsewhere on Penn's campus, there are some other notable stops:

- **Annenberg Center, 3680 Walnut Street.** The center isn't beautiful, but it has a nice outdoor space with places to sit and rest.
- **Sansom Row, Sansom Street between 34th and 36th Streets.** Within the row are many places with outdoor tables, including:
- **The White Dog Café, 3420 Sansom Street, 215-386-9224.** Featuring contemporary American cuisine, and American wines and beers. You can bring your dog on-leash to sit outside here, and outdoor seating is available from April to October. If you'd like to know why it is called the White Dog: In 1875, Madame Helena P. Blavatsky, a teacher, spiritualist, and eccentric, lived in the building. While ill with an infected leg, she had a transformative experience of some kind that led her to found the Theosophical Society, an organization for the promotion of brotherhood and the freedom of individual search and belief. She then dismissed her doctors and had a white dog sleep across her leg at night, which allegedly cured her. The café has a gift store next door (The Black Cat) that sells bowls and other doggy items, along with handcrafted wares: you can visit the shop online at www.blackcatshop.com.

    The White Dog Café throws some cool summer block parties you and your dog might want to watch or attend:

    White Dog Café's Annual Liberty and Justice for All Ball (July). Enjoy an American heritage buffet dinner under a tent top, accompanied by Dixieland jazz. The entertainment after dinner includes a skit titled "The Birth of a Nation," which I've heard involves a pregnant woman and tap-dancing twins named Liberty and Justice.

    Café Chien Blanc's Annual Bastille Day Street Party (July 14). A Parisian accordionist strolls among guests enjoying a French dinner under a tent top. After dinner, everyone sings "La Marseillaise" and lights sparklers, which is followed by the storming of the Bastille to free imprisoned French poodles (white, of course!) by revolutionaries who then perform the can-can. After 10:00 p.m., you can dance to American and French songs spun by a deejay.

    El Perro Blanco's Annual Noche Latina Block Party (July). Come for a Latin American buffet under the tent top, and dancing to live Latin music under the stars.

    White Dog Café's Annual Rum & Reggae Caribbean Street Party (August). There's a Caribbean buffet dinner under the tent-top with exotic rum drinks. A reggae band will play, and there will be dancing in the street after 9:30 p.m.

- **Sansom Common.** This is a new retail center at 36th and Walnut Streets, and includes Barnes & Noble, Urban Outfitters, xando Coffee & Bar, and other shops. There are lots of tables on both sides of the street where you and your dog can sit together. Penn is in the process of constructing other pedestrian-friendly areas as well: the Sundance Theater complex at 40th and Walnut Streets in Hamilton Square is planned to have a small street plaza, including a café and garden.

Other places of note:

▶ **The Old Veterinary Hospital, Old Quadrangle, 3800 Spruce Street,** built in 1904.

▶ **The Veterinary Hospital of the University of Pennsylvania, 3900 Delancey Street.** A wonderful place, not so much for the architecture, but for what they do there. I saw an electrocardiogram of Georgie's heart there, and it was an amazing sight. Her heart was in good shape, too, which was very nice to know. At the 39th Street entrance to the hospital, there is an interesting painted steel piece called *Life Savers*, by Billie Lawless.

(Drexel University)

Drexel University, centered around 32nd and Chestnut Streets (where the original building stands), is the second university of University City. There are interesting buildings here, including the Abbotts Building, on Chestnut Street just east of 31st Street, and the Centennial National Bank, built in 1876 (of course), a beautiful Frank Furness building at the corner of 32nd and Market Streets.

(❖ WEST PHILADELPHIA)

Before the universities grew, West Philadelphia had a history all its own, and vestiges—actually, much more than just vestiges—remain. There are several National Historic Districts in West Philadelphia, full of housing stock you can't find anywhere else in the city. For detailed information on the districts, contact the University City Historical Society, 40th Street and Woodland Avenue, 215-387-3019, or visit their Web site at www.liberty net.org/uchs—a wonderful site with terrific information.

Of course, your dog's favorite place in West Philadelphia, outside of University City, will be:

▶ **Clark Park, bounded by 43rd and 45th Streets, and Baltimore and Woodland Avenues.** Open all hours, with benches, tables, and 9 acres of trees, grass, and paths. There's a life-size statue of Charles Dickens here with Little Nell, a character from *The Old Curiosity Shop*. There are also phones, lights, water, and trash cans. In the upper part of the park there's a Gettysburg Stone, and a Veterans Day ceremony traditionally is held there. The park is not fenced, but a lot of people bring their dogs here to play. And they have fairly frequent events at which your dog on-leash is welcome:

Clark Park Music & Arts Festival (June). This is a summer solstice festival featuring local music, puppet theater, craftspeople and vendors, and more.

Clark Park Harvest Festival (September). Lots of music, food, and craft vendors, and lots of free kids' entertainment. If you'd like more information, call 215-382-0461, or send e-mail to clarkparkfest@email.com.

Clark Park Bark in the Park (October). Sponsored by the Friends of Clark Park, this is for dogs, their human guardians, and anyone who loves dogs. There will be contests, information on care and training, and raffles.

Bartram's Gardens

You and your dog have got to make a trip here. Located at 54th Street and Lindbergh Boulevard, these are the oldest surviving botanical gardens in the U.S. Established in 1728, the 44-acre park has remained virtually unchanged for two centuries. It is a National Historic Landmark, and attracts garden enthusiasts from around the world. The grounds are open from dawn to dusk, all year, they are free, and your dog can come with you to see them: just be careful in the historic areas. May and June are good months to go to see the azaleas and rhododendrons blooming.

Various events held at Bartram's Gardens that you and your dog might want to come back for include the **Schuylkill River Festival (June), Bartram's Fall Festival (October)**, and the **Holiday Greens Sale (December)**. For information, call 215-729-5281.

You and your dog can stay in the area at:

▶ **Korman Suites at International City the Mews and Chalets, 8400 Lindbergh Boulevard, 215-365-3100.** See full description on page 24.

Philadelphia on the Edge

Other points west that you and your dog may want to visit include:

▶ **Cobbs Creek Park, along the Cobbs Creek, partially bounded by the Cobbs Creek Parkway.** Managed by the Fairmount Park Commission. There's more park across the creek, in Delaware County.

▶ **St. Joseph's University, 5600 City Avenue, 215-660-1000.** Founded by Jesuits in 1851, this is a very open campus, with some great architecture, and you are welcome to join others walking their dogs as you sightsee.

If your dog needs to do some shopping, you can go to:

▶ **PETCO, 4508 City Avenue, 215-878-3203.** All the items you would expect from this one-stop pet supply emporium.

🐾 NORTHEAST PHILADELPHIA

One thing that the Northeast has in abundance is fantastic parks. Some of these include:

▶ **Hunting Park, Logan.** Located between Wingohocking and Lycoming Streets, and Old York Road and Darien Street. Very pretty.

▶ **Tacony Creek Park, Olney.** This park follows the Tacony Creek to the Frankford Creek and is crossed by Rising Sun Avenue. It is a beautiful park in a diverse area.

▶ **Eden Hall (Fluehr) Park, Torresdale.** Grant Avenue, I-95, and Convent Lane bound it; the entrance is off Grant Avenue. This is a 61-acre community park that used to be part of a country estate, and then was a convent and school. A Gothic Revival chapel, built in 1852, remains. There is also an ice house that was built in the late 1700s.

▶ **Burholme Park, Fox Chase.** Located along Cottman Avenue, between Fillmore Street and Central Avenue, this is a particularly wonderful site. There are 70 acres surrounding the Ryerss Library and Museum, an Italianate 1859 mansion with an absolutely gorgeous widow's peak with stained glass windows: on a sunny morning, they are amazing. There's a pet cemetery with headstones on the west side of the mansion under a tree, so you know you are on property that was once inhabited by animal lovers. The estate was ultimately turned over to the city and opened in 1910 by the Fairmount Park Commission. Dogs on-leash are permitted, and lots of dogs use this park. The mansion sits on a hill, providing some great views. There are lots of benches to rest on here, and plenty of parking. This is definitely a favorite of my entire family, human and canine.

▶ **Pennypack Creek Park.** Verree and Pine Roads cross the park, and Bloomfield Avenue bounds the northwestern portion. Operated by the Fairmount Park Commission, the park covers 1,334 acres, and encloses the Pennypack Creek, which runs for 22 miles down to the Delaware River. There are trails for hiking, jogging, and horseback riding, and people also fish, swim, and canoe here. There are areas for more active recreation, and picnic areas with barbecue pits. As in other places, people do take their dogs off-leash to swim in a shallow place in the creek, but technically, dogs should be on-leash. There are the usual park benches, parking areas, phones, water, and trash cans.

▶ **Benjamin Rush State Park.** Located along Roosevelt Boulevard, at Southampton Road, this is the only state park within Philadelphia proper. Although it is mostly undeveloped, with a mixture of open fields and woodlots, the park contains the world's largest community gardens, as well as hiking trails, a model airplane field, and soccer fields. Pets on-leash are welcome.

▶ **Glen Foerd, 5001 Grant Avenue, 215-638-7003.** This is a waterfront estate with 18 acres of exotic trees, a lily pond, and riverfront oaks that are over 300 years old. There is also a statue, thought to be of the family dog, near the dog's tombstone, which has a very loving inscription. The mansion here is gorgeous, originally built in 1850, and added to in the Edwardian style in 1902–03. Your dog on-leash is welcome to walk around the grounds with you as long as you clean up, and the grounds are open from dawn to dusk, except when the mansion has been rented for private affairs (Friday evening, Saturday, or Sunday). There are some events here at which dogs on-leash are welcome, including:

Summer Concerts. Bring a blanket or lawn chair and your dog and listen to the music along the river. The concerts are free, but donations are appreciated.

Glen Foerd Regatta (June). The Racing Fleet of the Delaware River Yacht Club opens this regatta. This is a ticketed event at Glen Foerd, but you might be able to watch from somewhere nearby as well.

Annual Old-Fashioned Country Fair (September). Admission is charged. Call 215-632-5330 for more information.

There are pet supply stores that will allow you to shop with your dog in Northeast Philadelphia:

▶ **PETCO, 4333 Roosevelt Boulevard, 215-535-9132,** and **3595 Aramingo Avenue, 215-535-9847**
▶ **PetsMart, 4640 Roosevelt Boulevard, 215-743-9602.** In December, this store offers to take photos of your pet posing with Santa, and gives you two, including one in a snowflake ornament.

When your dog has finished shopping, you both need to go to:

▶ **Blue Ox Brauhaus Restaurant, 7980 Oxford Avenue, Fox Chase, 215-728-9440.** The Blue Ox has been in business for over 25 years, and is a family-owned German restaurant. They have outdoor seating from May to the end of September or the beginning of October. They love dogs (owner Walter Grund has an Akita named Wolfgang). They will offer your dog ice water, and a marrow/rib bone if your dog is large. On Tuesdays, they have live blues music in the outdoor café.

There are also a few doggish events in the Northeast you might want to check out:

▶ **Canine Companions for Independence, CCI Awareness Day (May).** CCI's open house, featuring puppy demonstrations. You can't take your dog, but you might learn of ways you can help out CCI. They are always looking for puppy-raisers. Also keep an eye out for their fundraising pet photo events—"Bunny Paws" in the spring, and "Santa Paws" in December, usually at a PETCO or PetsMart store. They have held these events in Warminster, Pennsylvania, as well as in Pennsauken, New Jersey. They also raise funds through the **Philadelphia Area Champions Dog Walk-a-thon.** For more information, call 215-602-2093, or visit www.libertynet.org/cci.
▶ **Richmond Street "Olde Village" International Festival (October).** Held in the 2900 and 3000 blocks of Richmond Street (just south of Allegheny Avenue). You and your dog on-leash can enjoy music, food, and entertainment of all kinds.
▶ **Hero Scholarship Fund Show and Carnival (November).** This is an arena show put on by the Philadelphia Police and Fire Departments. The show features the motorcycle drill team, performances by the police horses, and demonstrations by the K-9 Corps. You can't bring your dog, but you might want to come anyway, and see what the K-9 Corps can do. Not to mention that it's a worthy cause.
▶ **Dog Lover's Holiday Bazaar (November).** Held in the Pennsylvania Army National Guard Armory at 2700 Southampton Road (Roosevelt Boulevard and Southampton Road). You can have your dog's picture taken with Santa here (call to make a reservation), but the highlight of the bazaar is the 50 to 60 vendors offering breed novelty items, dog supplies, and gifts for dog lovers. Canine rescue groups attend, and there is a timed obedience match on Saturday, as well as other regularly scheduled events in a center ring. On Sunday, by appointment, you can have your dog take the Canine Good Citizen test and/or the Therapy Dog International test. Donations requested at the door benefit the Women's Humane Society Building Fund. You can bring your dog to the entire event, as long as you also bring a way to clean up

after him or her. The Dog Lover's Holiday Bazaar is put on by the Greater Philadelphia Dog Fanciers Association, Inc. For more information, call 215-338-6870.

You and your dog can stay overnight in the Northeast at a variety of **Korman Suites**. See full description on page 24. Locations include:

Apartment Center E, 6242 Roosevelt Boulevard, 215-289-1100
Rushwood, 10825 East Keswick Road, 215-632-5858
International City Townhouse, 8201 Bustleton Avenue, 215-365-2500
Winchester, 2600 Welsh Road, 215-969-7330
4901 Oxford Avenue, 215-533-6567
Caster Gardens, 5051 Oxford Avenue, 215-289-1100

Finally, it is possible to take some walking tours of Northeast neighborhoods. The Foundation for Architecture leads two tours through Frankford: "18th-Century Frankford" and "Victorian Frankford." They also lead a tour through Tacony emphasizing the late 1800s. Contact the Foundation for Architecture for more information at 215-569-3187. Your dog on-leash can take the tours with you as long as they are outdoors only.

Montgomery County

Montgomery County in general is extremely dog-friendly. From the Main Line to the more rural outreaches, the number of fast food restaurant drive-throughs that will give you "something for the dog," bank drive-up windows that keep doggy treats just in case you have a dog in the car, and shop owners who may invite you and your canine companion inside will surprise you. It constantly surprises me. And virtually every town and borough and local community in the county puts on some terrific parades and festivals that you and your dog can enjoy together, as spectators or as participants.

❧ EASTERN MONTGOMERY COUNTY

The first thing you and your dog need to know about the eastern portion of Montgomery County is that the same trail that leads along the Schuylkill in Philadelphia County extends over 11 miles through Montgomery County. The **Schuylkill River Trail** is planned to extend for 25 miles eventually, but for now, you can go from the Philadelphia Museum of Art to Valley Forge National Historical Park, passing through a bunch of places along the way. Restrooms, drinking fountains, picnic tables, and 911 phones are available along the trail in Montgomery County near Valley Forge National Historical Park, Norristown Farm County Park, Norristown's Riverfront Park, Bridgeport, and Conshohocken's Spring Mill Park. Dogs are permitted on the trail on leashes not exceeding 6 feet, they must be attended to at all times, and, of course, you must clean up after your dog. For more information on the Schuylkill River Trail, contact the Pennsylvania Department of Conservation and Natural Resources (DCNR) at 888-PA-PARKS or visit www.dcnr.state.pa.us.

☙ NORTHEASTERN MONTGOMERY COUNTY

Jenkintown Borough

Although as a borough it dates only to 1874, as a village Jenkintown was already established by 1759. In the era of stagecoaches, it was a stopping place for lines traveling between Philadelphia and New York. Today, Jenkintown retains a comfortable, hospitable feel, and you and your dog can do some great window-shopping here along Old York Road and West Avenue, perusing antiques, art, gifts, jewelry, and more. There are places along the way to get takeout food, and there are benches along Old York Road where you can sit with your dog and enjoy your bite to eat or some coffee. Or you and your dog can grab a bite together at:

▶ **Fill A Bagel, 424 Old York Road, 215-887-8577.** If you sit outside here, your dog can sit with you, and outdoor seating is available as long as the weather permits. They will give your dog water on request—they even keep a bowl of water available for passing dogs.

While you're hanging around Old York Road, your dog can go shopping at:

▶ **Pet Valu, The Shops at the Pavilion, 323 Old York Road, 215-572-6349**

There are some annual Jenkintown events that you might want to attend with your dog. Keep your eye on the local papers for the **Jenkintown Memorial Day Parade (May)**, the **Jenkintown Fourth of July Parade**, and **Santa Claus Night (December)**.

There's only one thing missing in Jenkintown—a nice, doggish park. And Abington Township, which surrounds Jenkintown Borough, unfortunately does *not* permit dogs in *any* of its parks. But have no fear! There's a Montgomery County park along the eastern edge of Abington Township, where your dog on-leash is welcome:

▶ **Lorimer County Park.** Located on Moredon Road near Huntingdon Pike, Lorimer Park contains over 230 acres of woods and meadows, along with impressive rock outcroppings, including famous Council Rock. You can hike, picnic, or cross-country ski here with your dog. There are 6 miles of hiking trails, as well as bridle trails. The park's land was bequeathed to the county in 1938 by George Horace Lorimer, once the editor of the *Saturday Evening Post*, and there are some tremendous trees here, as well as a portion of the Pennypack Creek and some smaller streams. Park facilities include picnic tables, grills, a multipurpose field, and modern restrooms. The park is open from 8:00 a.m. to sunset. If you want to extend your hike, cross the border into Philadelphia's Pennypack Creek Park (see "Northeast Philadelphia" for more information).

Rockledge Borough

While you're in the area, you and your dog might want to check out Rockledge Borough. This little town has some great historic sites packed into a small area. You'll definitely want to take your dog to see:

▶ **Hollywood.** Centered around the intersection of Cedar and Fox Chase Roads, Hollywood is a neat little enclave of adobe-style homes emulating early-20th-century California houses.

Glenside

Glenside is a special area within Abington Township (though parts of it seem to sprawl into Cheltenham Township) that has quite a bit to offer dogs and their owners. Centered on Keswick Avenue and Easton Road is Keswick Village, a cluster of shops, trees, street lamps, and brick sidewalks that make for a very nice area to walk around. There is plenty of great window-shopping here: antiques, jewelry, boutique items, gifts, and more.

You and your dog will find plenty of places to get takeout coffee, bakery items, pizza, and deli foods in Glenside. If all else fails, you can always get something at:

▶ **Rita's Water Ice, 520 North Easton Road.** There's no outside seating here, but they are dog-friendly, and will grant any requests you may have on behalf of your dog.

There are some great, dog-friendly events in Glenside you and your canine pal may want to return for:

▶ **GYAC Day Parade and Special Keswick Village Sale Day (April).** The Golden Dog-Friendly Rule is that if it's outside and on public property, you and your dog can enjoy it together.
▶ **Glenside Fourth of July Parade.** A nice, small-town, patriotic display you and your dog can enjoy watching together.
▶ **Glenside Annual Car Show (August).** A very big show—hot rods, classic autos, trucks, and motorcycles, with food, amusements, bands, and a deejay. Admission is free. For information, call 215-887-9084. Dogs on-leash are permitted.

Cheltenham Township

One highlight of Cheltenham Township is its lovely, well-maintained parks. According to the township code, your dog on-leash can go into any of the following parks (some of the best for canines and their owners), whether you're a Cheltenham resident or not:

▶ **Coventry Park, New Second Street and Coventry Avenue, Melrose Park.** There are about 2 3/4 acres of open space and natural area here.
▶ **High School Park, High School Road and Montgomery Avenue, Elkins Park.** This is a 7-acre, passive-recreation area.
▶ **Grove Park, Lynnwood Avenue near Cherry Lane, Glenside.** Almost 3 acres of passive-recreation and open-space areas.
▶ **Ralph Morgan Park, Glenside Avenue near the Jenkintown Train Station.** This park has 5 1/2 acres of passive-recreation areas, open space, and a natural area.
▶ **Robinson Park, Greenwood Avenue and North Bent Road, Wyncote.** This is a 4-acre park that includes a pond, a fountain, and a passive-recreation area.

▶ **Parkview Road Park, Parkview Road, Cheltenham.** Open space and natural areas total-ing over 13 acres.

▶ **Tookany Creek Park, Tookany Creek Parkway, Cheltenham.** One of the best area parks, with a passive-recreation area, natural areas, jogging trails, and more. Kleinheinz Pond, near Tookany Creek Parkway east of Beryl Road, is kept stocked for fishing, and there is parking and a fountain there. During the spring and fall, on five Sundays, Tookany Creek Parkway is closed to traffic to allow walkers, joggers, cyclists, and in-line skaters to use the parkway between 1:00 p.m. and 4:00 p.m.

▶ **Edward Hicks Parry Bird Sanctuary, Chelten Hills Drive, Elkins Park.** Almost 13 acres of open space and natural areas dedicated to providing a habitat for birds. You are permitted to bring your dog into the sanctuary, as long as you use a leash.

▶ **George A. Perley Bird Sanctuary, Glenside Avenue and Rices Mill Road, Glenside.** Open space and natural areas totaling over 8 acres. The same rules regarding dogs apply as for the Edward Hicks Parry Bird Sanctuary.

And if you are a Cheltenham resident, you and your dog can also make use of these cool places:

▶ **Curtis Arboretum, Church Road near Greenwood Avenue, Wyncote.** This property is the former estate of Cyrus H. K. Curtis, the famous Philadelphia publisher. There are over 45 acres to explore here, including two ponds and an arbor. There is also a stone memorial and a tree grove, which were established to honor Cheltenham residents who died in World War II. Curtis Hall, on the arboretum property, is lovely. You can come to **summer concerts** in the arboretum, and to a **harvest festival** in October.

▶ **Rock Lane Park, Rock Lane, Elkins Park.** Almost 2 acres of passive-recreation areas, open space, and natural areas.

There are a couple of annual events that take place in Cheltenham parks you might want to keep in mind when looking for entertainment for yourself and your dog:

▶ **Annual Kite Flying Contest, Curtis Arboretum (Spring).** You and your dog will have a great time watching area kids trying to get their kites up and up and up.

▶ **Kleinheinz Pond Fishing Derby, Tookany Park (Spring).** Over 200 area children partici-pate. Go and watch—you'll have a blast, and your dog always likes going to the park.

Hatboro Borough

Hatboro Borough, all 1.2 square miles of it, is both historic and fun, with about 60 shops and almost 20 restaurants and pubs in the central business district. Hatboro has been getting a facelift through the "Main Street Hat-boro" program, which began in 1995, adding Victorian streetlights, brick pavers, and plantings to York Road, Hatboro's main street. The borough is also extremely dog-friendly. There are benches to sit on here, and places to pick up a bite to eat or some coffee. Hatboro is really sprucing up, and a stroll up York Road will also afford you a small walking tour of historic buildings, such as the Old Mill Inn, Union Library, and the Nathaniel Boileau House.

If you and your dog are in need of a park, here are a couple your dog will like best:

▶ **Eaton Park, West Moreland Avenue.** The park has a pedestrian trail and a picnic pavilion.

▶ **Memorial Park, also on West Moreland Avenue.** There's a picnic area in this park.

And there are dog-friendly events galore in Hatboro!

▶ **Easter Egg Hunt (March/April).** You and your dog will have a blast watching, if the two of you are anything like me and my dogs.

▶ **Hatboro's "Summer Fun" Sidewalk Sale (July).** Stroll the York Road Business District, and enjoy the entertainment, food, and shopping.

▶ **Moonlight Memories Car Show (July).** This is one of the biggest outdoor car shows in the region: 500 classic cars and street rods, along with a food court and oldies music. It's free, but it will be crowded, so keep that in mind when deciding whether it's something your dog is up for.

▶ **Dog Days of Summer Dog Show (August).** One of the reasons we love Hatboro. Sponsored by the Greater Hatboro Chamber of Commerce, this is a wonderful opportunity to show off your dog and enjoy dog-related activities.

▶ **Annual Hatboro Arts Festival (September).** There's a juried art show, live music, theater and dance performances, and great food and drinks available.

▶ **Hatboro Halloween Stroll (October).** Dress up your dog and come out to watch!

▶ **Annual Holiday Parade (End of November).** This parade keeps growing and growing. There's always a theme, and there are floats, bands, fire trucks, and more to welcome Santa Claus to town.

▶ **Annual Christmas Tree Lighting (December).** Held at the Union Library of Hatboro. It's free, so grab your dog and an ornament for the tree and enjoy!

▶ **The Holiday Stroll (December).** Santa Claus is on hand to get shoppers in the holiday spirit, and there are drawings for prizes offered by merchants.

If you want to, you and your dog can even stay overnight in Hatboro:

▶ **Homestead Village, 537 Dresher Road, 215-956-9966.** Your dog is welcome on the lower floor, for a $100 nonrefundable fee. They have grounds where you can walk your dog.

Huntingdon Valley

Your dog will absolutely want to be taken to:

▶ **Ruck/Pennypack Preserve, 2955 Edge Hill Road, 215-657-0830.** Headquarters of the Pennypack Ecological Restoration Trust, the preserve includes acres owned by the Natural Lands Trust. Restrooms are available at the Pennypack Trust headquarters, and there is parking for 30 cars. The Pennypack Trust oversees the 26-acre Pennypack Center and the 600-plus acres of the Pennypack Wilderness, along with other property in the Pennypack Creek Watershed area in Montgomery County. There are 2 miles of trails through woodlands and meadows at this preserve, and a small pond. You and your dog on-leash can use the three multipurpose trails (and please don't go off them): **Creek Road Trail, Pennypack Creek Trail,** and **Pennypack Parkway.** Open daily from 8:00 a.m. to dusk.

While you're in the Huntingdon Valley area, your dog may want to stop by:

▶ **Pet Fantasy, 1960 County Line Road, 215-953-9959.** You and your dog can shop together here. They offer treats, and take pet pictures with Santa in December. What else does owner Darian Schaef want you to know? "Most customers I know on a personal basis. . . . I am a small business owner and for this reason [customers] and their pets . . . receive personal attention and educated answers."

And, of course, there's the old standby:

▶ **Pet Valu, 2138 East County Line Road, 215-942-7922**

You and your dog can stay overnight in Huntingdon Valley at:

▶ **Korman Suites at Meadowbrook, 1700 Huntingdon Pike, 215-947-0101.** See full description on page 24.

(Horsham)

There are some truly great places to take your dog in Horsham Township. For instance:

▶ **Graeme Park, 859 County Line Road.** Administered by the Pennsylvania Historical and Museum Commission, this park and National Historic Site contains the only surviving residence in the commonwealth of a colonial governor, Sir William Keith (governor from 1717 to 1726). It was later renovated into an elegant country house by Keith's son-in-law, Dr. Thomas Graeme. You and your dog on-leash can view and explore the grounds and the exterior of the mansion, for which there is no charge. You can also bring your dog to the events held in Graeme Park, as long as you know your dog's limitations regarding crowds and noise, and come prepared to clean up. For more information on the events, call the park at 215-343-0965. Events include:

Native American Cultural Festival (Spring)

Fourth of July Celebration

Scottish Heritage Festival (July). Celebrate the Keith and Graeme heritages with traditional games, music, dance, and crafts. Admission is charged. Be aware that there will be bagpipe bands, along with the occasional jet from the Willow Grove Naval Air Station, so the noise level might bother some dogs.

Hands on History Day (August). Crafts, games, colonial music, and more let you explore life in the 1700s. Admission is charged.

There are also some other dog-friendly events in Horsham:

▶ **Concerts in the Park (Summer).** Held in **Carpenter Park, Kohler Park,** and **Deep Meadow Park,** all on Horsham Road, and in **Meetinghouse Road Park, Jarret Road Park, Maple Park** on Brumar Drive, and **Hideaway Hills Park** on Marietta Drive. For more information, call 215-643-3131.

▶ **Horsham Day (First Saturday in June).** Some 8,000 people come to this all-day event. Carpenter, Kohler, and Deep Meadow Parks are joined by footpaths, and there are all kinds of activities and entertainment: softball games, funnel cakes, sports for adults, a rock music fest for young people, and more. The day culminates in fireworks—you might want to take your dog home before the big bangs start to go off, unless your dog is okay with that kind of noise.

▶ **New Year's Eve 5K FunRun (December 31).** Held in Carpenter Park, Horsham Road. For details, call 215-674-4545.

Gwynedd Valley

One of the great things about Lower Gwynedd Township is that it encourages developers to include trails in their development plans. You and your dog can look for one trail off Penllyn Pike, near the Wissahickon Creek. And you and your dog will also want to go to:

▶ **The Gwynedd Wildlife Preserve, Natural Lands Trust, 640 South Swedesford Road.** There are 240 acres of rolling open meadow and woodlands to explore and romp through with your dog here, including 4 miles of maintained trails. There are guidebooks available, and you can park at Evans Mill on Swedesford Road. Picnicking, bicycling, and swimming are prohibited in Natural Lands Trust preserves. Your dog must be on-leash, and be aware that some preserves have a hunting program in November and January: signs are posted when the preserves are closed.

Play, eat. Play, eat. It's a dog's life. So if you and your dog are hungry (and you *know* your dog is), try:

▶ **The Station Café, 521 Plymouth Road, 215-542-9893.** This is a BYOB restaurant offering Mediterranean gourmet dishes for lunch and dinner. They have outdoor seating from spring to fall, as long as the weather is warm, and your dog can sit there with you "as long as [there is] no disturbance to other customers." Which makes sense to me.

Willow Grove

There's a great event in Willow Grove, at the Naval Air Station:

▶ **Country Fair (September).** At Route 611 and County Line Road. Handmade crafts, food, and entertainment, all in an open field where your dog on-leash is welcome.

There's a great pet supply store in Willow Grove:

▶ **Pet Diner, Upper Dublin Shopping Center, 215-659-8020.** Dogs on-leash (and all other animals) are welcome to come inside, and the staff will give them treats. Everyone on the staff has experience that allows them to give good nutritional advice. The store is carpeted, only top-quality merchandise is stocked, and it is all 100 percent guaranteed. They have events irregularly, so keep an eye on the store for pet portraits, flea-dipping, obedience training, and other programs, all of which are done by professionals brought in for the purpose.

And there's also an old standby:

▶ **PETCO, 41 North York Road, 215-659-9916**

(Fort Washington)

Fort Washington straddles Whitemarsh and Upper Dublin Townships, and is a very fun place to explore. Wonderful sites are tucked in all over the place. Along Bethlehem Pike, there are some nice historic buildings, including:

▶ **Clifton House, 473 Bethlehem Pike, 215-646-6065.** Built in 1801, and now the headquarters of the Historical Society of Fort Washington. Formerly the Sandy Run Tavern, it was built on the site of an 18th-century stagecoach stop. In the Gay Nineties, Clifton House was used as an exclusive resort for Philadelphians. You and your dog can tour the grounds and admire the house from the outside.

There are also some great historic homes in the area, some quite interesting architecturally, along Church Road and the streets across the Upper Dublin Township line. And your dog will want to take you to see:

▶ **The Highlands, 7001 Sheaff Lane, 215-641-2687.** This is a beautiful, 44-acre estate with extensive gardens and a 1796 Georgian mansion, built as a summer house by a Quaker lawyer, and now a National Historic Site. The Highlands is open seven days a week, from 9:00 a.m. to dusk. Admission is charged. Dogs on-leash are perfectly okay on the grounds. Among the events at the Highlands you may want to come back for are the **Glyndebourne Musical Concert (June)** and the **Highlands Craft Show (October).**

▶ **Hope Lodge, 553 Bethlehem Pike, 215-646-1595.** This Georgian estate and National Historic Site was built in the 1740s by Samuel Morris, a Quaker grist mill operator. It is one of the best surviving examples of Georgian architecture in the area. There are extensive herb and flower gardens, and dogs on-leash are permitted on the grounds. Visits to the gardens and grounds are free. You can't, however, bring your dog to events at Hope Lodge.

And then there are parks in Fort Washington—great *doggish* parks:

▶ **Mondauk Manor Park, Camphill Road between Susquehanna Road and Highland Avenue.** This is the only one of Upper Dublin Township's 36 parks to which you can bring your dog—but they are considering putting a dog park here. So all you Upper Dublin dogs get together and rally for this, okay? Let "Off-leash Play!" be your battle cry.

▶ **Fort Washington State Park, 500 Bethlehem Pike.** This was the site of the Continental Army's northern defense line against the British in 1777. There are several sections along the Wissahickon Creek and Sandy Run, totaling 493 wonderful acres. The Pennsylvania Militia held positions along the ridge on Militia Hill. The Flourtown Day Use and Militia Hill Day Use Areas have over 300 picnic tables between them, and in season (Memorial Day to Labor Day) a mobile food vendor makes the rounds. You and your dog can hike $3\frac{1}{2}$ miles of trails of moderate difficulty, or meander the half-mile, self-guided nature trail in the Militia Hill Day Use Area. You can come for winter sports here, and you don't have to worry about hunters mistaking your dog for a deer or a bear, because hunting is not permitted. Finally, if Fort Washington State Park doesn't provide enough room for you and your dog to play in, the park ties into county land, where the Green Ribbon Preserve Trail follows the Wissahickon Creek. You and your dog are welcome to travel along the Green Ribbon Preserve Trail. (For more information on the trail, see "Ambler Borough," below.)

▶ Between Fort Hill and Militia Hill of Fort Washington State Park, there is a great historic spot, **Mather Mill**. This stone grist mill was built about 1684, and operated for two centuries. Future restoration of the mill is planned. In the meantime, dogs are permitted on the grounds, and there are special events you may want to come back for, including:

Summer Concerts.   Bring a lawn chair or blanket and your dog. Admission is charged.

Annual Gala of Trees (End of November/December).   Features more than 30 decorated trees. Admission is charged, but dogs on-leash are welcome. For information, call 215-646-1595.

▶ There's a **Fort Washington Expo Center, 1100 Virginia Drive (exit 26 off the Pennsylvania Turnpike), 215-641-4500,** which holds an event you may want to go to, although you can't bring your dog with you:

Horse and Pet Expo (March).   Includes horse demonstrations, bird shows, and dog and cat presentations. Admission is charged.

So, your dog wants to do some more shopping? He or she just hasn't been able to find the perfect toy? Try one of these:

▶ **Pet Diner, 901 Bethlehem Pike, Springhouse, 215-654-9779,** and **1937 Norristown Road, Maple Glen, 215-643-2024.**   See full description on page 49.

▶ **Pet Valu, 1866 Bethlehem Pike, Flourtown, 215-836-0906.**   You can bring your dog inside here, of course.

(Ambler Borough)

Ambler Borough, in the middle of Upper Dublin Township, is a lovely, small place to walk around with your dog. The business district is very nice, and you and your dog can get some great window-shopping in along Butler Avenue, Ambler's main street. There is also plenty of takeout food available, or you and your dog can go to:

▶ **Trax Café, 27 West Butler Avenue, 215-591-9777.**   You can get lunch and dinner here, and it is BYOB. Outdoor seating is available from April to November 1, weather permitting, and they will provide water for your dog on request. They also have "veal bones throughout the year. We are very dog-friendly!"

Ambler puts on one great dog-friendly event that your dog will *not* want to miss:

▶ **Annual Dog Days of Summer (August).**   You and your dog can parade down Butler Avenue and compete in seven categories. Along with the parade, there are sidewalk sales, and booths with information on area vets, kennels, animal rescue operations, and pet stores. The event is sponsored by Ambler Main Street. For more information, call 215-641-1071. Ambler also puts on some other events, including an **auto show** and an **Oktoberfest**, so keep an eye out for those.

Nearby, there's a great place to go for a walk or a run or a romp:

▶ **Temple University, 580 Meeting House Road.** Dogs on-leash are welcome on the 187-acre grounds of the Ambler campus, which includes woodlands, fields, an arboretum, and nurseries. Avoid taking your dog into the formal gardens behind Dixon Hall—although I didn't see any signs, the official word is that dogs aren't permitted there. There are picnic areas on campus where you can eat takeout food you've picked up in Ambler, or you can get a small snack from the vending machines in College Hall, where there are also restrooms.

There is another terrific place in Ambler to take your dog:

▶ **The Wissahickon Valley Watershed Association (WVWA), Four Mills Barn, 12 Morris Road.** The barn is an 1891 structure designed by Horace Trumbauer, and built of Upper Dublin stone. It was once part of a 93-acre estate: the estate mansion used to stand on the other side of Morris Road, but only the service wing, now a private residence, remains. In 1966 the owners of the land surrounding the barn donated 50 acres to the Natural Lands Trust. Those acres now make up the Four Mills Nature Reserve, part of the Wissahickon Creek Green Ribbon Preserve, and wide open for you and your dog on-leash to enjoy. On the Four Mills Nature Reserve lands are many trails, open to the public from dawn to dusk. Get some excellent exercise exploring the paths and streams with your dog, along with a different view of the Wissahickon than you can get in Fairmount Park.

The WVWA, the Natural Lands Trust, and the Pennypack Ecological Restoration Trust work together to preserve open space along the Wissahickon Creek. The **Wissahickon Creek Green Ribbon Preserve** extends along the Wissahickon from Lansdale to Fairmount Park in Philadelphia. Besides the Four Mills Nature Reserve, the Green Ribbon Preserve includes Upper Gwynedd Park, Penllyn Woods, Penllyn Natural Area, Fort Washington State Park, and the Andorra Natural Area. The **Green Ribbon Preserve Trail** travels 21 miles through natural, wooded lands, following the creek. In Montgomery County, the trail is rustic and grassy, fairly flat, and easy to walk along.

Besides the Green Ribbon Preserve, there are 600 acres of natural area safeguarded by the WVWA in Montgomery Township, Lansdale Borough, North Wales Borough, Upper and Lower Gwynedd Townships, Whitpain Township, Ambler Borough, Upper Dublin Township, Whitemarsh Township, and Abington and Springfield Townships. For more information, call 215-646-8866, or e-mail wvwa@aol.com.

(Lafayette Hill)

Lafayette Hill is a terrific, dog-friendly place in Whitemarsh Township, very close to the Wissahickon Gorge and Chestnut Hill. There's a cluster of good shops and other places to check out along Germantown Pike in Lafayette Hill, including antique shops, gift shops, convenience stores, clothing shops, and boutiques. And great places you and your dog can get a bite to eat include:

▶ **Bruno's Restaurant, 9800 Germantown Avenue, 215-242-1880.** This is a wonderful place to enjoy friendly, family-style food and beverages. Outdoor seating is available year-round, and they will provide water or ice for your dog on request. As they remind you, "We are close to Fairmount Park." So keep them in mind before or after you and your dog get your exercise.

▶ **General Lafayette Inn & Brewery, 646 Germantown Pike, 610-941-0600.** This brewpub and bed and breakfast offers fine dining, and it has outdoor seating from April to October, where you and your dog can sit together. There is direct access from the parking lot to the beer garden. Beyond the garden is lawn and open space your dog can explore, and the inn will provide your dog with a bowl of water on request.

Once you've eaten, your dog can go shopping:

▶ **Pet Diner, 422 Germantown Pike, 610-832-0350.** See full description on page 49.

❧ SOUTHEASTERN MONTGOMERY COUNTY

Plymouth Meeting

Plymouth Meeting is convenient to a lot of surrounding dog-friendly delights. So it's good that there's a place in Plymouth Meeting where you and your dog can stay overnight:

▶ **The Inn at Plymouth Meeting, Germantown Pike and the Pennsylvania Turnpike, 610-825-1980.** There are no restrictions regarding pets, and no extra charge. And they have grounds where you can walk your dog.

Conshohocken

Conshohocken, along the Schuylkill River, is a great place for you and your dog to go exploring. Along Fayette Street there's nice window-shopping, a good selection of takeout food places, and benches to sit on while you eat. There are takeout places along Butler Pike as well, but Fayette Street is nicer. You and your dog can also grab a quick bite to eat at:

▶ **Dairy Queen, 1662 Butler Pike.** They have outdoor seating from March to October, and you are welcome to sit there with your dog. They will provide water for your dog on request.

▶ **Rita's Water Ice, 201 West Ridge Pike.** From March to October there is curb seating to which patrons can bring dogs on-leash. They will provide ice or a small cup of custard for your dog, usually free of charge. "We welcome all pet owners to our establishment."

Or, if you and your dog are tired of walking around and want to hang out for a real meal, there's a fabulous place you can cool your heels (or pads, depending on who you are):

▶ **Spring Mill Café, 164 Barren Hill Road, 610-828-2550.** Owner and chef Michèle Haines describes the food she prepares as "French provincial cuisine with Mediterranean flavors and Cambodian dishes." The café has outdoor seating on a deck, on its porch, and next to the Spring Mill Creek, and the owner is a wonderfully friendly dog lover. Patrons who sit outside may bring dogs on-leash, and outdoor seating is available "any time the weather is suitable." On request, the staff will provide your dog with water, ice, and "brioches, as a treat." The café is open for breakfast, brunch, lunch, tea, and dinner, every day from 9:00 a.m. to 10:00 p.m. Bring cash—the café does not accept credit cards.

Michèle, who has a beautiful Great Dane, would also very much like you to know that "we do a dog walk for lupus every year on Bastille Day. I would like people to participate with their dogs. Merci." The annual Bastille Day Dog Walk in Center City benefits the Lupus Foundation of Pennsylvania and Delaware (see full description on page 20).

(Norristown)

Norristown was laid out on the Schuylkill River in 1704. The 12-square-mile borough has been perking along as the county seat for quite a while. And it is working on giving itself a new look through a façade enhancement program. Take a stroll with your dog around the Central Norristown National Historic District, roughly bounded by the Stoney Creek and by Lafayette, Walnut, and Fornace Streets. Or explore the West Norristown National Historic District, bounded by the Stoney Creek and by Selma and Elm Streets. There are also some lovely buildings along Main Street.

If you want a quick bite to eat, there's always:

▶ **Rita's Water Ice, 1727 Markley Street.** They have outdoor seating from March to October, and you can sit with your dog. They will provide water or water ice in a dish if the owner requests.

Looking for parks? Try:

▶ **Riverfront Park.** Two miles of the Schuylkill River Trail pass through here, so you can extend your exercise time, if you and your dog want to, by continuing along the trail.

▶ **Elmwood Park, along Harding Boulevard.** This 110-acre park includes picnic areas, a hiking trail, fishing in the Stoney Creek, historic structures, a fountain, restrooms, and plenty of parking. There is also a food concession in season. Elmwood Park hooks up with Norristown Farm County Park as well, so you and your dog can romp virtually forever (in dog time, anyway).

▶ **Norristown Farm County Park, 2500 Upper Farm Road.** This park features 700 acres of fields, woods, pasture, and meadows. Fishing is permitted in the Stoney Creek. There is a working farm and over 5 miles of multi-use trails, as well as picnic areas scattered throughout the park. You can walk, run, cycle, in-line skate, cross-country ski, or ice skate here. I don't know if your dog can do that last one.

And there is a tank along Harding Boulevard that I know your dog will want to take a look and a sniff at (at least, mine did—we have a thing about tanks).

Norristown holds many events and festivals that you and your dog can come back and enjoy:

▶ **St. Patrick's Day Parade (March).** Bands, Irish dancers, veterans, floats, and more will pass along while you and your dog cheer. For information, call 610-277-4924.

▶ **Outdoor Concert Series at the Memorial Band Shell in Elmwood Park (Summer).** The concerts are held on Sundays, beginning in June and lasting through Labor Day weekend. Bring a lawn chair or blanket (the snack bar will be open) and enjoy. Admission is free.

▶ **Norristown Family Celebration (June).** Enjoy crafters vending unique items, live entertainment on stages, entertainers strolling the streets, food vendors of all kinds, and more.

▶ **Annual Car Show (October).** Enjoy music, food, fun, and more.

▶ **Push Back the Darkness (October 30).** A borough-wide evening walk around town. Dogs are especially good at pushing back darkness, so take yours and go to it!

▶ **Norristown Halloween Parade (October)**

▶ **Tree-Lighting Ceremony (December).** The tree is lighted on the Norristown Borough Hall patio, and you can join in Christmas carols led by a choir.

Finally, if your dog would care to do some shopping before going home, stop by:

▶ **Pet Valu, Audubon Square Shopping Center, 2650 Egypt Road, 610-650-7790**

You and your dog can stay overnight in Norristown at:

▶ **Korman Suites at Marshall Wood, 450 Forrest Avenue, 610-272-8542.** See full description on page 24.

(Plymouth Township)

Plymouth Township has some great parks, and you and your dog are welcome in all of them. You can get a complete brochure, map, and usage guidelines at the Plymouth Township Community Center, 2910 Jolly Road, or call 610-277-4312. The best Plymouth parks to visit with your dog include:

▶ **Bicentennial Park, Belvoir Road.** Adjacent to the Plymouth Township Municipal Building, this is a natural area for passive recreation, with picnic tables, a walkway, and park benches.

▶ **Colwell Park, Hillcrest Road.** Besides the multipurpose court, basketball court, and play apparatus, there are natural areas for you and your dog to explore.

▶ **Community Center Park, located behind the community center at 2910 Jolly Road.** The park has a recreational field, a small picnic area, a parking area, and a multipurpose trail, as well as natural and open areas. And Community Center Park has "mutt mitts" stocked for easy clean-up. Annual events are held here as well, and they don't turn dogs on-leash away. Come and check out events such as:

   Fall Fest (October). A family fest including pumpkin decorating, scarecrow making, hayrides, pony rides, and more. Bring your family-friendly dog to this fun event.

▶ **East Plymouth Valley Park, Germantown Pike.** Contains baseball fields, tennis courts, basketball courts, a football field, picnic tables, park benches, a pond area, play equipment, and restrooms. A concession stand operates when leagues are in session.

- **Harriet Wetherill Park, Narcissa Road.** This is an undeveloped natural area with informal trails.
- **John F. Kennedy Park, Fairfield Road and Lucetta Street.** Besides playing fields, there is a scenic natural area with a walking trail, open play space, a pavilion, picnic tables, and park benches.
- **Plymouth Hills Park, Camelot Drive and Arthurs Court.** An undeveloped, natural area. Explore!
- **Plymouth Meeting Park, Sierra Road and Blue Ridge Road.** Open space for passive recreation.
- **Sandwood Park, Sandwood Road.** Has grass, trees, and shrubs on one side of the park, an open area on the other. Perfect for you and your dog.

If you and your dog want to pick up some supplies while you're in the general area, stop at nearby:

- **Pet Valu, Norriton Square, 55 East Germantown Pike, 610-277-5090**

Blue Bell

There are a few things you and your dog might find of interest in Blue Bell:

- **Whitpain Police Association's Blue Bell Bike Race (June).** Come out and enjoy the competition. The proceeds benefit the Montgomery County Salvation Army Capital Campaign and Eagleville Hospital.
- **Rita's Water Ice, 926 DeKalb Pike.** Patrons sitting outside may bring dogs on-leash. There is outdoor seating from March to October. They will provide water or water ice in a dish if the owner requests.
- **Pet Valu, Center Square, 1301 Skippack Pike, 610-239-8175**

And you can stay here overnight with your dog at:

- **Korman Suites at Meadow Wick, 1707 Meadow Drive, 610-275-5265.** See full description on page 24.

Upper Merion Township

Upper Merion Township is a wonderful playground for you and your dog. Simply fantastic. The township has 20 parks, all of which are dog-friendly. Dog training classes are held in the park adjacent to the Upper Merion Township Building. Some of the best area parks for your dog are:

- **Bob White Park.** Has playing fields, a passive-recreation pathway, and natural areas in a total of 21.22 acres.
- **Executive Estates Park.** Has playing fields, a picnic area, natural areas, a pedestrian bridge, a monument, and restrooms (9.13 acres).
- **McKaig Nature Education Center.** Has trails and natural areas (90 acres).
- **Mount Pleasant Park.** A small, natural area (1.23 acres).

▶ **Natural Lands Trust 1.** A small, natural area (5 acres). Picnicking, bicycling, and swimming are prohibited in Natural Lands Trust preserves.

▶ **Natural Lands Trust 2.** Has natural areas (20 acres).

▶ **Schuylkill River Boat House Park.** Has natural areas and a boat launch (1.63 acres).

▶ **Sweetbriar Park.** Has playing fields, a picnic area, a pedestrian bridge, and natural areas (28.18 acres).

▶ **Upper Merion Community Center Park.** Has natural areas, a pedestrian bridge, a historic estate, and an arboretum (4.8 acres).

▶ **Volpi Common.** Has natural areas (3.48 acres).

▶ **Walker Park.** Has playing fields, a picnic area, a multi-use path, a pedestrian bridge, natural areas, and a monument (25.03 acres).

▶ **Upper Merion Township Building Park, 175 West Valley Forge Road, King of Prussia.** Has picnic areas, a multi-use path, a pedestrian bridge, natural areas, a pond, a monument, restrooms, and a bocce court (17.92 acres). During the summer, you and your dog will want to come back here for:

Concert Under the Stars. Upper Merion Township's King of Prussia Folk Music Summer Concert Series begins at the end of May and continues every Sunday evening until mid-September. Admission is charged, except for children and seniors. Bring a blanket or lawn chairs, a picnic, and your dog (as long as dogs are well-mannered, they are welcome). For more information, call 610-265-1071, or visit the series' Web site at www.umconcerts.org.

Upper Merion Community Fair (September). There's a 5K race, a senior fitness 1-mile walk, pony rides, arts and crafts, and more. Admission is free. For more information, call 610-265-1071.

If the Upper Merion parks aren't enough for you and your dog, try:

▶ **Gypsy Woods/Gulph Mills Preserve, Gypsy Road, King of Prussia.** Nine acres of wooded hillside, a stream valley, and a half-mile trail are leased to Upper Merion by the Natural Lands Trust.

And, of course, in Upper Merion is one of the best parks of all:

▶ **Valley Forge National Historical Park.** This wonderful, huge, and beautiful park commemorates and demonstrates the life of the approximately 12,000 Continental Army soldiers who struggled to survive here during the winter of 1777–78, after failing to shake the British out of Philadelphia in the Battle of Germantown. By February 1778, only 6,000 Continental soldiers were left. Enter Baron Friedrich Wilhelm von Steuben, who turned the soldiers who were left into an effective force that went on to ultimate success.

The park grounds are open daily, year-round, from sunup to sundown (6:00 a.m. to 10:00 p.m.), and the Visitors Center is open from 9:00 a.m. to 5:00 p.m., except on December 25. The grounds are free, and there are hiking trails, equestrian trails, and picnic areas galore. This incredibly historic place is wonderful for hiking, biking, walking, kite flying, running, cross-country skiing, and more.

The **Schuylkill River Trail**, an 11$\frac{1}{2}$-mile, class A paved trail along an old Pennsylvania Railroad right-of-way, begins at the Betzwood picnic area of the park and travels east to Philadelphia. A portion of the **Horse-Shoe Hiking Trail** also runs through the park, in the section of the park that extends into Chester County.

Dogs on-leash are permitted at the many events that take place at Valley Forge. Be cautious about events that involve the firing of guns, but you and your dog may want to revisit the park for:

French Alliance Day (May 1). A Revolutionary War reenactment.

The Dogwood Fair at Washington Memorial Chapel (May). Browse through attic treasures, attend a plant sale, and enjoy great food. Most important, a dog and pet show is part of the fair, with competitions in various fun classes, including a costume class. Call 610-469-6395 for more information.

March Out of Valley Forge (Weekend closest to June 19). A reenactment of the Continental Army's exit from Valley Forge. Costumed performers will reenact the event, and there is also a tea demonstration.

Carillon Concerts at Washington Memorial Chapel (Summer). Carillons consist of 23 or more cast-bronze bells played by keyboard. The Washington Memorial National Carillon, with 58 bells, is one of the world's largest. In total, the carillon weighs 26 tons, and covers almost five octaves. The low A minor (representing Illinois) weighs 8,000 pounds. The high G (representing Wake Island) weighs $13\frac{1}{2}$ pounds. In July and August, there are free concerts at 8:00 p.m. on Wednesdays. (From mid-September to mid-June, free recitals are given on Sundays after the 11:15 a.m. services.) Bring a blanket, lie under the stars with your dog, and enjoy wonderful music you literally can't hear anywhere else.

Valley Forge Signal Seekers Radio Control Model Airplane Club Fall Fun Fly. There are events throughout the day, including a candy drop for kids, gliders, helicopters, and a scale model airplane show. You and your dog on-leash are welcome to come and watch it all.

Annual DogWalk (October). Benefits the Spayed Club, which provides subsidized spaying and neutering to pet owners who can't otherwise afford it. Bring your dog on-leash and do the 3-mile walk along the Schuylkill River in the Walnut Hill section of the park for a worthy cause, then enjoy a veritable dog party. You and your dog can enjoy special activities and time for participating dogs to frolic with each other, as well as a training demonstration, agility demonstrations, and a Red Cross demonstration of pet CPR. Want more? Try pet photographs, a "Funny Match" dog show, and face painting (whose, I wonder?). Biscuits and water will be on hand for the dogs, and vegetarian cuisine from Fresh Fields will be available for you and the other humans. You can get a brochure and more information by calling 610-275-7486.

March into Valley Forge (December 19). Reenacts the entry of the Continental Army into Valley Forge for the winter.

There's another patriotic place in the area that you and your dog can visit, for a truly unique experience:

▶ **Freedoms Foundation at Valley Forge.** Dogs on-leash are welcome on this 105-acre campus. The Freedoms Foundation was founded in 1949 to promote responsible citizenship. The 52-acre Medal of Honor Grove has a 4.3-mile Walk of Honor in a nice wooded area, honoring all of the nation's men and women who have been awarded the Medal of Honor. Also on the campus are other monuments and statues, and the Independence Garden. The Freedoms Foundation is open Monday through Friday, from 9:00 a.m. to 5:00 p.m. For more information, call 610-933-8825.

Whew! After all that exercise you and your dog have just gotten in Upper Merion, you're probably looking for something else to do, right? Well, you could go get a bite to eat. Try:

▶ **Starbucks, 140 West DeKalb Pike, King of Prussia, 610-768-5130.** They offer gourmet coffee, other beverages, and some incredible pastries. They have outdoor seating when the weather permits, and you can sit there with your dog. They will give your dog water on request.

Or you and your dog could go shopping at:

▶ **PETCO, 145 West DeKalb Pike, King of Prussia, 610-337-4484**

Finally, since you're having such a great time in Upper Merion, you and your dog may want to stay overnight. You can, in King of Prussia:

▶ **Motel 6, Route 202, 610-265-7200.** They have no restrictions on pets, and no extra fees. There are grounds where you can walk your dog. It's sort of a no-frills place, but your dog won't care.

Lower Merion Township (Eastern Main Line)

Why is the Main Line known as the Main Line? Early on, it seems, it was difficult for horses to pull wagonloads of goods along the unpaved roads in the area. So someone came up with the idea of building rails along which horse-pulled wagons could glide. By 1832, there were rails from Philadelphia to Columbia (out by Lancaster), known as the "Main Line of Public Works." Horse-drawn stagecoaches were used along the rails as well. After only two years, however, steam locomotives came into use, and the Philadelphia and Columbia Railway ultimately became part of the Pennsylvania Railroad. The towns centered around the stations form the Main Line.

There is a lot of history along the Main Line that you and your dog can enjoy. I mention a few areas below, but there's just no way to mention them all. If you would like more information, contact the Lower Merion Historical Society, Ashbridge House, Rosemont, 610-525-5831 or 610-649-4000. And while you travel through Lower Merion, look for milestones from the stagecoach era, engraved with the distance to 2nd and Market Streets in Philadelphia: you and your dog will see quite a few.

Gladwyne/Pencoyd/Penn Valley

Gladwyne Village is at the intersection of Righters Mill Road and Youngsford Road. Stroll around with your dog and window-shop. Pick up some takeout food at Gladwyne Village Lunch, the Delaware Market, or Kimmey's Deli. There are tables and chairs at the Village Lunch where you and your dog can sit and eat together.

And enjoy the historic ambience! The two of you are sitting in a very historic area: the Merion Square Historic District, a 19th-century crossroads village including about 87 buildings of all types. This district was the main shopping center in Lower Merion Township in the early 1800s.

There are plenty of area parks that will allow you and your dog to walk around on grass:

- **Black Rock Road Site, Gladwyne.** The site includes 6 acres of undeveloped open space along Black Rock Road.
- **Eco Valley Nature Park, Pencoyd.** Located behind Lewis J. Smith Park and Swimming Pool, the park has almost 6 acres of undeveloped open space.
- **Henry Lane Park, Gladwyne.** Along Henry Lane, the park includes land across Conshohocken State Road, and has 22 acres of natural areas, as well as hiking and bridle trails.
- **Kenealy Nature Park, Gladwyne.** At Youngsford Road near the intersection of Lafayette Road, this is a beautiful natural area to hike through with your dog. There are bridle trails here as well.
- **Merion Square Road Site, Gladwyne.** At Old Gulph and Merion Square Roads, the site has 1.6 acres of undeveloped open space.
- **Mill Creek Valley Park, Pencoyd.** Along Mill Creek Road, Conshohocken State Road, and Hollow Road, this is an 88.6-acre nature park.
- **Pencoyd Park.** Along Woodbine Avenue, Centennial Road, and Greentree Lane, the park has almost 58 acres of undeveloped open space.
- **Rolling Hill Park, Gladwyne.** At 1301 Rose Glen Road, this 103-acre park has hiking and bridle trails, woodland, and open fields to play in, and there are lots of ruins here (Georgie and I love ruins, you will recall).

    The Lower Merion Conservancy holds its annual **Post-Thanksgiving Turkey Trot** here, on the Saturday after Turkey Day. It's more of a brisk walk than a trot. For more information, call the conservancy at 610-645-9030.
- **West Mill Creek Park, Penn Valley.** At Mill Creek and Old Gulph Roads, the park has almost 10 acres of nature park and a fitness trail.
- **Williamson Road Site, Gladwyne.** At Youngsford and Williamson Roads, the site has 3 acres of undeveloped open space.

Other recreational opportunities for you and your dog include:

- **Saunders Woods, 1020 Waverly Road, Gladwyne.** This is a Natural Lands Trust property, so feel free to enjoy it with your dog! There are 26 acres here, with 2 miles of trails through meadows, stream valley, and woodland. The stream feeds into the Schuylkill River. Guidebooks are available at the barn on site: the main house, the barn, and the springhouse are historic sites from the mid- to late 1800s that you can admire while you are here. There are also lots of wildflowers. Picnicking, bicycling, and swimming are prohibited in Natural Lands Trust preserves. Your dog must be on-leash, and be aware that some preserves have a hunting program in November and January: signs are posted when the preserves are closed.
- **Riverbend Environmental Education Center, 1950 Spring Mill Road.** The Riverbend Center is housed in a 1923 converted barn standing on 31 acres of natural area. There are foot and horse trails, 26 acres of woods, and open fields. Open from 8:30 a.m. to sunset, the

Riverbend Center is free. Best of all—it's private property and they will allow you to let your dog *off-leash* here! Enjoy a 2-mile walk through field, forest, pond, and creek habitats. For information, call 610-527-5234.

▶ **Woodmont, 1622 Spring Mill Road, 610-525-5598.** This 73-acre site has a shrine honoring the late evangelist Father Divine, as well as lawns, gardens, woodland, and lakes. Mother Divine still lives in the Victorian French Gothic manor house, but she is very gracious, and doesn't mind your dog on-leash coming to enjoy the site. There's a dog that lives here, but it is friendly, and inside most of the time anyway. This is a National Historic Site.

There are Gladwyne events you and your dog might want to attend:

▶ **Azalea Day Country Fair, St. Christopher's Church (May).** Held on the Saturday before Mother's Day. Features games, crafts, a plant sale, books, food, prizes, and more. For information, call 610-642-8920.

▶ **Gladwyne Memorial Day Parade and Festival (May).** Held in Gladwyne Village, rain or shine. Kids are invited to participate, dressed patriotically, walking or riding decorated bikes, along with the fire company and antique cars. After the parade there are bands, crafts, food, and more.

▶ **Christmas Parade (December).** The Gladwyne Fire Company escorts Santa on a tour of the Gladwyne area.

Bala Cynwyd

There is more history in Bala Cynwyd than you might think at first glance. The East Bala residential area was developed by the Lower Merion Realty Company between 1907 and 1913. The North Bala residential area was built between 1896 and 1913, and includes Colonial Revival and Shingle-style homes with large porches on small lots. And the South Bala residential area includes a wide variety of late-19th- and early-20th-century styles such as Queen Anne, Colonial Revival, Tudor, and Bungalow. You can do some great walking around Bala.

There's only one park in Bala Cynwyd your dog can use:

▶ **Cynwyd Station Park.** With not quite an acre of natural area, the park is located on Conshohocken State Road, near Montgomery Avenue.

You and your dog might want to come out for the following events:

▶ **Bala Cynwyd Fourth of July Parade**

▶ **Union Fire Station of Lower Merion's Annual Halloween Parade (October)**

▶ **Santa Paws, Saks Fifth Avenue (December).** You can bring your dog (or other pet) to be photographed with Santa for a donation to the Morris Animal Refuge. The refuge brings select animals available for adoption, as well. For information, call 215-735-3256.

Would your dog like to do some shopping while you're in Bala Cynwyd? You can take your dog to:

▶ **Pet Valu, Bala Cynwyd Shopping Center, 77 East City Line Avenue, 610-660-8682**

Merion, Narberth, and Wynnewood

Township parks where your dog on-leash is welcome in this large area of Lower Merion include:

▶ **General Wayne Park, Maplewood Avenue and Revere Road, Merion Park.** Dogs are permitted in a designated area north of the elevated path (behind the ballfields, in the wooded area).

▶ **Shortridge Memorial Park, Shortridge Drive, Wynnewood.** Dogs are allowed in an unmarked area bounded by the paved walkway entering from Parkview Drive, the west bank of the stream, and the wooded embankment behind the houses along Parkview.

You can also take your dog onto the grounds of the **Merion Tribute House, 625 Hazelhurst Road**, an English country manor built in the early 1920s as a memorial to Merion World War I veterans. It is a very elegant property of 8 acres, and the house has a lovely stone terrace. There's a good field where you and your dog can romp together.

You and your dog will absolutely have a great time in Narberth, "America's Small Town," with its attractive downtown area and lovely residential streets with homes ranging from Victorians to early 1900s bungalows and twins. It's a great place to walk with your dog and just look and look: no two houses are alike.

Want to take your dog shopping? In downtown Narberth there is a well-known treasure of a store:

▶ **Mapes 5 & 10, 228 Haverford Avenue, 610-664-2132.** One of the coolest stores on the Main Line. Are you looking for something? Anything? They have it, and at a very reasonable price. And they don't mind if you bring your dog on-leash inside.

Your dog can help you pick out a movie to rent at **Narberth Video, 241 Haverford Avenue, 610-664-4136.** After the two of you have chosen a film, your dog can head up to the counter for a treat.

Hungry? Although you can't take your dog inside **Albrecht's Gourmet Market, 701 Montgomery Avenue**, there are outdoor tables where you can sit with your dog and enjoy a bite to eat from inside the market.

Finally, Narberth puts on some terrific events for its size. You and your dog may want to come out for:

▶ **Narberth 5K Run (May).** This race benefits the Cystic Fibrosis Foundation. Come on out and cheer the runners with your dog! For more information, call the Narberth Borough Office at 610-664-2840.

▶ **Narberth Sidewalk Sale and Spring Festival (May).** Features music, performances, food, outdoor tables, and a health fair.

▶ **Memorial Day Parade (May).** Enjoy a traditional small-town parade complete with marching bands.

▶ **Narberth Fourth of July Parade.** In addition to a baby parade, there are games and contests at the Narberth Playground that you and your dog can at least watch from outside the fence.

- **Narberth Sidewalk Sale (October).** Sponsored by the Narberth Business Association; come for bargains, food, and more.
- **Narberth Halloween Parade (October).** This evening event is great to watch and possibly the biggest Halloween parade on the Main Line. Dress up your dog (Georgie has her very own witch's hat) and go see the kids parading in all their Halloween finery. As your dog will tell you, sniffing is always more interesting at night.
- **Holiday Festivities in Narberth (December).** Santa Claus takes the R-5 SEPTA line to Narberth's Station Circle at Haverford and Forrest Avenues, and hangs around for some caroling. Dress up your holiday dog and go enjoy the celebration.
- **Narberth Candlelight Night (December).** Participating stores serve refreshments, carolers walk up and down the candlelit street, and Santa will be there.

You and your dog can also head over to Wynnewood Road for something to eat and drink:

- **Irish Bread Shoppe, 75 East Wynnewood Road (at the SEPTA station), 610-642-0544,** has outdoor benches where you can indulge in some of the goods from inside the store.
- The **Wynnewood Shopping Center, 50 East Wynnewood Road,** has set up a lovely pocket of tables and chairs. Pick up something from Delancey Street Bagels or another of the center's options, and sit with your dog for a while.

Ardmore

Ardmore is a great place to hang out with your dog. Along Lancaster Avenue there are interesting shops and eating places to get takeout food. And even the shopping centers are historic:

- **Suburban Square Shopping Center, between Montgomery and Lancaster Avenues, 610-896-7560.** This is the country's oldest shopping center—right here, smack dab in the middle of the Main Line. With over 60 elegant specialty shops, this is a great place to go window-shopping, and there are large outdoor spaces here—with benches, and even tables and chairs—where your dog is welcome, including at events. Pick up some coffee at Starbucks, or something to eat from the farmers market or Baker Street, or dessert from TCBY Treats or Sweet Stuff (assuming there is someone to stay outside with your dog). Many of the non-food stores may let you bring your dog inside. And there are regular events, including:

    Summer Concerts at the Square. Free concerts in the Suburban Square courtyard, with all sorts of music.

    June Jamboree Sidewalk Sale at Suburban Square. Features clowns, music, food, and more.

    Annual Main Line Food Festival (September). Vendors in the courtyard serve samples, and there is entertainment.

    Halloween Celebration (October). There are pumpkins in the square! And you can exchange a receipt from the Ardmore Farmers Market or any Suburban Square merchant for one of those pumpkins. There's also a gravesite and jack-o-lantern display, along with other Halloween festivities.

Operation Santa Parade (December). On the Friday after Thanksgiving, the Suburban Square Annual Santa Parade leads Santa and his reindeer to the courtyard. Following this event, Santa, without the reindeer, is in Suburban Square every Saturday in December until Christmas. (You really need to go see the reindeer—they are beautiful, and smaller than you would expect from traditional Christmas renderings.)

If you've had enough of Suburban Square and want to go hang out somewhere else, try:

▶ **Manhattan Bagel, 50 West Lancaster Avenue, 610-642-0171.** Patrons who sit outside can bring dogs on-leash. Outdoor seating is available as the weather permits, from spring to fall. The staff will provide water or ice for your dog on request.

And don't forget to come out with your dog for these Ardmore events:

▶ **Lower Merion Township Memorial Day Parade (May)**
▶ **Ardmore Dog Show (September).** This fun family event will allow your dog to show off in 10 different categories, culminating in a parade and lots of treats.
▶ **Ardmore Holiday Celebration (December).** Held on F. Karl Schauffele Plaza, Lancaster Avenue, this is Ardmore's official tree-lighting ceremony, with free hot chocolate and cider. Bring your dog and an ornament for the tree.

Bryn Mawr

Bryn Mawr is a very dog-friendly town. I've seen dogs in all kinds of places in the Bryn Mawr area. From businesses to college campuses to events, your dog and you can have a great time in Bryn Mawr.

Here's a place for you and your dog to start:

▶ **The American College, 270 Bryn Mawr Avenue.** You and your dog can take a self-guided walk through this 45-acre campus, which is open daily from 7:00 a.m. to 8:00 p.m. There's a picnic area here. There's also a stream, paths, two ponds, 600 labeled trees, and the Goodwin Daffodil Hill.
▶ **Bryn Mawr College, 101 North Merion Avenue, 610-526-5152.** This parklike campus features Collegiate Gothic buildings designed to replicate the look of Oxford and Cambridge, and it is a truly incredible place. You can bring your dog on-leash onto the campus and take a tour. The grounds are open daily from dawn to dusk.

Have your dog and you had enough of college campuses? Well, go see:

▶ **Harriton House, 500 Harriton Road.** There is a 16$\frac{1}{2}$-acre park surrounding this 1704 house, and picnicking is permitted (though there are no tables). Dogs on-leash are permitted as well. Some of the fields here were the site of the Revolutionary War's Battle of Old Gulph Road.

Okay, okay, you and your dog have done enough walking and sightseeing. You're looking for a place to sit back and relax. I've got the perfect spots for you and your canine:

▶ **Food Source by Clemens, 663 West Lancaster Avenue, 610-581-7209.** You can pick up chef-prepared foods, gourmet items, coffee, exclusive chocolates, fresh produce, and other special goodies here, and then eat them outside with your dog at the tables and chairs set up next to the building. Outdoor seating is available as the weather permits. When asked if they provide any amenities for dogs (water, ice, treats), they replied: "This is a great idea and we will look into it." They do sell gourmet dog treats, so you can pick up something for your dog as well as for yourself.

▶ **Starbucks, 766 West Lancaster Avenue, 610-526-0650.** There are tables and chairs outside, next to the building, where you and your dog can enjoy coffee (or water) and some really incredible pastries.

▶ **xando Coffee and Bar, 761 West Lancaster Avenue, 610-520-5208.** Patrons who sit outside are allowed to bring dogs on-leash, and there are tables outside as long as the weather permits. "We will gladly give water and ice to our four-legged friends." If they aren't too busy, they will let you run in to order and have the staff bring the food out to you, so you don't have to leave your dog unattended. They "wish we could have dogs indoors!"

There are also a couple of places with benches outside that you and your canine can use:

▶ **The Point, 880 West Lancaster Avenue, 610-527-0988.** Serving items from coffee to lunch.
▶ **Walter's Swiss Pastries, 870 West Lancaster Avenue, 610-525-0824**

Then, when you've rested your feet and paws and are ready to go again, check out all the wonderful shops along Lancaster Avenue. If your dog would like to do some shopping, go to:

▶ **Bryn Mawr Feed & Seed Company, 1225 Montrose Avenue, 610-525-7011.** You can both come inside here.

Bryn Mawr also has some wonderful, dog-friendly events:

▶ **Bryn Mawr Neighbor Days (May).** This is a sidewalk sale with entertainment.
▶ **Bryn Mawr Open Air Concert Series (Summer).** Bring a blanket or lawn chairs, and enjoy great music with your dog.
▶ **Bryn Mawr Day (October).** Strolling street performers, bands, free soft pretzels and lollipops, demonstrations, information booths, and sidewalk sales.
▶ **Christmas in Bryn Mawr (December).** There's an official tree-lighting ceremony with caroling at the Community Center next to Ludington Library. And every Saturday in December, carolers perform along Lancaster Avenue in "the Village," and Santa is present for pictures at Bryn Mawr Trust.
▶ **The Charity Fun Run (December).** A 5-, 8-, or 10-mile run sponsored by the Bryn Mawr Running Company. Runners bring unwrapped gifts for infants to 20-year-olds, which are given to the Homeless Advocacy Project at the People's Emergency Center.

Rosemont

There's a college campus for you and your dog to visit in Rosemont (yes, there are a lot of those on the Main Line):

▶ **Rosemont College, 1400 Montgomery Avenue.** This 56-acre campus is lovely, with 18 interesting buildings, but none as interesting as the one constructed as a country home in

1891: Rathalla. This fascinating building was modeled on an early French Renaissance château, and features a large Victorian porch, round towers, and 52 carved grotesques on the exterior.

There are also a couple of great parks in Rosemont:

▸ **Austin Memorial Park, Lancaster, Airdale, and Norwood Avenues,** is a 2.3-acre nature park.

▸ **Riverbend** (headquartered in Gladwyne) maintains 45 acres of natural habitat on Latches Lane and Beech Road in Rosemont. You can enjoy this land with your dog as well.

Looking for a great, dog-friendly store? Go to:

▸ **Smith & Hawken, 1225 Montrose Avenue, 610-526-9314.** This is an excellent store to go browsing through for gardening tools and related items, and you can bring your dog on-leash inside.

And if you're looking for a place to get a bite, try:

▸ **Juice & Java, 1201 West Lancaster Avenue, 610-520-6244.** Besides juices and javas, they have pastries and sandwiches, and tables outside where you can sit with your dog.

As for events, Rosemont has one of the oldest parades in the country:

▸ **Rosemont–Garrett Hill Fourth of July Parade.** Technically, Garrett Hill is in Delaware County, but come out anyway and watch the parade with your dog. There will be drum and bugle corps, bands, baton twirlers, clowns, floats, and more.

🐾 CENTRAL MONTGOMERY COUNTY

The heartlands of Montgomery County are more rural in nature, but they have some really fun, dog-friendly towns. Let's get right to it.

Lansdale

Lansdale has a very nice downtown, with an interesting Main Street. Find a place to park and take your dog window-shopping. Rumor has it that quite a few of the shops in Lansdale will allow you to bring your dog inside. I don't know if it is true, but these rumors do have a way of panning out, and it never hurts to ask.

There's plenty of takeout food downtown, including **Rita's Water Ice,** the **Broadway Deli & Café,** or even **McDonald's.** Right on Main Street there is a great pocket park where you can sit and eat with your dog. There's a lot of concrete here, but there's also the coolest fountain Georgie and I have ever seen: a black globe that turns with the flow of the water. There's lots of seating for al fresco dining. Or you can go to one of these:

▸ **Dairy Queen, North Penn Marketplace, Sumneytown and Valley Forge Roads.** Patrons who sit outside can bring dogs on-leash. Outdoor seating is available all year, weather permitting. They will provide water, or a "kiddie cup of vanilla is perfect for our doggie customers." Anything else? "Pet birthdays—we can [reproduce] a picture of your pet on a cake, or even of the pet's owner!"

▶ **Freddy Hill Farms, 1440 Sumneytown Pike, 215-855-1205.** This is a great place—really a whole lot of places rolled up in one. They have an ice cream store, a deli, and a miniature golf course. While your dog can't play miniature golf with you, there is outdoor seating where the two of you can sit in warm weather and enjoy the goodies you got from the ice cream place or the deli.

▶ **Mother Bruce's Café, 312 West Main Street, 215-362-3001.** They offer gourmet, homemade dishes. They have one table and two chairs outside when the weather is above 65 degrees, and you can sit there with your dog. They will provide water or ice on request, and may offer your dog a treat. In November 1999, they began making dog cookies.

▶ **The Spice Smuggler, 219 West Main Street, 215-362-8893.** They offer ice cream cones, shakes, malts, espresso, soda, coffee, and tea. Outdoor seating is available spring through fall, and your dog can sit with you here. Do they offer any amenities for dogs? "Not at present, but—hey, why not?"

Or try the nearby:

▶ **Colmar Dairy Queen, 2620 North Broad Street, Colmar (north of Lansdale).** They have benches outside year-round, and your dog can sit there with you. "We give dog bones through the drive-through and cups of water on request."

Looking for a place for your dog to go shopping? Try one of these:

▶ **Pet Valu, Towamencin Village Square, 1758 Allentown Road, 215-412-0610**
▶ **Lansdale Feed & Pet Supply, 1100 North Broad Street, 215-362-1387.** You can bring your dog inside here. They offer pet grooming and inexpensive nail trimming for all animals. They have pet photo days, usually around Thanksgiving. Dog training classes are available throughout the year. "We are experienced with dog behavior and nutrition and are very willing to help customers make the right choices for their pets. We have an extensive pet food/treat/toy selection!"

Lansdale also has some great, dog-friendly parks. Among them are:

▶ **Lansdale Park, along Whites Road.** A pretty nice place, and dogs on-leash are welcome. **Summertime concerts** are held here, so keep an eye out for them.
▶ **Memorial Park, Main and Line Streets.** This is right in the center of town, and very pretty, with monuments and lovely green lawns. Events held here include:
   Annual Play in the Park (Spring/Summer). Area theater groups perform in the park in this series. For more information, call 215-368-1691.
   Lansdale Festival of the Arts (August). A juried fine-art and crafts show, which also has a marionette theater, chamber music, and jazz.

Speaking of events, Lansdale holds a great one that you and your dog won't want to miss:

▶ **Lansdale Mardi Gras Celebration and Parade.** Held on the Saturday before Thanksgiving (I know—the date seems a bit off). Includes bands, Boy Scout troops, and more. The Valley Forge Kennel Club has participated in this one. Bring your dog and have a good time.

You and your dog can also pick up a little history while you're in Lansdale. There are a lot of nice, older houses, so take a stroll and explore. You should also stop by:

▶ **The Jenkins Homestead, 137 Jenkins Avenue.** Circa 1795, this house was the center of a 100-acre farm, and it is the oldest existing building in Lansdale. Dogs on-leash are permitted on the grounds (which are significantly less than 100 acres now).

You and your dog can stay overnight in Lansdale at:

▶ **Korman Suites at Morgandale, 1203 Cross Hill Court, 215-368-5021.** See full description on page 24.

Kulpsville

Kulpsville is just to the southwest of Lansdale, and along Forty Foot Road is a great place where your dog and you are always welcome:

▶ **Kulpsville Antique and Flea Market, 1375 Forty Foot Road, 215-361-7910.** You and your dog on-leash are free to browse through this outdoor flea market. Food is available. And they even have events:
Pet Parade (Spring/Summer). All pets are welcome. There are demonstrations of the basics of obedience training, pet items for sale, and free samples from pet-related vendors.
Summer Festival (July). Features family activities, food, and lots of fun. Admission is free.

And if you and your dog are having a good time in this area of Montgomery County, you can both stay overnight at:

▶ **Holiday Inn, Sumneytown Pike and the Pennsylvania Turnpike, 215-368-3800.** There are no restrictions, but they require a $25 deposit. There are grounds where your dog can take care of any necessary business.

Collegeville/Trappe

Collegeville got its name from:

▶ **Ursinus College, Main Street between 5th and 8th Avenues, 610-409-3200.** Founded in 1869, and coed since 1881. This is an interesting campus, and there is a lot of outdoor sculpture to enjoy, including a nice copy of Philadelphia's famous *LOVE* sculpture. There are also some great buildings, and a mall area. You are welcome to stroll the grounds with your dog on-leash, as long as you clean up (of course).

Also in Collegeville is a great source of activities for younger dog owners:

▶ **Montgomery County 4-H, Penn State Cooperative Extension, 1015 Bridge Road.** Montgomery County 4-H offers a spring obedience training course for young handlers of dogs, and a year-round Friendly Paws 4-H Dog Club for kids to learn about dogs and their care. They also have a 4-H Seeing Eye Puppy Club for youths who want to raise or train dogs that will go on to become Seeing Eye dogs, working with Seeing Eye in Morristown, New Jersey. And the whole family can enjoy:

Montgomery County 4-H Fair (August). Held at the 4-H Center on Route 113 in Skippack. The fair is free, but there is a parking fee. You can enjoy music, food, crafts, cloggers, educational displays, pet and animal shows, and other activities. In 1999 there was a Seeing Eye Puppy Obstacle Course (outdoors), a 4-H Seeing Eye Puppy Demo (in an activity tent), a Pet Show (open to all youths, not just 4-H members, inside an activity tent), and a 4-H Dog Obedience Show (in an activity tent), followed by canine junior handling. Can your dog on-leash come with you to the fair? Well, yes. This is the official word: "We really do prefer that people do not bring their pets unless they are showing in the pet show. We have not forbidden dogs to attend, but people are often unthinking and want to take their dogs with them into the animal tents, and this can easily frighten the rabbits, poultry, cats, and even the goats and sheep who do not know these dogs. There are also the issues of animal health and owners who do not clean up after their dogs in a responsible manner." So, if you and your dog can behave, and follow the rules, you *can* go together. For information, call 610-489-4315.

What else can you do with your dog in Collegeville? Go get a Christmas tree!

▶ **Boswell's Cut-Your-Own Christmas Tree Farm.** In business for over 50 years, they actually have two sites you can go to: Mill Road Farm (between Collegeville and Evansburg Roads) and Bridge Road Farm. Here your dog can help you choose the perfect tree.

You can go shopping with your dog at:

▶ **Agway Collegeville Yard-Garden-Pet Place, Park Avenue and Route 29, 610-489-2521.** You and your dog on-leash can shop both inside and outside here.

In nearby Trappe, you and your dog can get a bite to eat at:

▶ **Trappe Dairy Queen, 345 West Main Street.** Outdoor seating is available all year, and your dog can sit there with you. They will provide your dog with water, or ice cream treats with the owner's permission—"no chocolate is ever given to any animal."

And after eating, your dog can go shopping at:

▶ **PETCO, 130 West Main Street, 610-489-9830.** You can bring your dog inside, and they will provide a doggy treat. They hold adoption days, and twice a year will clip your dog's nails for a $2 donation.

You and your dog can play in a variety of area parks:

▶ **Central Perkiomen Valley County Park, Plank Road between Routes 29 and 73, Collegeville.** The park extends over 500 acres along the Perkiomen Creek, with ice skating, cross-country skiing/sledding, bridle trails, and woodlands, open fields, and wetlands. There's an old mill house here—a lovely, turn-of-the-century summer retreat (it can be rented out for private parties). This is really a hiker's paradise, with lots of scenic trails: one trail follows the Perkiomen Creek through heavy woods; another is an old Reading Railroad right-of-way used by mountain bikers. Picnicking, fishing, boating, and canoeing are other ways you can enjoy this park. The park is open daily from 8:00 a.m. to sunset.

▶ **Eagleville Park, Parklane Drive, Eagleville.** There are jogging trails and play areas here. The park is open daily from dawn to dusk. And come back for:

Lower Providence Funday (September). Dogs on-leash are permitted to come with you to enjoy the music, petting zoo, antique car show, crafts, and other activities. Admission is free.

▶ **Lower Perkiomen Valley County Park, 101 New Mill Road, off Egypt Road, Oaks.** The park is on the opposite side of the Perkiomen Creek from Mill Grove, the Audubon Wildlife Sanctuary. You can't take your dog onto Mill Grove lands, but you can spot many of the same birds in Lower Perkiomen Valley Park. There are 30 acres of multipurpose fields here, about 160 picnic tables, restrooms, and open fields—a total of 107 acres to enjoy. You can walk, jog, cycle, or in-line skate with your dog here, and cross-country ski or sled in the winter. Fishing and boating are permitted on the Perkiomen Creek. The park is open daily from 8:00 a.m. to dusk. For more information, call 610-666-5371. And in the summer, there are **band concerts** on Sundays. The schedule varies, so call the park for information.

▶ **Upper Schuylkill Valley County Park, Route 113.** The park has 60 picnic tables, grills, and a shaded area along the Schuylkill River. Fishing is permitted, as are sledding and ice skating in the winter, although at the doer's risk. Hikers can follow a river trail to Mont Clare.

Mont Clare

The best thing in Mont Clare, as far as your dog is concerned, is:

▶ **The Schuylkill Canal Recreation Area.** The Schuylkill Navigation Canal, Oakes Reach Section (north and east banks of the Schuylkill, from PA 113 to Lock 61) is on the National Historic Register. Along the canal, which extends about $2^1/_2$ miles through Mont Clare and Port Providence, there are towpath trails you and your dog can walk. There is also a historic lock and an 1836 lock house, picnic groves, 3 miles of riverside and woodland trails connecting to other trail networks, and an herb garden. The area is centered on a remnant of the Schuylkill Navigation system of dams, pools, and canals built in the early 1800s to make the river navigable from Philly to the coal regions 100 miles north. Of 60 miles of hand-dug canals, only the Mont Clare Schuylkill Canal area and Manayunk's canal remain. Bring your dog back for:

Annual Canal Day (Last Sunday in June). This is a gala celebration on the banks of the canal, with an art show, trail run, fishing derby, canoe race, live music, food, crafts, and games.

Luminaria (December). The locktender's house will be decorated and hundreds of candle luminaria will light the towpath to the house.

Skippack Village

Skippack is not only a great Victorian town (actually, it was settled in 1702, and during the American Revolution, Continental troops encamped here, but the atmosphere today is definitely Victorian), it's both tourist- and dog-friendly. You can have a really great time here with your dog; come stroll the streets. Skippack welcomes visitors to such an extent that there are restrooms visitors can use at the following locations: Dutch Cottage Tavern, Skippack Roadhouse, Justin's Carriage House Restaurant, Floral and Hardy, and behind Skippack Travel. You can park anywhere. There are lots of places to sit outside and rest with your dog, and about 70 shops and restaurants. For more information and a free guide, call 610-584-3074, or visit the Skippack Village Web site at www.skippackvillage.com.

If you would like to go to a restaurant where you can sit with your dog, try:

▶ **Back Porch Café, 610-584-7870.** This restaurant offers fine dining, with outdoor seating from May to September. Dogs on-leash are permitted to sit with you outside. The staff will provide your dog with water on request.

▶ **Mal's American Diner, 610-584-0900.** This restaurant offers family dining, and also has outdoor seating from May to September. The management is the same as for the Back Porch Café, and therefore the policies regarding dogs are also the same. And according to the owner of these restaurants, "Most of the shops in [Skippack] Village are okay with dogs."

Come back to Skippack for the marvelous and fun dog-friendly events:

▶ **President's Day Weekend (February).** Three days of shopping and celebrating.

▶ **Skippack Spring Fest (May).** At this weekend fest, over 100 artists and crafters offer their items for sale, while Victorian dancers wander the street before giving a formal performance. There are kids' activities, and all the good things that go into a good street festival.

▶ **Skippack Festival of the Arts (June).** This juried show of arts and crafts was inaugurated in 1999, and it is great fun! You'll find food booths along the way, and there is live music.

▶ **Skippack Under the Stars (June, July, August, and September).** Held one Friday night each month. Enjoy a night in a country village. Admission is free.

▶ **Fourth of July in Skippack.** A village parade, fun, and food at an outdoor barbecue. Admission is charged.

▶ **Skippack Super Sales (September).** A weekend event.

▶ **Skippack Days (October).** Includes entertainment and arts and crafts.

▶ **Holiday Open House (November).** On Black Friday (the Friday after Thanksgiving), the shops in Skippack Village stay open until 9:00 p.m. and offer complimentary treats and drinks. The village is decorated for the winter holidays.

▶ **Illuminaire Nites (December).** Skippack Village glows with candlelight every Wednesday and Friday from the beginning of December to the last Wednesday or Friday before Christmas.

▶ **Lighting of the Village Tree (December).** The Skippack Village Christmas tree is located in front of Floral and Hardy. Come and celebrate the official lighting with carolers, Santa, and more.

Looking for a park? There's one heck of a park nearby:

▶ **Evansburg State Park.** The park consists of 3,349 acres in south central Montgomery County, between Norristown and Collegeville, along the Skippack Creek. You can reach it by following

Germantown Pike. There are meadows, old fields, mature woodlands, play fields, picnic areas, and trails here, available to you and your dog daily from 8:00 a.m. to sunset. Evansburg offers activities that include fishing, hunting/dog training (the hunting areas are clearly marked), hiking, biking, picnicking, winter sports, and horseback riding. There's an eight-arch stone bridge spanning the Skippack Creek on Germantown Pike: built in 1792, this is the oldest bridge in continuous heavy use in the U.S. There are restrooms and water available at Evansburg, as well as a nature center. This is a beautiful park, with the remains of mill buildings and homes from the 1700s and 1800s.

If your dog would like to do some shopping after you've enjoyed yourselves in the Skippack area, try:

▶ **Creatures Feeds & Needs, 3411 Skippack Pike, 610-584-8874.** Do they permit dogs inside? "Permit it? We prefer it. All the dogs are offered treats (with their parents' permission). We always fawn over them as much as we can. Most of the time we know the dogs by name and refer to their people as Rover's mom or dad." This shop has photos with Santa for all pets, and holds a Halloween parade and costume contest. "We also hold a raffle at least once a year to raise money for our no-kill rescue." Other comments: "Our focus is on health and nutrition. If you have any questions about your dog's behavior, food, skin/haircoat or other issue, we will probably be able to provide effective, natural advice. Our gorgeously restored barn is also a fun place just to see." And beyond that: "We are located in a village of shops outside Skippack. Most of the shops are antique and gift shops, and they all allow well-behaved dogs to shop with their parents." Want more info? E-mail them at creatures@p3.net, or visit their Web site at www.creaturesneeds.com.

When December comes, don't forget to take your dog to:

▶ **Boswell's Cut-Your-Own Christmas Tree Farm.** Bridge Road Farm is on Route 113 between Routes 73 and 29.

In nearby Worcester, you may want to stop by:

▶ **The Peter Wentz Farmstead, Schultz Road (off Route 73), 610-584-5104.** There are over 90 acres on this historic farmstead. Dogs are allowed on the grounds, but only in the upper portion near the main parking lot (there are fields there), not where the farm animals are. Still, the 1758 Georgian mansion is beautiful and a nice example of a blending of architectural styles by second-generation Germans. Closed Mondays and some holidays. Admission is free. They have some events during the year, including:
   Muster Day (June). Enjoy 18th-century Pennsylvania's arts and crafts, and a reenactment of a mustering of farm citizens in preparation for war. Admission is free.

Just to the north of Skippack is Harleysville, and:

▶ **The Mennonite Heritage Center, 565 Yoder Road, 215-256-3020, www.mhep.org.** You can bring your dog on-leash onto the grounds here, as well as to events, such as:
   Annual Apple Butter Frolic (October). You and your dog can come and enjoy folk craft demonstrations, Pennsylvania-German food, stage programs, and old-fashioned games. Admission is charged, except for children under 12.

❧ WESTERN MONTGOMERY COUNTY

Schwenksville

Take your dog to:

▶ **Green Lane Park, Route 29, Green Lane.** Formerly the Upper Perkiomen Valley and Green Lane Reservoir Parks, the combined park features cross-country skiing, sledding, camping, picnicking, bridle trails, a nature center, and gardens. There are a total of 3,200 acres of woods and fields here, and three large lakes: Green Lane Reservoir, Deep Creek Lake, and Knight Lake. At Deep Creek and Knight Lakes you can fish and boat, and rental boats are available. There's lots of hiking throughout the park for you and your dog to enjoy, as well as 400 picnic tables, and restrooms. Bring your dog back to the park for these great events:

    Band Concerts (Summer). Held on Sundays.

    Row Boat Regatta (July 4). You can borrow rowboats for free to enter this holiday boat regatta, but you have to decorate your boat! Or you and your dog can just stand on the sidelines at the Deep Creek Lake Pavilion and watch. Prizes are awarded for the most patriotic and creative boats.

If you and your dog are looking for another event to go to in the area, try:

▶ **Upper Perkiomen Fourth of July.** This event is combined with Community Awareness Day, and held in **Goshenhoppen Park in East Greenville.** You can enjoy puppet shows, music, amusement rides, and a craft show, as well as a firefighters' water battle, home-run derby, baby parade, band concert, and fireworks in the evening.

The final thing you and your dog might want to do in the area is stop by:

▶ **Pennypacker Mills, 5 Haldeman Road at Route 73 (Skippack Pike), Schwenksville, 610-287-9349.** An 18th-century colonial mansion on a 135-acre gentleman's farm. This is county property, and technically dogs are not permitted on the grounds, but people do bring them and the staff doesn't kick them off the property, I've been told. However, dogs are definitely *not* permitted at events held here, like the Civil War Reunion, because of gunfire. So, I guess if you want to bring your dog on-leash to see the Colonial Revival mansion, you can. The house and grounds are beautiful. Closed Mondays. Admission is free.

Limerick

There are a couple of cool places to take your dog in Limerick:

▶ **Stone Hills, Limerick Township, 610-827-0156 (for directions).** This is a Natural Lands Trust property. There are 12.6 acres with a half-mile trail. Along the way you can admire the bridge, mature forest, the creek, and rock outcroppings. There is on-site parking. Picnicking, bicycling, and swimming are prohibited in Natural Lands Trust preserves. Your dog must be on-leash, and be aware that some preserves have a hunting program in November and January: signs are posted when the preserves are closed.

▶ **Sunrise Mill, Swamp Creek Road (where Limerick Township meets Upper and Lower Frederick Townships), 610-584-0222.** The mill buildings—a 1767 grist and saw mill along the Swamp Creek, and a house and bank barn from the mid-1800s—are under restoration. Besides these picturesque structures, there are 200 acres to explore with your dog.

And your dog can go shopping at:

▶ **Pet Valu, Royersford Center, 70 Buckwalter Road, 610-792-9294**

(Pottstown)

Pottstown was founded in 1752 by ironmaster John Potts. The downtown area and the neighborhoods nearby made it onto the National Register of Historic Places in 1985, and there are two local ordinances protecting the exteriors of over 1,000 homes and buildings. Although the town is a bit spread out, it is very interesting. There is a pavilion with a lovely clock downtown. Along Hanover and King Streets are nice historic homes, churches, and other buildings. The official Old Pottstown National Historic District is bounded by South, Race, Bailey, Adams, Lincoln, Beech, and Manatawny Streets, plus High Street between Hanover and Franklin Streets.

You can pick up food or coffee at various places along the way, and there are two major parks included in Pottstown's five square miles along the Schuylkill River: **Riverfront Park** along the Schuylkill, and **Memorial Park** along the Manatawny Creek. Dogs on-leash are permitted in both, and there are smaller parks as well.

There are also plenty of places to get some takeout food, and:

▶ **Pottstown Dairy Queen, 1390 North Charlotte Street.** Outdoor seating is available from March to November, and your dog can sit there with you. They will gladly give you water or ice for your dog.

There are some annual events in Pottstown that you may want to check out with your dog:

▶ **Suburban Cable Bicycle Race (June).** The race goes through the downtown area.
▶ **Annual Pottstown Rumble (June).** This is a volleyball tournament in Memorial Park. Great fun to watch with your dog!
▶ **Annual Preservation Pottstown 5K Race (June).** You and your dog can watch hundreds of runners in this race that benefits local historic preservation efforts.

You and your dog may also want to check out:

▶ **Pottsgrove Manor, 100 West King Street, 610-326-4014.** A 1754 Georgian mansion owned by John Potts, the founder of Pottstown. Troops from Valley Forge foraged for food and other supplies in the Pottstown area while John's son, Pennsylvania militia colonel Thomas Potts, was living in the mansion. There are events held here from time to time, such as:

Camp Pottsgrove (September). Commemorates George Washington's army encampment during the fall of 1777. There are programs throughout the day, including a self-guided tour of the encampment area. Admission is free. For information, call 610-326-4014.

Your dog can go shopping in Pottstown at:

▶ **Pet Valu, Pottstown Center, 223 Shoemaker Road, 610-718-9970.** You may bring your dog on-leash inside the store. They will offer biscuits. Anything else? "Wide selection of dog items, very competitive prices."

And your dog can shop with you at:

▶ **Dilworth Lawn Ornaments, 124 Shoemaker Road, 610-970-9583.** Small dogs are permitted inside.

There are several choices of places where the two of you can pick up a Christmas tree in the Pottstown area:

▶ **Coventree Farm, 661 Ebelhare Road, 610-287-5983.** Your well-mannered dog on-leash can come with you to help get a tree.
▶ **Kutz Christmas Tree Farm, 10001 Cadmus Road, 610-469-0321.** Your dog can help you select a blue spruce or a Douglas fir. If you go in the evening, they have a lighting display.
▶ **Westlake Tree Farm, 2421 North Hill Camp Road, 610-469-6913.** On weekends, the farm has a no-pet policy, but if you and your dog on-leash want to go on a weekday, when there are fewer people around, they may relax the policy. Give them a call before you go.

You and your dog are welcome to stay overnight in Pottstown at:

▶ **Comfort Inn, Route 100, 610-326-5000.** There are no restrictions on pets, but a $25 deposit is required. They have grounds where you can walk your dog.
▶ **Days Inn, High and Manatawny Streets, 610-970-1101.** They will charge your dog a $10 fee per night. There are grounds for walking your dog.

Bucks County

Bucks County is chock-full of beautiful countryside, lovely towns, and parks—*lots* of parks! It's a great big, dog-friendly playground. If you aren't lucky enough to live there (or even if you are), pack up your dog and go see what Bucks County has to offer!

Let me start with a couple of general items. There is one particularly wonderful place you should keep in mind as you and your dog enjoy yourselves in Bucks:

▶ **Delaware Canal State Park.** Extending from Bristol to Easton, the Delaware Canal is the only remaining early- to mid-19th-century, continuously intact canal in the country. Five feet deep, it was used to move anthracite from the Upper Lehigh Valley to Philadelphia and New York, and thus was crucial to the Industrial Revolution in the United States.

The last paying boat went through in 1931, and the state park was established in 1940. Besides the canal and towpath, the park includes portions of the Delaware shoreline, and 11 river islands that together have been designated as a natural area. The canal is a National Historic Landmark, while the 60-mile towpath is a National Heritage Hiking Trail that follows the Delaware Canal its entire length, and provides access to the Delaware River at six public recreation areas. There are picnic areas, restrooms, and lots of things to see and do along the way. As you travel through Bucks, remember that you can pick up the towpath virtually anywhere you please along the Delaware River: among other places, it passes through Morrisville, Yardley, Washington Crossing Historic Park, New Hope, Centre Bridge, Point Pleasant, Tinicum, and Erwinna, on its way to Easton.

Enjoy this unique recreation area with your dog. It is a beautiful and fascinating place that really lets you experience history. Hike or jog along the towpath, picnic where you please, or just rest at one of the river access areas and watch people launching canoes. You and your dog can also canoe on the river (assuming your dog is used to that kind of thing, and both of you are wearing life vests—yes, they do make them for dogs, and yes, dogs need them just as humans do) and head over to the river islands to explore. Treat the islands with respect, and carry out what you carry in. For more information on Delaware Canal State Park, visit the Pennsylvania Department of Conservation and Natural Resources (DCNR) Web site at www.dcnr.state.pa.us, or call 888-PA-PARKS. You can order a recreational guide for the park from the DCNR.

Even more information on the canal and park can be obtained from the Friends of the Delaware Canal: 215-862-2021, www.fodc.org. They also sponsor an annual event that might be of interest to you and your dog:

Annual Canal Walk (End of September/beginning of October). Walk all 60 miles of the towpath if you and your dog can handle it, or walk one or two of several different segments. For more information, contact the Friends of the Delaware Canal.

You and your dog should also know that all Bucks County parks are dog-friendly, as long as your dog is on a leash no longer than 6 feet, and you don't take him or her into any overnight areas (camps or cabin areas).

LOWER BUCKS COUNTY

Bensalem

Although there aren't lots of ways in particular that your dog and you can enjoy Bensalem, there are a few. First, you can check out a couple of historic places:

▶ **Growden Mansion.** Growden Mansion, also called Trevose, is either an original mansion from the late 1600s or a rebuilding from circa 1740 (the evidence is inconclusive). Either way, it is an early example of Palladian architecture in the Delaware Valley. Sited on 12 acres bounded by East Drive, Valley Drive, and the road behind Durham Place, the mansion and outbuildings are interesting and lovely in their own way. Take a walk around the grounds with your dog on-leash.

▶ **Pen Ryn Mansion on the Delaware, 1601 State Road, 215-633-0600.** Pen Ryn is a privately owned museum and banquet facility, carefully restored and very interesting to look at. It sits on 100 riverfront acres, and has some lovely gardens. The **Delaware River Access Area,** managed by the Bucks County Department of Parks and Recreation, surrounds Pen Ryn. Only about 8 acres of the area are developed, but those acres include about 2,000 feet along the river, with picnic facilities. It is open from sunrise to sunset. Have a picnic with your dog, and watch boats being launched onto the Delaware River.

When you've finished enjoying yourselves at Growden and Pen Ryn, you can take your dog shopping at:

▶ **PETCO, 2355 Street Road, 215-245-7133.** Keep an eye out for events the store may sponsor from time to time.

Then take your dog to play in:

▶ **Neshaminy State Park, Dunks Ferry Road.** Dunks Ferry Road, which forms the east boundary of this 330-acre park, is one of the oldest roads in the commonwealth. This is a great park, with picnic facilities, fishing, swimming, food service, and Delaware River access for boating. There are several hiking trails, including the **River Walk Trail,** for which you can pick up a brochure at the park office. For more information, visit the Pennsylvania Department of Conservation and Natural Resources (DCNR) Web site at www.dcnr.state.pa.us, or call 888-PA-PARKS.

If you are looking for events in Bensalem, I know of a couple:

- ▶ **Memorial Day Parade (May).** Sponsored by the Bensalem Chamber of Commerce.
- ▶ **Annual Tree Lighting (December).** Held at the Township Municipal Complex. You and your dog can join madrigals and a choir in caroling and await Santa's arrival.

For more details on these events, contact Bensalem Township, 2400 Byberry Road, 215-633-3600, or visit their Web site at www.bensalemtownship.org, which should also keep you up-to-date on other events that may happen.

If you and your dog need a place to stay in Bensalem, try:

- ▶ **Comfort Inn, 3660 Street Road, 215-245-0100.** There are no restrictions, but dogs are charged $10 per night.
- ▶ **Korman Suites.** See full description on page 24. Korman Suites has the following locations in Bensalem:

    Korman Suites Apartments, 1459 Neshaminy Valley Drive, 215-752-5400
    Korman Suites–Country Lights, 3300 Neshaminy Boulevard, 215-752-5347
    Korman Suites at Village Square East, 180 Willow Court, 215-245-6888
    Korman Suites at Village Square West, 370 Redwood Court, 215-639-5000

Bristol Township

Among the highlights you and your dog will find in Bristol Township are some very pretty parks, including:

- ▶ **Oxford Valley County Park, Hood Boulevard and Oxford Valley Road.** There are woodlands here; trails for hiking, walking, jogging, or biking; open field areas; and the 9-acre Lake Caroline. **Chickenfoot Park**, a part of Oxford Valley County Park, is a natural area recognized as significant by the Nature Conservancy.
- ▶ **Silver Lake County Park and Nature Center, 1306 Bath Road.** There are 393 acres here for you and your dog to explore. The Silver Lake Nature Center, part of the park, is one of the few nature centers I have found that is dog-friendly: your dog can come with you to explore its 235 preserve acres, including 170-acre Delhaas Woods, through which there are several miles of trails. Silver Lake County Park is adjacent, and there are two lakes there, as well as more great trails. You can boat, fish, hike, picnic, or just plain enjoy yourselves. The park is open daily from sunrise to sunset, and there are restrooms available.

To the immediate north of Silver Lake County Park is:

- ▶ **Black Ditch County Park, Mill Creek and Bloomsdale Roads.** There are 80 acres of hiking opportunities here for you and your dog to enjoy.

All that hiking is bound to make you and your dog hungry, and you can eat together nearby at:

▶ **Ted's Lakeside Deli, 803 Bath Road, 215-788-5188.** Not only is it a deli, it's also a dairy bar. They have several benches and tables outside, year-round, and your dog is welcome to sit there with you. They will offer your dog ice or water, and if you want, you can get your dog a hot dog. And, they say, "Once we made a grilled cheese for a beagle. He devoured it!"

Levittown

Levittown is famous because it was the first planned community in the country, built just after World War II to house returning GIs. It's a very interesting place, and worth a ride or walk around to see. You'll notice right away that the streets are in alphabetical sections. When you and your dog have finished admiring the community, you can explore a couple of local county parks:

▶ **Frosty Hollow County Park, New Falls Road.** Open from sunrise to sunset, there are 95 acres of woodland to hike through here. You can also picnic if your dog would like to.
▶ **Queen Anne County Park, New Falls and Woodbourne Roads.** Mostly undeveloped woodland, this park is available for exploration from sunrise to sunset.

Does your dog need to go shopping? Try:

▶ **Bristol Feed & Grain Company, 1415 Elkins Avenue, 215-943-6343.** You can bring your dog in here to get supplies, and they will provide treats. They custom-fit leashes and harnesses. They also have a scale to weigh dogs.

Bristol Borough

This is a very fun place to explore with your dog. Four of the borough's five wards are on the National Historic Registry. Historic Mill Street is the main business district of Bristol Borough, and it is very pretty, lined with Bradford pear trees, with sidewalks of brick. There are plenty of benches where you can stop and rest with your dog, and several restaurants where you can get some takeout food. The buildings along Mill Street reflect a range of architecture.

Okay, your dog is tired of walking around and wants to find a large, grassy area. You can take your dog into any Bristol Borough park, and the best places to go are:

▶ **Spurline Park.** This is a mile-long swath of land that runs through the borough, from Mill Street to Trenton Avenue, following what was once a main line of the Pennsylvania Railroad. There are plans to extend this park.
▶ **Memorial Fountain and Park.** Located at Pond and Beaver Streets, this is a small park, but it contains one remaining section of railroad track, commemorating Abraham Lincoln's stop in 1861 on his preinauguration journey to Washington, D.C.

▶ **Bristol Marsh.** Located next to the municipal parking lot to the right at the end of Mill Street. There are signs at the south end of the lot, and you can look for the observation deck. The marsh includes 11 acres managed by the Nature Conservancy, with a buffer of 7 acres of adjacent land. It is one of the last remaining freshwater tidal marshes along the Delaware River in Pennsylvania. The marsh ecosystem and wetland plants can be studied from both the viewing platforms and a nature trail.

Delaware Canal State Park's towpath begins in Bristol, at **Grundy Park**, where, I'm told, old buttonwood trees form the shape of a *B*. Bristol Borough has the last water-filled sections of the canal. You and your dog can go see the **Bristol Lagoon** near the end of the canal: there is a gazebo overlooking the lagoon off Jefferson Avenue. The lagoon was recently restored as part of the five-year restoration plan for the Delaware Canal.

There are a few borough events that you and your dog may want to make a point of coming back for:

▶ **Annual Historic Bristol Day (Third Saturday in October).** Join the festivities: your dog on-leash is welcome at anything that is going on outside. For information, call 215-781-9895.

▶ **Christmas Caroling and Tree Lighting (End of November).** Held at 131 Mill Street. Put on your dog's reindeer antlers and jingle bells, and come join the celebration.

▶ **First Night® (December 31).** The first First Night® happened in Boston in 1976. The goal of the celebration is to offer a nonalcoholic visual and performing arts festival featuring local artists on New Year's Eve, right up to midnight. While some events take place indoors, where your dog probably cannot go, there are outdoor venues, including streets, sidewalks, public open spaces, and even storefront windows. Wear a hat, paint your face, dress up—be creative, that's the point. To enjoy the celebration, you buy a First Night® button that helps support the cost of putting on the festival. It's a great way to bring in the New Year, and you and your dog won't wake up with a hangover.

If you and your dog would like to stay overnight, there's a place nearby:

▶ **Days Inn, Route 13 (Bristol Pike) and the Pennsylvania Turnpike, Bristol, 215-788-8400.** You can stay here with your dog if you are willing to pay a $5 fee per night. There are grounds available for walking your dog.

(Falls Township)

Falls Township may at first glance appear to be typical suburban sprawl. That first glance is wrong. There is history here—marvelous history. Take a look at the gem of Falls Township (in my humble opinion):

▶ **Historic Fallsington, 4 Yardley Avenue, Fallsington, 215-295-6567.** This is a 300-year-old village that is absolutely wonderful to visit: walking amidst its 90-some buildings is like stepping right into colonial America. And the coolest part is that people really live here! What a beautiful little pocket of history in the middle of commercial strips, big roads, suburban houses, and industry. And it is *very* dog-friendly.

You can take your dog on-leash along on the formal tours of the village offered by Historic Fallsington, Inc. You can also take your dog into the Historic Fallsington Information Center (in the Gillingham Store, a general store opened circa 1910) to get a brochure and map for a self-guided tour. The center is open Monday through Saturday from 9:00 a.m. to 5:00 p.m., and Sunday from noon to 5:00 p.m., from the beginning of May to December 24 (closed Memorial Day weekend); after December 24, Monday through Friday from 9:00 a.m. to 5:00 p.m.

There are wonderful, dog-friendly events in Historic Fallsington to come back for:

Historic Fallsington Opening Day Celebration (May). Held on the Saturday before Mother's Day, this free event includes demonstrations of colonial skills, and a perfectly timed Mother's Day flower sale.

Historic Fallsington Day (Second Saturday in October). Admission is charged for this event, but you can see historical reenactors, crafters, and American Indian dancers all day in Meetinghouse Square.

Historic Fallsington Christmas Tree Lighting and Caroling (Second Sunday in December). Come to Meetinghouse Square to sing carols around the tree. This event is free.

Before you leave the area, take your dog for a walk in **Fallsington County Park**, right next to Historic Fallsington, at Tyburn and Trenton Roads.

While you're in Falls Township, your dog may want to stop at one of these stores to pick up some supplies:

▶ **PETCO, 110 Lincoln Highway, Fairless Hills, 215-943-6440**
▶ **PetsMart, 220 Commerce Boulevard, Fairless Hills, 215-949-9602**
▶ **Pet Valu, Queen Anne Plaza, 511 Oxford Valley Road, Fairless Hills, 215-946-5571**

And there is one last park you and your dog can visit:

▶ **Falls Riverfront Park.** Located next to Pennsbury Manor (where your dog is not allowed), this is a bit out of the way, but if you and your dog are up for a longish and sometimes strange journey, head here. You can reach it by taking the right-hand fork of Pennsbury Road rather than going to the manor site. Before you get there, you'll drive through some pretty unusual landscape created by the USX Corporation. The park itself is along the Delaware, and there are areas to walk around and picnic. Our dogs liked it, but it is a bit isolated.

Morrisville

Morrisville is a nice, largish town along the Delaware River, and the Delaware Canal towpath goes right through the middle of it. It's a nice place to take a stroll with your dog.

If you and your dog like it in Morrisville, there are some annual events you may want to come back for:

▶ **Memorial Day Parade (May)**
▶ **The River Festival (Summer).** This is held in **Williamson Park, along Delmorr Avenue**. For information on this or any other event, contact the Borough of Morrisville, 35 Union Street, 215-295-8181. Your dog on-leash is permitted at Williamson Park.

▶ **Labor Day Picnic/10K Run (September).** This is also held in Williamson Park, with pic-nicking, games, classic cars and fire engines, arts and crafts exhibits, music, food, and more.

Just north of Morrisville is:

▶ **Falls of the Delaware County Park.** You and your dog can walk along the towpath right out of Morrisville and into this park. There are 125 acres here along River Road, adjacent to the Delaware River and Delaware Canal State Park. It is undeveloped, but open from sunrise to sunset. It's a lovely place to explore.

Yardley Borough

Yardley was incorporated as a borough in 1895, and it is yet another great place to walk around and explore with your dog. If you want to know what you are looking at as you stroll around town, you can get a walking tour brochure for a small fee from the Yardley Historical Association, 46 West Afton Avenue, P.O. Box 212, Yardley, PA 19067, 215-493-9883. The historic highlights you can enjoy in Yardley include:

▶ **The Delaware Canal.** Yes, the towpath is here. The canal runs between Main Street and the Delaware River. Our dogs enjoyed Yardley's section of the towpath very much.

Are you and your dog hungry? You can pick up some takeout food from a variety of places in Yardley. Or you can get something to eat together at:

▶ **Charcoal Steaks N' Things, 11 South Delaware Avenue.** You can get breakfast, lunch, and dinner here—from cereal and omelets to burgers, to soup and a sandwich, to entrées like steak or crab cakes—and take your meal out to the riverside picnic area, where there are tables with umbrellas and a terrific view of the river. It's a great place to hang out, and you are free to BYOB. If you'd like more information, call 215-493-6394, or visit their Web site at www.bucksnet.com/charcoalsteaks. (Sometimes there are even coupons on the site that you can print out and use toward your meal.)

Annual Yardley events that are pretty cool include:

▶ **Memorial Day Parade (May)**
▶ **Yardley Canal Festival (June).** Among other entertainment, this new festival is planned to include a decorated canoe parade. Definitely something you and your dog will enjoy.
▶ **Harvest Day (Last weekend in September).** Over 160 vendors and crafters are spread out along Canal and Main Streets, as well as along the canal. There is also plenty of food and entertainment.
▶ **Old-Fashioned Christmas (Early December).** There's a tree-lighting ceremony, followed by a parade featuring bands, floats, singers, and more. Clowns, antique cars, and wandering minstrels are also on hand. And there are hot chestnuts and popcorn available.

For more information on these events, contact Yardley Borough, 56 South Main Street, 215-493-6832. And if it's December, head to:

▶ **Shady Brook Farm, 931 Stony Hill Road, 215-968-1670.** You and your dog will love their 250-acre drive-through light show.

(Langhorne Borough)

Langhorne Borough is a small, 18th-century village: very pretty with nice old buildings. There are Georgian and Craftsman-style buildings for your dog and you to admire, as well as a variety of Victorian homes. A self-guided walking tour brochure put out by the Historic Langhorne Association is available at Judy's Corner, 127 South Bellevue Avenue, 215-757-6158. The Langhorne National Historic District is bounded by Summit and Marshall Avenues, Pine Street, Richardson Avenue, and Green Street.

While you're walking around with your dog, you may want to know about the following:

▶ **Memorial Park, along West Maple Avenue.** In case your dog should have a need.
▶ **Langhorne Coffee House, 102 South Bellevue Avenue.** They have benches outside where you can sit with your dog.

Langhorne Borough puts on some wonderful annual events, including:

▶ **Memorial Day Parade (May).** Sponsored together with Langhorne Manor Borough.
▶ **Bucks County Folksong Concert Under the Stars (June).** This takes place at Langhorne Heritage Farm, on Route 213 (Maple Avenue). Bring a blanket and your dog on-leash, and enjoy the music together. Call 215-757-0471 for details.
▶ **Caroling (December)**

For details on these events, contact Langhorne Borough, 114 East Maple Avenue, 215-757-3768.

If your dog would like to do some shopping, you can head to:

▶ **Pet Valu, The Shoppes at Flowers Mill, 154 North Flowers Mill Road, 215-741-7070.** They will give dogs on-leash a treat to sustain them while shopping. They sometimes have pet photo days: check with the store for dates. They also donate food to animal shelters, so they are good folks.

And you and your dog can stay together in the Langhorne area at:

▶ **Red Roof Inn–Oxford Valley, 3100 West Cabot Boulevard, 215-750-6200**

There are two great county parks very close to Langhorne:

▶ **Playwicki County Park.** Located north of West Maple Avenue, and west of Langhorne Borough, there are 33 acres here along the Neshaminy Creek. Two stone-arched railroad bridges cross the creek right next to the park, forming a picturesque background. You can hike and picnic and fish here with your dog, from sunrise to sunset.
▶ **Core Creek County Park.** Located between Tollgate, Woodbourne, and Langhorne-Yardley Roads and the Bridgetown Pike, this is a terrific place to spend a half-day or even an entire

day. There are 1,200 acres for you and your dog to enjoy, including 156-acre Lake Luxembourg (boating is permitted, but only boats with electric motors are allowed). There are bridle trails, hiking and biking trails, jogging paths, playgrounds, picnic areas, restrooms, athletic facilities, and more. And you and your dog will definitely want to come back for some of the really cool events held here:

Olan Turner Memorial Kite Day (May). Features kite workshops for kids, professional kite demonstrations and sport kite exhibitions, giant kites, and more. There is no entrance fee. Bring a chair, a blanket, a picnic lunch, and your dog on-leash, and sit back to enjoy the festivities. For information, call 215-757-0571.

Annual International Day Festival (September). The festival celebrates ethnic diversity through music, crafts, games, and food. You and your dog on-leash can enjoy cultural music from Scotland, Brazil, Trinidad, India, Spain, Puerto Rico, and Poland, Jewish music, world dance, Italian puppet theater, African-American Stilt Ballet performances, and more. Admission is charged.

Annual Bucks County Antique Car Show (September). Benefits the Churchville Nature Center. Admission is charged, but parking is free. For more information, call 215-357-4005.

Annual Cornell Pumpkin Festival (October). Sponsored by the Churchville Nature Center, the festival features crafts and games, pumpkin painting, a magician, nature exhibits, and more. Admission is charged. A highlight is the Great Pumpkin Weigh-in. Dogs on-leash are welcome.

Hulmeville

This is a small town, but it has some great National Historic Sites that you and your dog can look for, such as the Hulmeville Inn, Johnson's Hall, and the old Hulmeville Schoolhouse. Take a stroll around with your dog. And if you happen to be in Hulmeville at the time, you can take in annual events such as the **Christmas tree-lighting ceremony**, or the warm-weather **All-Hulmeville Flea Market**.

Newtown Township

Newtown Township parks are open to your dog on-leash, as long as you clean up (of course). There's also a place to take your dog shopping:

▶ **Pet Valu, Village at Newtown Shopping Center, 2814 South Eagle Road, 215-504-7170**

And you can even take your dog to do some produce-picking in Newtown Township:

▶ **Active Acres, 881 Highland Road, 215-860-6855 or 215-579-7766.** Dogs on-leash are permitted during the day (though not for nighttime events). You and your dog can pick your own strawberries and pumpkins here. Call to find out when the time is ripe.

Newtown Borough

This is a great historic town, with over 400 shops and businesses. It's a wonderful place to explore. As you walk around, you and your dog can do lots of window-shopping, and there are plenty of benches to rest on or enjoy some takeout food. The local **Starbucks, 100 South State Street,** has benches in front. If you want to know what you're looking at as you stroll the streets of Newtown Borough, you can get a walking tour brochure and map from the Newtown Historic Association, Court Street and Center Avenue, 215-968-4004.

Here's a taste of the annual events that you and your dog will absolutely want to come back for:

- **Newtown Car Show & Sidewalk Sale (July).** You can bring your dog to enjoy this event, which is exactly what it sounds like. Call 215-968-3611 for details.
- **Annual Market Day (September).** Held along historic Court Street, Mercer Street, and Centre Avenue. Browse through 50 exhibitors of crafts such as pottery, dried flowers, textiles, jewelry, painting, photography, woodworking, and needlework. Live entertainment, including music and colonial juggling, will amuse you and your dog the entire day. Admission is free.
- **Newtown Halloween Parade (October).** Put on your costume (and your dog's) and take part, or at least watch.
- **First Night® Newtown (December 31).** First Night® is a different sort of New Year's Eve celebration, with the focus on the arts, not alcohol. Newtown first put one on in 1998. It was a great success, and a wonderful showcase for local arts and artists. While some venues are indoors, there is plenty going on in the street and even in shop windows, so you and your dog should be able to have a fun time. Live performances of dance, music, and more will be offered right up until midnight. You can attend by buying a First Night® button. It's a great way to bring in the New Year.

Lower Southampton

There are a couple of great, dog-friendly events here:

- **Independence Day Parade (July).** Lots of bands, antique and race cars, floats, a baby parade, and more.
- **Gibson Road Antique Fire Association Fire Engine Muster (September).** Held at 4900 Street Road in Trevose. You and your dog on-leash can enjoy over 100 firefighting vehicles from all eras, as well as a Dalmatian contest, a flea market, games, live music, and food. The event is free. Call 215-245-1545 for more information.

Dogs are permitted in Lower Southampton parks at present, but keep an eye out: the township is considering prohibiting them because of owner irresponsibility. For more information, contact Lower Southampton Township, 215-357-1235.

Your dog can go shopping in Lower Southampton at:

- **Pet Valu, Feasterville Shopping Center, 1045 Bustleton Pike, Feasterville, 215-942-4567**
- **PETCO, 97 East Street Road, Feasterville, 215-354-0820**

And if you and your dog want to stay overnight, try:

- **Red Roof Inn–Trevose, 3100 Lincoln Highway, 215-244-9422.** AAA-approved.

Northampton

You and your dog may want to spend some time exploring the Churchville National Historic District. This district extends into both Northampton and Upper Southampton, along Bristol Road, Bustleton Pike, and Cornell and Knowles Avenues. Then come back to Northampton for some good events:

▶ **Northampton Days (September).** There's a parade, a bike rally, a car show, a petting zoo, craft displays, a closing concert, and—a dog show! Admission is free.

▶ **Halloween Happening (October).** Includes a children's concert, costume parade, crafts and games, and a painted or carved pumpkin contest. It's a chance for you and your dog to dress up and see who looks better.

Your dog can go shopping in Northampton at:

▶ **Lick Your Chops, 700 2nd Street Pike, Richboro, 215-322-5266.** You and your dog can browse through pet supplies of all kinds, and they have treats available for your dog. In October, they have a pet fair, and in December, photographs with Santa.

And the two of you can go to pick a pumpkin or get a holiday tree at:

▶ **Bryan's Farm, 2032 2nd Street Pike ($2^1/_2$ miles north of Richboro), 215-598-3206.** In December, you and your dog can choose from blue and white spruce, or Douglas fir trees, and also pick up some greens. The farm offers wagon rides to the trees. "A lot of people bring dogs," they told me, and dogs have even gone on hayrides.

There are also some truly wonderful parks in the area:

▶ **Churchville County Park, 501 Churchville Lane, Northampton Township.** The park has 172 acres across Churchville Lane from the Churchville Nature Center, at which dogs are not permitted. You can hike and picnic in the park, and there are equestrian trails. Open from sunrise to sunset.

▶ **Tyler State Park.** This is a really great park along the Neshaminy Creek. There's plenty of parking, $10^1/_2$ miles of paved biking trails, 4 miles of gravel hiking trails, and 9 miles of equestrian trails. You and your dog can use all the trails, but stay alert for other users who may be bigger and faster. There are some wonderful picnic areas here, with restrooms. There is also access to the Neshaminy Creek, where your dog may want to splash around with new canine and human friends on a hot day. The park has a total of 1,711 acres. In the winter, you can come back with your dog and do some cross-country skiing.

Upper Southampton

Upper Southampton has a great park of its own:

▶ **Tamanend Park.** Located along 2nd Street Pike, there are 105 acres here that you and your dog on-leash are welcome to explore. There are hiking trails and a nature center. Obedience and puppy kindergarten classes are held in the park, too.

Southampton also puts on a really great festival that you and your dog on-leash can attend:

▶ **Southampton Days Country Fair (July).** This event starts off with a Fourth of July parade with bands, floats, and a baby parade. Then there's a country fair in Tamanend Park, with a craft show, bingo, games, amusement rides, and a magician. The festival wraps up with fireworks and music. Admission is charged. The fireworks start at 9:30 p.m., so unless your dog couldn't care less about the noise, you might want to go home before then. For information, call 215-355-1714.

And if your dog needs to do some shopping while you're in Southampton, stop by:

▶ **Pet Diner, 454 2nd Street Pike, 215-364-5686.** See full description on page 49.

(Upper Makefield)

Before you get to the major attraction in Upper Makefield, you and your dog might want to do some exploring. At the intersection of River and Browns-burg Roads, there's the Brownsburg Village National Historic District. The Dolington Village National Historic District is at the intersection of Route 532 and Mt. Eyre Road (Washington Crossing Road). You might want to park somewhere and take a sightseeing walk with your dog. Then, of course, you will both want to head to:

▶ **Washington Crossing Historic Park.** The park is open Tuesday through Saturday from 9:00 a.m. to 5:00 p.m., and Sunday from noon to 5:00 p.m.; it is closed Mondays and some holidays. Administered by the Pennsylvania Historical and Museum Commission, this is a National Historic Site: the site of Washington's Christmas Eve crossing of the Delaware River in 1776 to march on Trenton and win a crucial battle with the Hessians occupying that city. There are 13 historic buildings in this 500-acre park, and a hill (the site of Bowman's Tower) that provides some stunning views. The park has two sections, about $3^1/_2$ miles apart: the McConkey's Ferry Section and the Thompson's Mill Section. To enter some areas, a small admission fee is required. For more information, visit the Pennsylvania Department of Conservation and Natural Resources (DCNR) Web site at www.dcnr.state.pa.us, or call 888-PA-PARKS. You can order a recreational guide for the park from the DCNR. The park office can be reached at 215-493-4076.

   Besides hiking, touring, picnicking, and admiring the Delaware River here, you and your dog can enjoy some interesting events (some of them involve loud noises and bangs, so know what your dog can handle and use your judgment). The events change from year to year, but have included:

   Gingerbread Days, George Washington's Birthday Party (February)
   Sheep Shearing at the Thompson-Neely House (May)
   Colonial Day Encampment (May). Admission is charged, but dogs on-leash are permitted.
   Fourth of July Celebration. Includes demonstrations of colonial crafts, and cannon salutes by Coryell's Ferry Militia. Admission is charged.
   British/Hessian Encampment (July)

Encampment Weekend (August). Commemorates the Revolutionary War military encampment at the historic village of Taylorsville. Features military tacticals as well as demonstrations of open-hearth cooking, blacksmithing, rifle crafting, paper making, and cannon training for members of the reenactment community. Admission is charged, but dogs can come on-leash.

Pennsylvania Heritage Day (October). Call 215-493-4076 for details.

Durham Boat Drill (Early December). Free.

Washington Crossing Reenactment Dress Rehearsal (Mid-December). Call 215-493-4076 for times. Admission is charged.

Washington's Crossing (December 25). You and your dog can watch hundreds of reenactors in Continental military uniforms cross the Delaware in replica Durham boats.

❁ CENTRAL BUCKS COUNTY

Warwick Township

You and your dog can enjoy some great parks here:

▶ **Moland House Park, 1641 Old York Road, Hartsville.** Moland House is a historic farmhouse currently undergoing restoration. The plan is to restore it to its appearance in August 1777, when Washington used it as his headquarters. Stop by and take a stroll around to see how things are going.

▶ **Dark Hollow County Park.** This is a 650-acre, undeveloped park along the Neshaminy Creek. Walk along the creek, get your paws wet, but try not to disturb the people trying to fish. The park is open from sunrise to sunset.

Other parks in Warwick Township that you and your dog might want to visit include: **Guinea Lane Park (Guinea Lane), Hidden Pond Park (Long Pond Drive),** and **Hampton Chase Park (Dark Hollow Road).**

Warminster

Warminster has some wonderful parks that you and your dog will want to check out. All Warminster parks permit dogs on-leash, as long as you clean up. The parks are open from 7:00 a.m. to dusk. The parks your dog will like best include:

▶ **Barness Park, Log College and Gorson Drives.** This park has 14 acres of walking trails and nature areas.

▶ **Ivy Woods, Kirk Road, off Jacksonville Road.** Ivy Woods has 12 undeveloped acres you and your dog can explore.

▶ **Kemper Park, Valley and Sinkler Roads.** This is a lovely park along the Little Neshaminy Creek. There are 30 acres, with a fitness trail, walking trails, nature areas, picnic areas, a playground, and active-play areas. In May, the **Annual Rubber Ducky Regatta** is held on the creek. My dogs and I love these kinds of events. Bring a blanket, picnic by the creek, and watch the race with your dogs.

▶ **Log College Park, Log College Drive.** Along with active-play areas, the park's almost 27 acres include nature areas for you and your dog to enjoy.

▶ **Munro Park, Newtown Road, off Bristol Road.** This 36-acre park has active-play areas, nature areas, picnic areas, refreshments, and restrooms.

▶ **Recreation Center, 1101 Little Lane.** There are 13 acres here of mostly active-play areas, but there are restrooms, and in the summer, **concerts** on Wednesday evenings. Bring a lawn chair or blanket, and enjoy. Karen B. Whitney, Warminster's director of parks and recreation, brings her dog Kelsey, an eight-year-old yellow Lab, to "volunteer" at the recreation center, which my dogs and I think is just great.

And if your dog needs to pick up some supplies, you can head to:

▶ **PETCO, 624 York Road, 215-443-5225.** In the past, this store has held a dog wash to benefit Canine Companions for Independence. For more information on this event, call 215-602-2093.

▶ **PetsMart, 934 West Street Road, 215-773-9170**

And you and your dog will no doubt enjoy the following Warminster events:

▶ **Warminster Township Memorial Day Parade (May).** After a ceremony at the township building, the parade begins.

▶ **Annual Puppy Promenade (September).** Sponsored by the Warminster Department of Parks and Recreation and PETCO. Dog owners and dogs can take a 1-mile walk with Kelsey the Rec Dog, for a small participation fee. All are welcome, owners will receive a keepsake photo, and participating dogs will get a treat bag. Your dog (and you) can dress up for the costume parade, or come just for the walk. Preregistration is required.

Ivyland Borough

Ivyland doesn't have a lot of amenities, but it is an interesting place, and you and your dog might want to take a walk or drive around it. There are historic landmarks like the Ivyland Hotel, the Hobensack Mill ruins, and blocks of homes mostly over 100 years old. Ivyland is one of the largest intact Victorian villages in the county, and possibly the state: it was laid out in squares in the 1870s as a summer escape for visitors to the Philadelphia Centennial Exhibition. The developer, unfortunately, went bankrupt.

Warrington

There are lots of parks for you and your dog to enjoy in Warrington, including:

▶ **Palomino Park, on Palomino Drive**
▶ **Valley Glen Park, on Appaloosa Drive**
▶ **Willow Knoll Park, on Oxford Drive**
▶ **Barness Park, on Bristol Road**
▶ **Igoe Porter Wellings Park, on Bradley Road**
▶ **Lower Nike Park, on Bradley Road**
▶ **Bradford Dam Park, on Folly Road**

What else can you do in Warrington?

▶ **Concert Series (June to August).** Held at Barclay Elementary School, 2015 Palomino Drive. Every summer there is a free concert series that both you and your dog on-leash can enjoy. Bring chairs or a blanket, and hear music of all kinds. For information on the schedule, call 215-343-9350.

Finally, you and your dog can get a bite to eat together at:

▶ **Warrington Dairy Queen, 1111 Easton Road.** Outdoor seating is available from March to October, and your dog can sit there with you. Not only that, but all of their products are reduced-fat.

Rushland

You and your dog are welcome to spend some time at:

▶ **Rushland Ridge Vineyards Winery, 1521 Route 413, 215-598-0251.** There are 22 acres to the vineyards, which are open Saturdays from noon to 6:00 p.m., and Sundays from noon to 4:00 p.m.

Buckingham

There are scattered historic areas around Buckingham Township that you and your dog may want to explore. Forest Grove National Historic District, centered on the intersection of Forest Grove and Lower Mountain Roads, is one place the two of you might want to check out. There's also Spring Valley National Historic District, centered on Mill Road and U.S. Route 202, and Wycombe Village National Historic District, bounded by Township Line, Mill Creek, and Forest Grove Roads, Cherry Lane, and Park and Washington Avenues.

When your dog is ready to head to a park, try:

▶ **Holicong Park, Holicong Road and Route 202.** There are **summer concerts** here. Pack a picnic and your dog and go enjoy them.
▶ **Hansell Park, Route 413 and Hansell Road**

Lahaska

There is great shopping in Lahaska:

▶ **Peddler's Village, Routes 202 and 263.** This is a 42-acre complex of shopping, dining, and entertainment. Brick paths and landscaped gardens provide the setting for regular outdoor events, and they will let you bring your dog on-leash onto the premises, though the village doesn't emphasize itself as dog-friendly. Peddler's Village is open Monday through Thursday from 10:00 a.m. to 6:00 p.m., Friday and Saturday from 10:00 a.m. to 9:00 p.m., and Sunday from 11:00 a.m. to 6:00 p.m. From mid-November through December 23, the hours are Monday through Saturday from 10:00 a.m. to 9:00 p.m., and Sunday from 11:00 a.m. to

6:00 p.m. The village is closed on Thanksgiving, Christmas, and New Year's Day. There are all kinds of shops here where you and your dog can at least do some great window-shopping. For more information, check out the village Web site at www.peddlersvillage.com.

A particularly good time to come to Peddler's Village is during one of the many events put on during the year. These are family events, so be sure your dog can handle crowds with kids:

Annual Strawberry, Flower & Garden Festival (May). Enjoy fresh strawberries and preserves while you peruse exhibits from area nurseries, garden clubs, landscapers, floral artists, nature clubs, and more. There are demonstrations and live entertainment. Admission is free.

Fine Art & Contemporary Crafts Show (June). Features a juried outdoor exhibition and sale. There is also live music. Admission is free.

Teddy Bear's Picnic (July). Fun for all ages, with parades and competitions, repairs for injured bears, teddy bear vendors, and live music. Admission is free.

Country Sidewalk Sale (August). At this event, Peddler's Village merchants offer outdoor bargains.

Scarecrow Festival (September). Watch scarecrow-making workshops, pumpkin painting, and a carved, painted, and decorated jack-o-lantern and gourd art contest. Features live music and other entertainment. Admission is free.

Scarecrow Competition and Display (Mid-September to the end of October). See larger-than-life scarecrows displayed outdoors, with categories such as "Extraordinary," "Contemporary," "Traditional," "Amateur," and "Whirligig."

Apple Festival (November). Craftspeople, country apple butter, live music, medicine shows, marionettes, and more are part of this free fall festival.

Grand Illumination (November). Held on the Friday before Thanksgiving. The lights are turned on, outlining the village buildings in white and the trees and shrubs in lovely colors. Reindeer with Santa and a sleigh are also lit, followed by a sing-along, free hot mulled cider, and the opportunity to toast marshmallows over an open fire. The lights remain up through December, so come on out and enjoy them with your dog some evening, even if you can't make the initial illumination.

Country Christmas Weekend (First weekend in December). Features a parade, during which Santa arrives in a horse-drawn carriage (he stays through Sunday and listens to children's requests). Peddler's Village is decorated Victorian-style, with lots of greens. At the village gazebo there's a gingerbread display through the beginning of January: in the past it has included such creative exhibits as the Statue of Liberty, the Eiffel Tower, and even a structure made of dog biscuits.

▶ **Penn's Purchase Factory Outlet Stores, 5861 Lower York Road (Route 202), 215-794-0300, www.pennspurchase.com.** This shopping village features manufacturers' direct items, from apparel to crafts to furniture to housewares and gifts. According to Penn's Purchase management, "Dogs are allowed in the center. It is up to each store if they are permitted inside." In case this interests you as it interests me, there's a Big Dog Sportswear Outlet here. Penn's Purchase holds promotional events during the year that in the past have included:

Halloween Costume Contest (October)

Holiday Carolers (November–December). Strolling carolers in Victorian costume will help get shoppers in the proper holiday mood.

And when you and your dog are tired of shopping, head to:

▶ **Buckingham Valley Vineyards and Winery, 1521 State Route 413, 215-794-7188.** You and your dog can take a self-guided tour of the vineyards and picnic outside at one of the winery's tables. Open Tuesday through Friday from noon to 6:00 p.m., and Sunday from noon to 4:00 p.m. This is a family-owned business founded in 1966. You and your dog should be aware that they have a somewhat protective Doberman. For more information, call them, or you can visit them online by going to www.pawine.com and following the link.

Solebury Township

Check out the Carversville National Historic District at the intersection of Carversville and Sugan Roads. It's an interesting place that people seem to love. If you and your dog like it, come back for:

▶ **Carversville Founders Day (June).** A celebration of the area. Call 215-297-8054 for details.

You and your dog might also want to explore the Upper Aquetong Valley National Historic District. This district extends along Meeting House and Aquetong Roads, between Sugan Road and U.S. Route 202.

There are some parks in Solebury that your dog might also want to check out, including:

▶ **Magill's Hill Park, Chapel and River Roads**
▶ **Pat Livezey Park, Hagan and Parkside Drives**

There are **summer concerts** in these parks; for more information, contact Solebury Township at 3092 Sugan Road, 215-297-5656.

And you and your dog on-leash are welcome to come select a holiday tree together in Solebury at **Tuckamony Christmas Tree Farm, 6320 Upper York Road (Route 263), 215-297-8447.**

New Hope Borough

New Hope Borough is a very lively center of artists, craftspeople, and antique and other specialty shops and services along the Delaware Canal. There are over 30 restaurants. And the place is full of history. Even the information center is housed in an 1839 building (once the town hall and jail). Most important, New Hope is *very* dog-friendly. Some of the shops make a point of having a sign that says "no pets" or "pets must be on leash," so I suspect that quite a few shops and galleries will let you bring your canine friend inside. If there's a shop that intrigues you with its window display, lean in and ask.

The New Hope Village National Historic District is loosely bounded by Old Mill Road and Stockton Avenue, and by Ferry, Bridge, Mechanic, Randolph, Main, Coryell, and Waterloo Streets. Springdale National Historic District is bounded by Mechanic Street and by Old York, Stoney Hill, and

South Sugan Roads. You and your dog will have a great time walking around. You can get a brochure describing the sights at the New Hope Information Center, 1 West Mechanic Street. Landmarks include:

▶ **The Delaware Canal Locktender's House, 145 South Main Street.** Built in the 1800s and restored. (Yes! The **Delaware Canal State Park towpath** is here—take a walk with your dog but stay out of the way of the mules: New Hope offers mule-drawn barge rides.)

You and your dog can shop together at:

▶ **Bow Wow, Main Street, 215-862-9871.** You can definitely bring your dog on-leash into this pet-oriented gift shop.

Then go find a place to have a meal together—there are lots of places to choose from in New Hope. Here are the ones I know for sure:

▶ **C'est La Vie, 20 South Main Street, 215-862-1956.** This French bakery and café offers croissants, pastries, breads, cakes, light lunch fare, and hot and cold, nonalcoholic drinks. The café is set back from the street, overlooking the Delaware River. They have outdoor seating as the weather permits, generally from early spring to late fall or early winter. If you sit outside, your dog can sit with you "as long as the dogs do not interfere with other patrons' enjoyment or safety." What else would C'est La Vie like you to know? "During busy times, we'll often put a bowl of water out. Otherwise, we're happy to oblige if a customer requests water for their pet."

▶ **Giuseppe's Pizza and Family Restaurant, 473 Lower York Road (Route 202), 215-862-1740.** You can get wonderful takeout Italian food here, and sit at their outdoor tables to enjoy it with your dog. They will provide water for your dog on request.

▶ **Havana, 105 South Main Street, 215-862-9897.** The patio bar here is great for people-watching, and the kitchen prepares "world-style cuisine." You can dine outside with your dog from April to October, and the patio bar has a heater, so it is open all year. Havana features live jazz, R&B, and funk music. They will provide your dog with a bowl of water, ice, or a dog treat. They do have one request, however: "No pit bulls!" Sorry.

▶ **Landing Restaurant, 22 North Main Street, 215-862-5711.** Features American regional cuisine, with casual dining for lunch, and casual fine dining for dinner. Patrons who sit outside can have their dogs on-leash sit with them. Outdoor seating is available from April to November. The restaurant will provide water, ice, food, "anything the dogs need. . . . We encourage dogs!"

▶ **Paradise Found, 137 South Main Street, 215-862-4990.** They have an outdoor deck where you can sit with your dog, for whom they are happy to provide water. You can enjoy soft pretzels that are baked on the premises, as well as water ice, ice cream, hot dogs, nachos, and ice-cold drinks in warm weather, with hot cider, coffee, soup, stew, and chili added to the selection in the fall.

▶ **Wildflowers Restaurant and Garden Café, 8 West Mechanic Street, 215-862-2241.** This special place offers American food and, on weekends, Thai cooking. Patrons who sit outside can bring dogs on-leash, and outdoor seating is available from March to December, weather permitting. They will provide water for your dog, and you can order a "dog's meal." They also comment, "Cats are welcome, too, but no gorillas!"

Festivals, your dog is saying, where are the festivals? Here they are, and plenty of 'em:

- ▶ **Winter Carnival (First week of February).** This event is held jointly by New Hope and Lambertville, New Jersey (just across the Delaware River).
- ▶ **New Hope Summer Antiques Show (June).** Held on the grounds of New Hope–Solebury High School. Features over 100 antique and collectibles dealers. Admission is charged.
- ▶ **Grand Fireworks Display (July).** If your dog is sensitive to fireworks, you should probably leave before the culminating event. For information, call 215-862-5030.
- ▶ **New Hope Auto Show (August).** Held on the grounds of New Hope–Solebury High School. Features over 1,000 cars (vintage 1900 to 1975), an automotive flea market, a Parade of Champions, music, entertainment, food, and more. Admission is charged. This show has been going on for over 40 years, so it's pretty big, and crowded: that means they don't encourage you to bring your dog. On the other hand, they won't kick you out if you do. If this event sounds all right for your dog, don't be shy. For more information, call 215-862-5665, or visit www.newhopeautoshow.org.
- ▶ **New Hope Fall Antiques Show (Last weekend in September)**
- ▶ **New Hope Outdoor Arts and Crafts Festival (First weekend in October).** Features contemporary and traditional arts and crafts, including painting, sculpture, and photography by artists from all over the country. Takes place throughout the borough, and you are free to browse with your dog on-leash. Sponsored by the Greater New Hope Chamber of Commerce, 215-862-5880.
- ▶ **Holiday Festivities/Santa Arrives (End of November).** Held at the Logan Inn, South Main Street.
- ▶ **Daniel Bray's Crossing (December).** Sponsored by the Washington's Crossing Re-enactors Society. This is a reenactment of Washington's December 14, 1776, crossing from New Hope to Lambertville, New Jersey, to ask Hunterdon County's Captain Daniel Bray to commandeer boats for the Continental Army's Christmas Day attack. You and your dog on-leash are welcome to watch. For more information, call 215-862-2050.
- ▶ **Monroe Crossing Reenactment (December).** Sponsored by Coryell's Ferry Militia. This is a colonial dress commemoration of Lieutenant James Monroe's troop crossing of the Delaware on Christmas Day 1776, downriver from Washington, on a mission of keeping enemy soldiers from calling for backup upon Washington's attack. Your dog on-leash is welcome to come with you to watch. For more information, call 215-862-2050.
- ▶ **Christmas Time in Bucks County (Mid-December).** Admission is charged. For more information, call 215-862-5082.

What else can you do in New Hope? Well, you and your dog can stop by:

- ▶ **New Hope Winery, 6123 Lower York Road, 215-794-2331, www.newhopewinery.com.** Dogs on-leash are permitted on the grounds here, but they prefer that you do not bring your dog inside the winery. They do have outdoor wine tastings in warm weather.

And you and your dog have lots of choices for a place to stay overnight together in New Hope:

▶ **Aaron Burr House.** Pets are welcome at this seven-room, Victorian bed and breakfast on a lovely corner in New Hope. It has two sister houses, **Umpleby House** and **Wedgwood House**, making for 18 rooms in all, and there's a room for you and your dog in each house. There are some rules, but otherwise your dog is welcome to come and meet the innkeepers' dog, Jasper. There's a $20-per-day charge for your dog to stay. For more information, call the **Wedgwood Historic Inns** at **215-862-2570,** e-mail **stay@new-hope-inn.com,** or visit **www.new-hope-inn.com.**

▶ **Best Western Inn, 6426 Lower York Road, 215-862-5221.** You can stay here with your dog, if he or she is 45 pounds or less, for a $20 charge per night. They have grounds on which you can walk your baby.

▶ **New Hope Motel in the Woods, 400 West Bridge Street, 215-862-2800.** There is a 50-pound limit on size, and they will charge a one-time fee of $25, but they have a 5-acre property where you can walk your dog. Note that they have a two-night minimum stay (three nights for holiday weekends).

There is another thing to know about New Hope:

▶ **Hal H. Clark County Park** is nearby, on **River Road (Route 32).** There are 27 acres here to explore with your dog, with some historic features.

Point Pleasant

Point Pleasant is exactly what it sounds like. There are some historic sites here that you and your dog may want to see. The Point Pleasant National Historic District, centered on River Road and Point Pleasant Pike, is very explorable.

If you and your dog enjoy Point Pleasant, come back for:

▶ **The Point Pleasant Fall Festival (October).** Held in the Village of Point Pleasant. For more information, call 215-297-8672.

And if that isn't enough, you and your dog will really enjoy the opportunities for pure recreation around Point Pleasant. Try these:

▶ **Prahl's Island.** Located 1 mile north of Point Pleasant, and accessible by boat or canoe, this is undeveloped county parkland you can explore with your dog.

▶ **Tohickon Valley County Park.** Located on Cafferty Road, 1 mile north of Point Pleasant. There are hiking trails and picnic areas here, as well as fishing and boating along the Tohickon Creek. There are also interesting geological formations to take in as you wander the landscape. Restrooms are available.

▶ **Ralph Stover State Park and "High Rocks."** Located at State Park and Stump Roads, and extending on either side of Tohickon Valley County Park, this is a 45-acre parcel. Besides hiking trails, it has restrooms and very nice, shaded picnic areas with fireplaces and water. The "High Rocks" section was donated by James A. Michener, and there are spectacular views here, with a 200-foot sheer rock face. You and your dog will love this park.

Doylestown Township

There's more to Doylestown Township than Doylestown Borough. Check out the Wheelright Building, on Edison Road off Route 611, in the historic Village of Edison. Also check out Highland Farm on East Road, $^1/_4$ mile from East State Street: this was Oscar Hammerstein's home from 1940 to 1960, and is where he wrote the lyrics for *Oklahoma!*

If you have kids as well as a dog, look into the **Bucks County 4-H,** run through the Penn State Cooperative Extension Office, Neshaminy Manor Center, 1282 Almshouse Road, 215-345-3283. Pet care and other dog-related programs are usually part of the curriculum, and this is a great way to get your children involved with the family pet.

Doylestown Township also has some very nice parks, including:

▶ **Sauerman Park, Sauerman Road**
▶ **Turk Parks I and II, Turk Road, off Almshouse Road**
▶ **Central Park, off Wells Road.** This park has 108 acres to enjoy. For more information, contact the township, 425 Wells Road, 215-348-9915.

Doylestown Borough

Doylestown was named after William Doyle, who built a tavern, about 1745, on the corner of Main and State Streets. In 1813, the township became the county seat, and the borough was incorporated in 1838. Between 1838 and 1900, a lot of beautiful structures were built, and many still stand. Because the borough had no source of water power, industry never really came to Doylestown, and as a result it grew to be a residential and professional community centered around the county offices and courthouse.

The official word is, "The borough is very dog-friendly." Your dog is allowed to be with you in all public areas in Doylestown Borough, as long as you keep your pup on-leash, and make sure you clean up. Maybe that's why Doylestown is the home of the **International Greyhound Center,** that marvelous organization that rescues retired racers and finds them good homes. Keep the IGC in mind if you're thinking about acquiring a new canine member for your family: you'll be surprised at what sweet couch potatoes these dogs tend to be.

You and your dog can stop by the Central Bucks Chamber of Commerce at 115 West Court Street, 215-348-3913, and pick up a walking tour brochure that will take you on three separate journeys through the borough's past and present. Or you can just start walking and explore. Doylestown Borough is approximately two miles square, and has over 1,200 buildings on the National Register of Historic Places along major streets and through alleyways. One of Doylestown's many highlights (a favorite of my dogs' and mine) is:

▶ **The Mercer Museum, 84 South Pine Street (at Ashland Street).** Built approximately 1914 of reinforced concrete to house Dr. Henry Chapman Mercer's collection of early American tools and artifacts, this is one of the three buildings that make up the famous "Mercer Mile." It is a National Historic Landmark. You can bring your dog on-leash onto the grounds. And you and your dog can come back for a variety of events held in the Mercer Museum Quadrangle, including:

Mercer Folk Festival (May). Early American crafts, food, and more.

Firefighting Day (June). This is an outdoor exhibition of antique pumpers, hose carriages, and ladder wagons by private collectors and area fire departments. Admission to the grounds is free.

Annual Outdoor Film Festival "Under the Stars" (Summer). Begins the first Tuesday in July and runs for six weeks. Bring lawn chairs or a blanket, picnic food, and your dog. A very reasonable admission is charged.

German Summerfest (July). Sponsored by the Friends of the Bucks County Historical Society. Features music, dance, and refreshments. Admission is charged.

Early American Bicycling Demonstration (September). The AWheelmen@ ramble the grounds of the Mercer Museum. Admission may be charged.

Twelve Trees of Christmas (December)

When you and your dog have admired enough historic sites (and sights), you can enjoy modern Doylestown. Main Street has very cool shops, a lot of places where you can pick up some takeout food or coffee, and lots of benches to sit on and enjoy what you've chosen to eat or drink, while your dog sits by you. You can also sit and eat with your dog at:

▶ **Dairy Queen, 318 North Main Street.** They have outdoor seating year-round.

▶ **Veterans Memorial Park, South Chubb Drive,** also has places where you can sit and picnic. This is a very nice park if your dog has some business to transact, or just wants to get off the pavement for a while. Other parks to look for include:

▶ **Chapman Park, East State Street, between Boro Mill Road and East Street**

▶ **The pocket park at State and Ashland Streets**

▶ **War Memorial Field, West State Street, next to Central Bucks West High School**

▶ **Burpee Park, East Oakland Avenue**

▶ **Community Fields Park, West Street, next to Doyle Elementary School**

▶ **Hillside Park, Hillside Avenue, off Main Street**

But if the two of you really want to go romp and have a good time, head for the other two pieces of the Mercer triumvirate of sites:

▶ **Fonthill, East Court Street and Swamp Road (Route 313).** This is Henry Chapman Mercer's reinforced concrete castle, and a National Historic Landmark. Fonthill was designed by Dr. Mercer from the inside out, making for a very interesting exterior (inside are 44 rooms, 32 stairways, and over 200 windows).

▶ **The Moravian Tile Works, Swamp Road (Route 313).** This Spanish Colonial Revival factory was designed by Dr. Mercer. The tile works are administered by the Bucks County Department of Parks and Recreation.

Fonthill and the Moravian Tile Works are surrounded by a wonderful **county park** that is both beautiful and a great place for you and your dog to spend time. There are 10 acres, open from sunrise to sunset daily, on which you can picnic, hike, or bike with your dog and admire the amazing buildings. There are gateways to the park along Old Dublin Pike that are gorgeous in themselves. And the trails beyond are very cool.

Come back to Fonthill and the Moravian Tile Works for many wonderful special events, including:

Shakespeare in the Park (June). Held at the Moravian Tile Works. For information, call 215-348-2788 or 215-297-5053.

Old-Fashioned Fourth of July Celebration. You and your dog can hang out at Fonthill and enjoy a bike parade, pony rides, antique bikes, fiddle music, a medicine show, and a 19th-century-style baseball game. A small admission fee is charged.

Annual Bucks County Pumpkinfest (October). This two-day event includes all sorts of fun festivities that benefit the Bucks County Council on Alcoholism and Drug Dependency, the Bucks County Historical Society, and Bucks County parks. You and your dog can watch artists carve giant pumpkins in the park, which will be lit at dusk. There is music, food, an awards ceremony, and more. Admission is charged.

Family Holiday Festivities (Mid-December). People will be sipping hot cider, taking hayrides through Fonthill Park, and enjoying other holiday entertainment. Come with your dog and soak up some of the cheer.

For more information on any of these events, call 215-345-6644.

Keep an eye out for these other Doylestown-area events that you and your dog may enjoy:

▶ **Bucks County Sculpture Show (April).** Held on the campus of Doylestown Hospital. Dogs on-leash can come to the outdoor part of the show. For information, call 215-348-3913.
▶ **Fun and Fitness Day (May).** Held on the Saturday of Memorial Day weekend.
▶ **Memorial Day Parade (May)**
▶ **Heart of Bucks Auto Show (July).** Held at Central Bucks West High School, and sponsored by the JAYCEES. A weekend of antique and classic cars, an auto flea market, music, food, and a crafts bazaar. Call 215-345-7937 or -8481 for more information.
▶ **Fall Arts and Crafts Fest (October)**
▶ **Santa Parade (November).** Held on the day after Thanksgiving.
▶ **First Night® (December 31).** From nightfall to midnight, throughout Doylestown there are a variety of venues where you can enjoy music, dance, theater, magic, and more. Although some venues are indoors, many aspects of this celebration are in the street, wide open and available for your dog and you to join in. Dress up, and watch the kickoff community procession. There are fireworks at midnight, so you might want to take your dog away from that area toward the stroke of the New Year.

Does your dog want to do some shopping? Go to:

▶ **Pet Valu, Mercer Square Plaza, 73 Old Dublin Pike, 215-489-7810**

And once your dog has gotten what he or she needed, both of you can go browsing through:

▶ **Grist Mill Craftsmen's Village & Market, 2087 Turk Road, 215-348-0596.** This is a craft village on the site of an 18th-century mill complex. Stroll around and examine outdoor and covered crafts, antiques, and collectibles. The market is held every Saturday, Sunday, and holiday, and dogs are allowed on all outdoor premises. Check it out.

Finally, while you're in the Doylestown area, there's a wonderful arboretum you can take your dog to:

▶ **Henry Schmieder Arboretum of Delaware Valley College, 700 East Butler Avenue (Route 202), 215-489-2283.** The arboretum was conceived in 1896 by Rabbi Joseph Krauskopf, who founded the college, and it covers the entire 60 acres of the main campus. There are thousands of plant species and specialty gardens. The best times to visit are in the spring and summer, but the arboretum is open daily, except holidays, from dawn to dusk. And it is free. A self-guided tour brochure is available, and your dog on-leash is welcome daily, and at all arboretum events, such as:

    Bucks Beautiful Garden Fair & Arboretum Plant Sale (March). All sorts of gardening-related items will be on display, along with professional floral exhibits. Admission is charged. For more information, call 215-348-3913.

    "A" Day—Country Fair and Educational Expo (April). This event is over 50 years old, and includes planting demonstrations, hayrides, farm tours, a petting zoo, games, live entertainment, and food, as well as livestock judging. For more information, call 215-489-ADAY.

New Britain

You and your dog will want to come here to see the Pine Valley Covered Bridge, 1842 Old Iron Hill Road. It is on the National Historic Register. It is also a lovely start to **New Britain Covered Bridge Park**, which our dogs loved. It's just a beautiful park.

Chalfont Borough

Chalfont is a pretty cool small town to stroll around with your dog. There are buildings with Victorian elements, and some shops and restaurants. In **Krupp Memorial Park, behind 40 North Main Street,** summer concerts are held. And in **Kelly Park, on Oak Avenue,** there's an iron bridge over a creek leading to great walking trails that you and your dog will enjoy.

    Better yet, the two of you should head to:

▶ **Peace Valley County Park.** Located on Route 313, between Ferry Road and New Galena Road, this is a gorgeous, 1,500-acre park—one of the largest parks in the region—with 356-acre Lake Galena in the middle. There are bridle trails, walking trails, a 3-mile biking/walking/jogging path, picnic areas, and more. Occasionally, events such as the following take place in Peace Valley County Park:

    Summer Concert (July). Admission is free.

    Canine Companions for Independence Snoopy's Dog Fest and Canine Education Fair (October). This is a walkathon, and more, to benefit CCI. For information on this event, call 215-602-2093 or e-mail cci@libertynet.org.

You and your dog can also visit:

▶ **Peace Valley Winery, 300 Old Limekiln Road, 215-249-9058.** The winery has grapes in August and September, and apples in September and October. It is open Wednesday through Saturday from noon to 6:00 p.m., and daily in December from 10:00 a.m. to 6:00 p.m. Stay for the tastings (your dog can sample some winery water).

You and your dog can get a snack at:

▶ **Petrucci's Dairy Barn, 205 East Butler Avenue, 215-794-3696.** You can get yourself something delicious from this ice cream shop and sit outside with your dog. Outdoor seating is available from March to December. The staff will give your dog water and doggy treats, and lots of petting. One day, they hope to have a "doggy fountain."

After your snack, your dog can go shopping at:

▶ **Pet Valu, New Britain Village Square, 4275 County Line Road, 215-997-1707**

☙ SELECTED POINTS IN UPPER BUCKS COUNTY

Bedminster

You and your dog need to go to Bedminster to enjoy recreation in some great doggish playgrounds:

▶ **Nockamixon State Park.** This park is huge—5,238 acres—with lots of trails and recreational opportunities. Lake Nockamixon, in the middle of the park, is large and lovely. There are restrooms, picnic areas, phones, and even a food concession in season. The day use area is open from 8:00 a.m. to sunset between April 1 and October 31. If you have hunting dogs, you can train them here from September, beginning the day after Labor Day, to March 31, in designated areas. Haycock Mountain in the adjacent State Game Lands is the second-highest point in Bucks County, and affords amazing views of Lake Nockamixon during winter and early spring (be careful during hunting season).

▶ **Stover-Myers Mill County Park.** Along Dark Hollow Road, east of Pipersville, this park contains a restored grist mill and sawmill built in 1800, and is a National Historic Site. There are hiking trails and picnic areas along the Tohickon Creek.

Dublin Borough

Stop with your dog at:

▶ **Dublin Dairy Queen.** You can sit outside with your dog from March to October. There is access to water for your dog outside in the back; the staff asks that you bring a dish or bowl with you for your dog.

Once you've gotten some sustenance, head for a unique site that both you and your dog will love:

▶ **The Pearl S. Buck House (Green Hills Farm), 520 Dublin Road (1 mile southwest of Route 313), 215-249-0100.** This is the prize-winning author's 1835 farmhouse, and a National Historic Landmark. Pearl S. Buck began an international foundation that places for adoption biracial children rejected by their country's agencies, and it is headquartered here at Green Hills Farm. Ms. Buck's grave is also here. The 65-acre grounds are lovely, and you and your dog on-leash are welcome to stroll them when the property is open (when it is closed, the grounds are gated). Call for more information. And bring your dog back for events such as:

Pearl S. Buck International Annual 5K Run and Kids' Sprint (May). There is other entertainment, such as classic cars to see, as well.

The International School of Performing Arts of Bucks County Music Festival (Summer). In the past, at least one of these concerts has been held outdoors at Green Hills Farm. Look for an event in August, in the evening.

Pearl S. Buck Holiday Festival of Trees (Mid-November through the end of December). You can't take your dog to see the marvelous decorations inside the house, but you will both enjoy the decorated grounds.

And if you're in the area at the time, stop by:

▶ **Dublin Community Day (June).** Held in **Borough Park.** Features food, games, fun, and more.

Tinicum

Going to Tinicum Township is really getting out there into the country. Tinicum Township doesn't own any parks, but it is dog-friendly in general: the township offices actually allow dogs inside. "Tinicum Township does have a leash law and has a kennel for housing lost dogs temporarily while we attempt to find their people. We currently have a Scout working toward his Eagle badge who will be replacing our dog kennel with a safe, clean, and comfortable kennel. (Not that we encourage people to lose their dogs.) . . . If [someone's] dog is lost in our area, they should contact the Tinicum Township Police (in addition to the SPCA) at 215-294-9158."

There are some great parks and other rural highlights in the area. The ubiquitous Delaware Canal State Park is here. And your dog will absolutely insist on going to:

▶ **Tinicum County Park, River Road (Route 32), north of Erwinna.** There are historic sites in the park, including the Erwin-Stover House, a Federal-style home built in 1800, with 1840 and 1860 additions. The park also has hiking and biking trails, and picnic areas. Boating and fishing are permitted. But the most important thing about Tinicum Park for your dog is all the wonderful rural and riverside acres with large, open fields for the two of you to romp through together.

Various events are held at Tinicum Park, and dogs on-leash are permitted at most of them:

Tinicum Park Polo Club Games (May 15 through October 30). Bring lawn chairs, a picnic, and your dog. A small admission per car is charged. For more information, call the

Polo Hotline, 609-996-3321. In June, the Bucks County Cup Polo Tournament is held. Polo matches are great fun to watch, even if you don't understand the rules.

Fourth of July Concert

Tinicum Art Festival (July)

Riverside Symphonia Concert Under the Stars (July). Features classical and pop music. Admission is charged, but dogs on-leash can come.

Tinicum Civic Association Outdoor Antique Show (First weekend in September). Dealers from all over the region gather around the park's historic farm buildings. The event is held rain or shine, and admission is charged.

Rockhill

There are good parks here, including:

▶ **East Rockhill Township Park, 1418 North Ridge Road.** Has 92 acres, including a pavilion, a soccer field, and a planned baseball field. **Friends and Neighbors Day** is held here, with the proceeds benefiting parks and recreation activities. Features food, children's games, and live music.

▶ **Three Mile Run Road, near Schoolhouse Road.** Provides 37 acres of open space and woodland for you and your dog to explore.

Sellersville

Sellersville is a very interesting town. Washington House, on Main Street, stands on a site that has been occupied by a tavern or restaurant since 1742. Sellersville legend says that when the Liberty Bell was transported from Philadelphia to Allentown to protect it from the British in 1777, the transporters stopped at the tavern that occupied the site at that time.

You can get some local takeout and go picnic with your dog in a very nice park, in the center of Sellersville, that is shared (in a way) with Perkasie. On the Sellersville side, it is called **Lake Lenape Park (North Main Street);** on the Perkasie side, it is **Menlo Park.** It follows the east branch of the Perkiomen Creek. A variety of events are held in the parks each year, as well as elsewhere in Sellersville, and as far as I could tell, there is no problem bringing dogs on-leash to these very friendly community events. Events change to an extent from year to year, so check with the borough to see what's happening, but here are some examples:

▶ **Sellersville Days (July 3–4).** Celebrating the anniversary of the incorporation of the Borough of Sellersville. July 3 features an all-day picnic and pig roast, with a band, a craft show, and fireworks. July 4 features a ceremony and a band concert. For more information, call 215-453-0694.

▶ **Pennridge Community Day (July).** An all-day event at Lenape Park, with fireworks at dusk.

▶ **Sellersville Halloween Parade (October)**

▶ **Sellersville Tree Lighting (December).** Held at the Sellersville Fire House. Includes choirs, a brass ensemble, cookies, and hot beverages.

Perkasie Borough

This is another nice small town, with gift shops, antiques, and restaurants. **Menlo Park, at Arthur Street and West Park Avenue,** contains a unique feature: the Perkasie Carousel. The carousel was purchased in 1951 to replace an original 1891 carousel, and the building housing it was built in 1895 and restored in 1995. The carousel is operated once or twice a month in summer, which can be a lot of fun to watch with your dog.

As for Perkasie events, you and your dog can enjoy:

▶ **Perkasie Olde Town Day (July).** Held along Church and Main Streets. Food, fun, and activities for all ages.
▶ **Summer Concert Series in Menlo Park (July).** You and your dog can hear big band, jazz, rock, and more. For more information on the series, call 215-257-5065.
▶ **"Under the Lights" Car Show (August).** Held in the Olde Towne area of Perkasie.
▶ **Fall Festival (October).** Includes a Civil War reenactment, Native American programs, scarecrow contests, jugglers, crafters, and more. For information, call 215-257-2908.
▶ **Pearls of Bucks Auto Show (October).** Dogs on-leash are permitted. For information, call 215-822-1818.

There are also some Perkasie businesses where your dog on-leash is welcome:

▶ **Rogers Road Stand and Garden Center, 255 Route 313, 215-257-6976**
▶ **Perkasie Dairy Queen, 200 Constitution Avenue.** This DQ has outdoor seating from April to October, where you can sit with your dog. They will provide water or ice for your dog on request. And some customers buy their dogs ice cream.
▶ **A.G.A. Farms, 1333 Elephant Road, 215-795-0660.** The farm has 100 acres, and there is plenty of parking. It is open daily from 9:00 a.m. to dusk. At holiday time, you can bring your dog on-leash to get a Colorado or Norway spruce, or a Douglas or Fraser fir.

Hilltown

Stop for some play or walk time in **Hilltown Civic Park on Route 152,** or **Blooming Glen Playground on Route 113**—both permit pets on-leash. The township is considering constructing an agricultural center and fairgrounds on Route 313 that would be available for dog shows, horse shows, and 4-H events.

Your final stop in Hilltown should be:

▶ **Hilltown Garden & Flea Market, Routes 313 and 113, 215-249-0488.** You and your dog on-leash are free to browse here together.

Revere

One last site you and your dog need to know about in Bucks County is:

▶ **Bucks County Horse Park, 8934 Easton Road (Route 611), 610-847-8597.** This is a private facility with a variety of events that include any kind of amateur horse-related competition you can think of, such as Thursday morning horse shows in summer, and dressage shows on Tuesday evenings. Dogs on-leash are permitted, although the staff prefers that the dog have some experience around horses. (This is not a problem for Georgie, who spent her first weeks in a stall right next to the horses on her birth farm, and had a nice perfume of manure when we brought her home.) In any case, call the park for information, if you are in the Upper Bucks area and think you might want to watch one of the events. They also have a Web site, www.buckscountyhorsepark.com.

The **Bucks County Polo Club**, formed in 1993, rents the horse park for matches. Call the club at 610-847-8228 for its schedule. The first match is in May, the last in October. And in August, the club puts on **"Pooches & Polo,"** an open dog show, along with a polo match. Polo matches are great to watch. They really are. And with a dog show added to the mix, this is something you and your dog won't want to miss.

New Jersey

The first thing you and your dog need to know about New Jersey is that it boasts the Pinelands National Reserve, a very special place that covers over a million acres, including parts of Camden and Burlington Counties. Created when glaciers dumped sand over the area, the Pinelands contain unique ecosystems that provide extremely important wetland and water resources, as well as many rare and endangered plant and animal species such as pitcher plants and the Pine Barrens tree frog.

You can explore the Pinelands with your dog in a variety of places, including along the Batona Trail, at Batsto Village, in Lebanon State Forest, at Whitesbog Village, at the Rancocas Nature Center, and at the Atsion Village and Recreation Area. These spots are covered in detail below.

🐾 CAMDEN COUNTY

Camden County has a lot of fine county parks, and your dog on-leash is permitted in all of them, even during events. The Camden County Department of Parks and Recreation holds quite a few events you and your dog might be interested in, including several summer concert series, and races and other competitions run throughout the summer. For more information, call the Department of Parks and Recreation at 856-795-7275 or visit www.ccparks.com.

Camden

There is a special historic site you and your dog might want to see in the city of Camden:

▶ **Pomona Hall, Park Boulevard and Euclid Avenue, 856-964-3333.** This 18th-century house is a National Historic Site. It is also the home of the Camden County Historical Society, in Parkside, a quiet residential area near Farnham Park. There are a couple of free events at Pomona Hall that you and your dog might want to come back for:

    Family Fun Day (April/May). Features open-hearth cooking and spinning demonstrations, and more.

    Civil War Day (May). Mid-19th-century soldier life is demonstrated.

Is your dog looking for a good park to hang around in for a while? The best ones in Camden for that purpose are:

▶ **Dudley Grange.** Bounded by Federal, 32nd, and Dudley Streets and Westfield Avenue. There are 20.6 acres here, and among various active-play areas, there is a 1.4-mile multi-purpose trail.

▶ **Farnham Park.** Bounded by Baird Avenue, Kaighn Avenue, and Park Boulevard. There are 22.3 acres here, with a fitness trail, a spray pool, a pavilion, and a nature trail.

▶ **New Camden Park.** Bounded by Wildwood Avenue, Park and Baird Boulevards, and Pine Street. The 23.84 acres here are adjacent to the Cooper River.

▶ **Dr. Ulysses S. Wiggins Waterfront Park,** along Mickle Boulevard. The park fronts the Delaware River, and you can park in the Waterfront Garage. There are 51.22 acres here for you and your dog to enjoy. You can take a stroll along the Wiggins Park Promenade, watch the boats at the marina, or bring a blanket and a picnic. You and your dog can also enjoy events here, including:

    Sunset Jazz Series (Summer). Free concerts. Call 856-216-2170 for more information.

    Mellon Jazz Festival (June). Held at various locations, but it usually includes a free concert at Wiggins Park. Call 610-667-3599, or check www.festival-productions.net for information.

    Waterfront Family Arts Festival (July). Features free performances and displays of all sorts of arts, beginning at noon.

    Fourth of July at Wiggins Waterfront Park. The festivities include a concert.

Collingswood

Collingswood is a nice town, with lovely residential streets and a historic business district with benches where you can rest with your dog. Take your dog to explore the Collingswood Commercial Historic District, along Haddon Avenue between Woodlawn Terrace and Fern Avenue, and adjacent areas along Collings Avenue.

After you've strolled around on the sidewalks, your dog will want to head for some parks. Try these:

▶ **Knight Park.** Bounded by Collings Avenue, Park Avenue, and Browning Road. There are Wednesday evening **concerts** here during the summer.

▶ **Newton Lake Park.** Located between Cuthbert Boulevard and the White Horse Pike. The 103.39 acres of this park extend through Haddon Township and Oaklyn, as well as Collingswood. It contains Newton Lake, picnic areas, a 1.5-mile multipurpose trail, and a boat ramp (for small boats only).

▶ **Cooper River Park.** Located between North and South Park Drives, Route 130, and Grove Street, in Collingswood, Pennsauken, Cherry Hill, and Haddon Township. The Cooper River runs through this 346.55-acre park, which also contains two bike/jogging trails, five picnic areas, the Jack Curtis Stadium, a boat launch area (no gas motors are permitted on the river), and—a dog-run! The **Cooper River Dog Run** is on Park Boulevard North. It is open 24 hours, it is fenced, and it has benches, bags for clean-up, trees, lights, trash cans, parking, and restrooms.

The Cooper River Park is home to the **Cooper River Yacht Club**, which sponsors races throughout much of the year. It's located on South Park Drive, and you might want to check out this club if you and your dog sail. Even if one or both of you don't sail, however, it is great fun to bring your dog to the river and watch the races, held every Sunday and many Saturdays from April to November. The races follow a selection of courses on the river between Route 130 and Cuthbert Boulevard. For more information, call the club at 856-869-9145, or visit users.erols.com/wolf6001 and follow the links.

Back in downtown Collingswood, the Collingswood Business & Professional Association sponsors all sorts of outdoor events you may want to take your dog to:

▶ **Easter Egg Hunt (March).** Kids hunt for eggs and get prizes for special ones. You and your dog on-leash can have a great time watching, and don't forget your dog's bunny ears.
▶ **May Fair & Arts and Crafts Show.** Features 5K and 10K in-line skating races, crafters, classic cars, food vendors, and entertainment onstage in the center of a 10-block area of Haddon Avenue.
▶ **Avenue Sale Days (July).** An old-fashioned sidewalk sale along Haddon Avenue.
▶ **Corvette Show (September).** Over 100 Corvettes to admire along Haddon Avenue, and sidewalk sale bargains to browse.
▶ **Santa's Arrival (November).** Santa's reindeer drop him off on top of the Collingswood Borough Hall, and a parade along Haddon Avenue follows.

Along Haddon Avenue through Collingswood, Westmont, and Haddonfield is another event you and your dog might want to check out:

▶ **Newton Colony/WXPN Arts & Music Family Festival (September).** All along the avenue there are live performances on Saturday, along with street performers, arts and crafts, a classic car show, and more. Admission is charged. On Sunday, the festival moves to The Island at Cooper River. For more information, call 856-663-9422, or visit the Web site at www.newtoncolonyartsbank.org.

Cherry Hill

Cherry Hill, covering 24 square miles, is pretty spread out, but the area still manages to be a community. You and your dog will want to make a point of admiring the cherry trees lining Chapel Avenue in the spring. And you might want to look for the following historic sites:

▶ **Bonnie's Bridge, 350 Wayland Road**
▶ **Samuel Coles House, 1743 Old Cuthbert Road**

▶ **Gatehouse at Colestown Cemetery, Kings Highway and Church Road.** A National Historic Site.

You and your dog will really want to come out for Cherry Hill community events:

▶ **Summer Family Concerts.** Free concerts held at Barclay Farmstead (see below).
▶ **Fourth of July Celebration.** Features entertainment and fireworks.
▶ **Annual Bass Fishing Tournament (July).** Held on the Cooper River.
▶ **Bass Fishing Tournament (September).** Held on Newton Lake.
▶ **Pumpkin Festival (October).** Held at Croft Farm (see below). The free festival includes pumpkin painting and a costume parade. Contact the recreation department at 856-488-7868 for more information.
▶ **Pets on Parade (October).** Held on a Saturday at the Garden State Discovery Museum, 16 North Springdale Road, Cherry Hill. Dress up your dog and take him or her to get an animal trick-or-treat bag. Free with admission. The Garden State Discovery Museum is a hands-on, interactive exploration museum for kids. For information, call 856-424-1233.
▶ **Fall Fair (November).** A celebration of arts and agriculture, with games, puppet shows, crafts, and music.

What else can you and your dog do in Cherry Hill? You can go to the park! There are lots of parks in Cherry Hill. Some of the best parks, as far as your dog is concerned, are:

▶ **Wallworth County Park.** Bounded by Brace Road and Kings Highway, in Cherry Hill and Haddonfield. There are 55.65 acres, with a pond, a picnic area, and a 1.2-mile multipurpose trail.
▶ **Maria Barnaby Greenwald County Park.** Bounded by Grove Street, Kings Highway, and Park Boulevard. With 47.21 acres, Greenwald Park fronts on the Cooper River and contains, among other things, a cross-country course, two picnic areas, and a 1.2-mile multipurpose trail.
▶ **Challenge Grove County Park.** Located along Borton Mill Road, at the corner of Caldwell and Brace Roads, this 17.7-acre park on the Cooper River has pavilions and picnic areas, a multipurpose path, restrooms, and even landscaped gardens.
▶ **Barclay Farmstead, 209 Barclay Lane, 856-795-6225.** The farmstead was first settled in 1684, and its 1816 mansion is a National Historic Site. The grounds are open year-round, and your dog on-leash is welcome to come with you to enjoy them. Feel free to picnic on the grounds. The farmstead is open Tuesday through Friday from 9:00 a.m. to 4:00 p.m. Admission is charged. Come back for special events held throughout the year.
▶ **Ashland Park, 3rd and Palmwood Streets.** There are walking trails here.
▶ **Croft Farm, Evans Mill Road.** This was once a working mill, and probably a station on the Underground Railroad. There's a plantation house and outbuildings that date to 1799. Not only is the site historic, there's a **Pumpkin Festival** in October (see above).

If your dog needs to pick up some supplies in Cherry Hill, you have your choice:

▶ **PetsMart, 2135 Route 38, 856-910-1400**
▶ **Pet Valu, Fashion Square, 1469 Brace Road, 856-216-8455**

Can you and your dog stay overnight in Cherry Hill? Try one of these:

▶ **Holiday Inn–Cherry Hill, Route 70 and Sayer Avenue, 856-663-5300.** With 186 rooms and six stories, the inn has two diamonds from AAA. They accept small dogs only.

▶ **Hilton at Cherry Hill, 2349 West Marlton Pike, 856-665-6666.** This 408-room, 14-story facility allows pets, with a $50 deposit.

▶ **Residence Inn by Marriott, 1821 Old Cuthbert Road, 856-429-6111.** The inn has 96 rooms, two stories, and exterior corridors. Pets are allowed, with a $25-per-night nonrefundable deposit, up to $100. They have a large grassy area where you can walk your dog.

Haddonfield

This is a 300-year-old town. In the 1850s, Philadelphians built vacation homes here, and in 1875, Haddonfield was officially incorporated as a borough. Haddonfield has been a "dry" town since 1873—no alcohol can be sold within borough limits. Today, the 2.9 square miles of Haddonfield are very pedestrian- and dog-friendly. If you take your dog on a stroll around the residential streets, you will see wonderful Victorians and other unique homes.

In the center of the shopping district along Old Kings Highway there's a clock dating from the 1800s. There are great shops and boutiques here for window-shopping with your dog, and some of the shops might even let you bring your dog inside.

Looking for some history? There are at least 400 buildings in the historic district, bounded by Washington, Hopkins, Summit, and East Park Avenues and Kings Highway, including most of those in the central business district along Kings Highway.

When you and your dog get hungry, you can sit together at:

▶ **La Patisserie Francaise, 101 Ellis Street, 856-428-0418.** This bakery also offers coffee, cappuccino, and more. Patrons who sit outside can bring dogs on-leash, and outdoor seating is available from April to October. Water for your dog is provided. "We like dogs!" they told me.

After the two of you have had a snack, your dog will insist on going to:

▶ **Velvet Paws, 107 East Kings Highway, 856-428-8889.** A wonderful pet boutique with great gifts for pets and their owners, or for animal aficionados. "There is always a bowl of fresh, clean water. Free dog treats. All dogs are always welcome."

And conveniently located nearby is:

▶ **Three Dog Bakery, 113 Kings Highway East, 856-857-1770, njthreedog@aol.com.** Of course you can bring your dog inside—it is, after all, a bakery *for* dogs! They will provide bowls of water and sample doggy treats. "We add no sugar or salt, chemicals, artificial preservatives, or animal fat to any of our products. We fresh-bake our treats using only wholesome, natural ingredients. We also sell treat jams, leashes, dog toys, T-shirts, bowls, collars, etc." They have an extensive selection of dog-delicious items for your dog to choose from. A percentage of the profits goes to help neglected and abused dogs.

Haddonfield holds frequent street festivals that you and your dog might want to attend:

- **Summer Evenings.** Open-air performances by brass bands and symphonies on Kings Highway, which is closed to traffic.
- **Fourth of July Celebration**
- **Antique Auto Show (Autumn)**
- **Christmas Tree Lighting (December).** Carolers stroll the streets in Dickensian garb.
- **First Night® Haddonfield (December 31).** Life-sized puppets and events for kids and adults are featured. There will be music of all kinds, street performers, and an ice carving at King's Court.

Dogs are permitted in all Haddonfield Borough parks and sites, and there are county parks here as well:

- **Pennypacker County Park.** Bounded by Kings Highway, Grove Street, and Park Boulevard, the 32.27 acres here contain Hopkins Pond, and front on the Cooper River. The park also contains the discovery site of the *Hadrosaurus foulkii*, a dinosaur find listed on the National and New Jersey Registers of Historic Places. The almost-complete skeleton was found in a marl pit in 1858, and the find helped establish the Academy of Natural Sciences in Philadelphia as a leading paleontological center for the rest of the century.
- **Hopkins Pond County Park.** Located off Grove Street, along both sides of Hopkins Lane, these 33.10 acres contain a tree trail as well as self-guided multipurpose trails around the park.

You and your dog can stay overnight in Haddonfield at:

- **Haddonfield Inn, 44 West End Avenue, 856-428-2195.** Dogs are permitted in one suite. You can walk your dog around the area, and don't forget the dog-run in Cooper River Park for more rambunctious exercise.

Haddon Heights

While you're in the general neighborhood, you may want to check out the Station Avenue National Historic Business District. It runs along Station Avenue, from 7th Avenue to the White Horse Pike. Or take a look at the White Horse Pike Historic District, bounded by 4th Avenue, High and Haddon Streets, East Atlantic Street, Kings Highway, and Green Street.

When you and your dog are finished touring, head to:

- **Haddon Lake Park.** Bounded by Station Avenue, 10th Avenue, Kings Highway, and the Black Horse Pike, the 78.82 acres extend into Audubon and Mount Ephraim. The park features Haddon Lake, as well as a 1.6-mile cross-country trail, a picnic area, and a 1.72-mile multipurpose trail.

Clementon

The Rutgers Cooperative Extension of Camden County is located here, at 152 Ohio Avenue. If you have kids, you might want to stop by and get information on the **Camden County 4-H**. Pet care, and in particular dog care, is part of the program. You can also call them at 856-566-2900.

Then take your dog to:

▶ **Silver Lake Park.** Located between Silver Lake Avenue, Ohio Avenue, Trout Run Avenue, and Higgins Avenue. There are 15.6 acres here and, of course, Silver Lake.

Berlin

Berlin has some great things to check out with your dog. For one, there's the Berlin Historic District, bounded roughly by Washington, East Taunton, and Haines Avenues, and including parts of the South White Horse Pike and Jefferson Avenue. You and your dog can take a walk around and look for landmarks.

When the two of you have finished doing the historic thing, take your dog to:

▶ **Berlin County Park.** Bounded by the White Horse Pike, Park Drive, and New Freedom Road. The Great Egg Harbor River runs through the park's 151.81 acres, along with a nature trail, 5 miles of hiking trails, active-play areas, and three picnic groves.

Does your dog want to go shopping? Take him or her to:

▶ **PetsMart, 215 Route 73 North, 856-753-9130**

And if it's December, and you and your dog want to get a Christmas tree together, go to:

▶ **Lucca's Christmas Tree Farm, 133 Penbyrn Road, 856-767-0189.** Dogs on-leash are permitted to come along when you go to get your tree. Be careful of young children, but otherwise the two of you should be okay.

Pennsauken

The first thing you can do here is take your dog to see historic sites, including:

▶ **Griffith Morgan Homestead, Griffith Morgan Lane, 856-665-1948.** Built circa 1693 in the Queen Anne style, this is the oldest sandstone house in Camden County, and a National Historic Site. Dogs on-leash are permitted on the grounds, so you and your dog can get a good look at the exterior.

If your dog needs to pick up some supplies, the two of you can go to:

▶ **PETCO, 7024 State Highway 70, 856-662-9692**

And the two of you can enjoy a variety of events at:

▶ **Cooper River Park.** Events include:
　　1st Day 5K, 2000-Meter Fun Run/Walk (New Year's Day). Held at Cooper River Park's Jack Curtis Stadium.
　　Cooper River Concert Series (Summer). Held at Jack Curtis Stadium, North Park Drive. Everything from country to opera, to jazz, to anything else you can think of. Admission is free.

Annual Dog Walk at Cooper River Park (September/October). This terrific walk, which starts at Jack Curtis Stadium, benefits the Animal Adoption Center, a no-kill shelter in Lindenwold. For more information on the center, visit their Web site at www.animaladoption.com, e-mail them at animaladopt@hotmail.com, or call them at 856-435-9116. You have to walk your dog anyway, right? Why not help this wonderful shelter: get some sponsors and raise some money for the center.

Turkey Day 5K (November). Held at Cooper River Park's Jack Curtis Stadium.

Merchantville

This is a lovely town, with nice streets and interesting houses. You and your dog can spend time here looking at lovely Victorian homes, or taking advantage of the window-shopping opportunities offered by the great shops along Centre Street. The Merchantville main business district includes books, antiques, gifts, crafts, and more. There are plenty of places to get takeout food. Next to Aunt Charlotte's Chocolates there's a small park with benches where you and your dog can rest. **Wellwood Park on Maple Avenue** is very nice, should your dog be looking for another park to check out, and there's also the **Merchantville Mile**, a wildlife preserve along the railroad tracks, starting at the gazebo and going west. What more could you and your dog ask for?

The Main Street Merchantville organization (856-665-6211, mainst@merchantvillenj.com) puts on quite a few events during the year, and your dog on-leash is welcome at all of them. The two of you can enjoy:

- **The Spring Arts Fair (May).** A juried art show along Merchantville's main streets.
- **Birthday Celebration and Picnic (First weekend in June).** Celebrating the 1874 incorporation of Merchantville. Bring your dog to enjoy the vendors, food, entertainment, and crafts.
- **Summer Sock Hop (July).** You and your dog can enjoy dancing, food, and classic cars, all in the fifties mode.
- **Antiques in August.** Browse with your dog through all kinds of items for sale.
- **Merchantville Harvest Food Fest and Folkart Craft Faire (October).** You and your dog can browse among craftspersons' booths, and sample the food offered by vendors. For information, call 856-665-6211.
- **Safe Halloween (October).** Candy bags for kids, and a scarecrow decoration contest hosted by downtown merchants. Bring your dog (appropriately dressed, of course) to see the kids in their costumes.
- **Tree Festival and Candlelight Shopping (December).** Includes a tree decoration contest in which merchants compete, displaying trees in their windows. Part of a four-week festival during the holiday season.

There's a very nice historic district to explore in Merchantville: the Catell Tract Historic District, bounded by North Chestnut Avenue, Cove Road, Rogers Avenue, and Leslie Avenue. Merchantville also contains the Oaks Historic District. This area is bounded by West Maple Avenue, Browning Road, Volan Street, and Oak Terrace. Take a walk with your canine buddy and explore.

Voorhees

There are 67 park areas in Voorhees. I'm not going to list them, but you and your dog will be glad they are there. Voorhees is adjacent to Cherry Hill, and there's a place here where you can stay overnight with your dog:

▶ **Hampton Inn, 121 Laurel Oak Road, 856-346-4500.** Pets are allowed, with no restrictions. The inn has 120 rooms and four stories. Located in the business district, it is a well-maintained property.

And your dog will no doubt want to do some shopping at:

▶ **Dr. Marc's Animal Crackers, Echelon Village Plaza, 1138 White Horse Road, 856-435-8090.** "We love dogs and cats and welcome them in our store. We are loaded with treats, toys, bandannas, and everything pets could love." They are also a veterinary center and grooming shop, and they offer pet care classes for free.

🐾 BURLINGTON COUNTY

Riverton

Located along the Delaware River, Riverton was one of the first planned residential communities, and the Riverton National Historic District is bounded by the river, Park and Thomas Avenues, and Fulton Street. There are 526 buildings in the historic district, including many stately Victorians. Take a stroll around with your dog. Admire the Riverton Yacht Club, a historic Stick-style building, and whatever might be going on around it.

When you and your dog are hungry, you can stop by:

▶ **Main Street Bakery Café, corner of Main and Broad Streets.** This is a bakery with an indoor coffee bar. They do not have outdoor seating at present, but they have "a place to hook up leashes outside the front door and [we] are always pleased to provide water and treats for dogs. We have several who visit daily." They also sell cakes in the shapes of some breeds of dogs.

Moorestown

This is a very pretty, historic town, with wonderful streets for dog-walking, and benches to rest on, so there's just no reason not to spend some time here exploring with your dog. The Moorestown National Historic District is bounded by Maple Avenue, Chestnut Avenue, Main Street from Zelley Avenue to Locust Street, and Mill Street, and includes many National Historic Sites.

Here's some really good news about Moorestown: the Moorestown Business Association puts on a lot of outdoor events, and dogs on-leash are permitted at all of them. You and your dog might want to come out for these:

▶ **Easter Egg Hunt (March).** Put on your dog's rabbit ears and go watch kids hunt for eggs.
▶ **Music on Main Street (May).** Bring your dog to sit (or lie) on the Community House lawn to enjoy the tunes.
▶ **Moorestown Day (June).** Come out with your canine to watch the Moorestown Rotary 8K race through Moorestown, browse through the wares of 100 vendors, enjoy entertainment, and get some great food.
▶ **Music on Main Street (September).** Held on the Community House lawn.
▶ **Moorestown Horse Show and County Fair (Weekend after Labor Day).** This event benefits the Memorial Hospital of Burlington County Foundation, and is held at Woodedge Stables, Borton Landing Road, for three days. On Friday evening, enjoy Country and Western Night, including steer wrestling and barrel racing. On Saturday and Sunday, the horse show and fair events take place: there are riding exhibitions, a magic show, cloggers, a petting zoo, a circus act, and more. Not only are dogs on-leash permitted, they are encouraged to come! The fair includes pet contests and other activities your pup will enjoy. Admission is charged.
▶ **Strawbridge Lake Festival (October).** A festival of arts and crafts in **Strawbridge Lake Park.**
▶ **Autumn in Moorestown (October).** A street festival on Main Street that includes fine arts, antiques, crafts, antique cars and classic Corvettes, and pumpkin painting all through Moorestown's business district. Bands and dancers of all different styles perform.
▶ **Candlelight Night (November).** The business district glows with candlelight, and the shopping is wonderful. Bring your dog and come enjoy the ambience.
▶ **First Night® Moorestown (December 31).** Main Street, from Chester Avenue to Church Street, will have musicians, dancers, artists, and actors performing at storefronts and other venues. Come out with your dog and celebrate a cultural and community New Year's Eve.

For more information on Moorestown events, contact the Moorestown Business Association, 856-727-3289, www.moorestown.com/mba.

Does your dog want to go shopping? Try:

▶ **PetsMart, 1331 Nixon Drive, 856-439-9899.** You can bring your dog inside (on-leash), and the staff will offer treats, water, and clean-up service along with a friendly greeting. They have a personal shopper service, and dates and times are posted for free playtime at the store (to participate, dogs must have rabies tags). Monthly events and contests are posted in the store. They have an annual Halloween costume contest and parade, and pet photos with Santa.

Burlington City

Burlington City proper, along the Delaware River, is a wonderful place to visit with your dog. Throughout downtown Burlington, on Union Street, and in Green Acres Pocket Park (along Union), there are benches and tables and other places to sit. Along High Street there are lots of places to get takeout food. And there is a fabulous public park and esplanade overlooking the Delaware, where you can walk with your dog.

The Burlington National Historic District, along High Street between Pearl Street and Federal Street, is one of the most beautiful areas my dogs and I have seen in our travels. Take a stroll around with your dog.

One of the events Burlington City puts on happens in the heart of the historic district, and it's a great one:

▶ **Annual Wood Street Fair and High Street Arts Festival (September).** Sponsored by the Colonial Burlington Foundation, this re-creation of a colonial fair features over 200 craft vendors lining the River Promenade, and there's an art show and an antiques/collectibles show along High Street. There's also food and free entertainment. For information, call 856-386-0200.

While you're downtown, you and your dog can stop to get a bite to eat at:

▶ **UMMM Ice Cream Parlor, 236 High Street.** Offering homemade ice cream and gourmet coffees. Are patrons who sit outside allowed to bring dogs on-leash? "You betcha." They have outdoor seating from April to December, weather permitting, and they will offer dogs anything that will make their visit more enjoyable. Any comments? "[Dogs] are customers also." More comments? "Dogs love ice cream too! Some just like the cones."

Burlington Township

Burlington Township puts on some events that might interest you and your dog, including:

▶ **Summer Concerts.** Held at **Green Acres Park, 851 Old York Road.**
▶ **Burlington Township Flea Market (September).** Held on Labor Day. Many vendors; food is available.
▶ **Burlington Township Community Day (October).** Held at Green Acres Park. Includes displays, food, a 1K fun run, a 5K race and fun run, and more.

Mount Holly

Settled in 1677, Mount Holly is the county seat of Burlington County, and contains a multitude of colonial and Victorian architecture. The Mount Holly National Historic District includes areas bounded roughly by Prospect, Elm, and Top-E-Toy Streets, the railroad tracks, and Madison and Clifton Avenues. Among the many historic sites you and your dog may see as you stroll through Mount Holly are:

▶ **Site of John Woolman's Shop, 47 Mill Street.** A bronze plaque on the southwest corner of the building honors John Woolman, an early citizen and abolitionist. You can also visit his house at **99 Branch Street**, about half a mile east of Mount Holly, with your dog on-leash and have a picnic on the grounds. Besides the 1783 house, there are gardens.
▶ **The Old Schoolhouse, 35 Brainerd Street.** This is the oldest schoolhouse in New Jersey, built in 1756. Dogs on-leash are allowed on the property, though not in the building.

As you explore Mount Holly, you and your dog can do some decent window-shopping, and you can also pick up some takeout food from a number of places, including anything from sandwiches to coffee. You'll find plenty of places to sit and enjoy a meal or snack together. You and your dog can also eat together at:

▶ **Robin's Nest Bakery & Café, 2 Washington Street, 609-261-6149.** They have outside dining here from April to October, weather permitting, and patrons who sit outside can bring their dogs on-leash. They will provide water or ice upon request. Cautions to dog owners: there are no immediate relief areas, and please have respect for other diners.

Mount Holly puts on some great events you and your dog won't want to miss:

▶ **About Last Night (End of each month).** Shops are open from 8:00 p.m. to 10:00 p.m., but even better than that, there are performers and visual arts to enjoy. While many of the performances and art are inside, where you can't bring your dog, a lot goes on in the streets as well, so come on out and mingle with the other shoppers and celebrators.
▶ **Mount Holly's Annual Ice Carving Festival (January).** Held downtown in Fountain Square. The carvings are judged by the National Ice Carvers Association. Bring your dog on-leash downtown to see some spectacular fantasies of ice.
▶ **Mill Dam Park Egg Hunt (March/April).** All Mount Holly residents are invited to participate. You and your dog can watch.
▶ **Dog Day Afternoon (September).** Held in Mill Race Village. Bring your dog to enjoy a day of doggishness, with vendors, free samples of pet items, pet training, races, and more. For information, call 609-267-9505.
▶ **Mount Holly Car Show and Cruise Night (October).** On High Street, you can see "flame-throwing hot rods," antique and classic vehicles, and muscle cars and trucks, dating to 1973 or before. You can also enjoy food and music. The event is free. Dogs on-leash are permitted, so cruise on out with your canine and enjoy the evening. Call 609-267-0077 for more information.
▶ **First Night® Mount Holly (December 31).** Inaugurated in 1999, Mount Holly's festival involves live music on three stages in the downtown area, street vendors, and Drumming in the New Year at midnight.

While you're in Mount Holly, and if you have kids, you might want to stop at the Rutgers Cooperative Extension of Burlington County, 122 High Street, to check out the county's **4-H program**. Pet care, including the care of dogs, is part of the program, so your dog-owning kid might want to participate. You can also call 609-265-5052 for more information.

You and your dog can stay overnight in Mount Holly at:

▶ **Best Western Inn, 2020 Route 541, 609-261-3800.** In this 88-room, two-story facility, they allow dogs under 30 pounds for a $5 charge. There are grounds around the inn that your dog can use as necessary.

Rancocas State Park

This is a special area in Mount Holly. The Rancocas Nature Center, 794 Rancocas Road, is a bird-watching mecca and educational center, with trails for bird-watching and light hiking. Rancocas Park itself has a total of 1,252 acres. There are 58 acres of natural area, containing trails that lead along the north branch of the Rancocas Creek and a freshwater tidal marsh, available for hiking, picnicking, and communing with nature with your dog on-leash. There is also a self-guided, interpretive trail. Part of the park is leased to the Powhatan Lenape Nation.

Eastampton

Near Mount Holly is another special place to take your dog:

▶ **Smithville Mansion Courtyards, Smithville Road, 609-265-5068.** This is a 19th-century manufacturing complex that includes an 1840s Greek Revival mansion on a 200-acre site along the Rancocas Creek. Many of the original estate plantings are still in place. This site is actually Burlington County's first park, founded in 1975, and open from sunrise to sunset. There's a lake here, and places to picnic. Your dog on-leash is welcome, including at outdoor events. Events you and your dog might want to come back for include:

Smithville Mansion Spring Celebration (March). Bring a picnic lunch and your dog and watch the children's egg hunt.

Summer Concerts. Bring a blanket and your dog on-leash to enjoy the music.

Annual Burlington County Earth Fair (June). Features entertainment, environmental demonstrations, and refreshments.

Summer Celebration Event (June). Bring a picnic lunch and your dog and enjoy the festivities.

Fall Festival at Smithville Mansion (September). There are antique cars and antiques vendors on the grounds, live entertainment of all kinds, community organization booths, crafts, and food. Admission and parking are free.

Mount Laurel

Mount Laurel got its name from the hill of the same name. Dogs are allowed in all Mount Laurel parks, and when I contacted the township, they were planning a dog-run: by the time you read this, it may already be in place.

Mount Laurel itself (the hill, I mean) is at the intersection of Hainesport–Mount Laurel and Moorestown–Mount Laurel Roads, and is New Jersey's smallest state park. Before 1844, it was used for semaphore and light-flash signaling to send stock reports from Wall Street to Philadelphia. Today, the mount has a Western Union microwave radio relay station on top.

Your dog can pick up a few things at:

▶ **Pet Valu in Town Square, 882 Union Mill Road, 856-802-9202**

Then the two of you can go to:

▶ **Zagara's, 4300 Briggs Road, 856-985-0727.** This is a specialty and natural foods market, with an outdoor café. Your dog can sit outside with you (outdoor seating is available from April to November). "We will accommodate *any* and *every* customer!" they said. And they sell both Iams and organic pet food.

You and your dog may want to return to Mount Laurel for:

▶ **The Mount Laurel Fall Festival (September).** Held in **Laurel Acres Park.** Includes crafts, a 5K race, a youth talent exposition, a Civil War demonstration, live entertainment, and lots of food.

And while you are in Mount Laurel, you and your dog may also want to stop by the **Rancocas Woods Village of Shops, Creek Road at I-295 (Exit 43), 856-235-1830.** More than 30 quaint shops are here, with antique shows, craft shows, and other special events year-round. Call for a schedule: your dog on-leash is welcome to attend these outdoor events with you.

Finally, you and your dog can stay overnight in Mount Laurel at:

▶ **Radisson Hotel, 915 State Route 73, 856-234-7300.** You and your dog can stay on the first floor for a $50 reimbursable fee. They have grass and fields for your dog to use as necessary.
▶ **Red Roof Inn, 603 Fellowship Road, 856-234-5589.** The inn has 108 rooms in two stories, with exterior corridors. Small dogs only.
▶ **Track & Turf Motel, 809 State Route 73, 856-235-6500.** This one-story, family-run operation has 30 rooms and exterior corridors. It is a well-maintained, though older, property. Pets are allowed, with no restrictions.
▶ **Summerfield Suites Hotel, 3000 Crawford Place, 856-222-1313.** This three-story, 116-room facility permits small pets, for a $100 to $150 fee. It has interior and exterior corridors, and three diamonds from AAA.

Medford

Dogs are permitted in all Medford Township parks, as long as they are on leashes, and you have to clean up after them, of course. The best news for your dog, however, is that **Freedom Park, on Union Street** (the newest Medford park, having opened July 3, 1999), includes a dog-run, as well as paved trails, two playgrounds, and two picnic pavilions.

Other Medford parks that your dog might be interested in include:

▶ **Bob Bende Park, on Route 541,** 3 miles north of the former Medford Circle
▶ **Bob Meyer Memorial Park, on Gravelly Hollow Road**
▶ **Cranberry Hall Park, behind the municipal center**
▶ **Medford Park, on Mill Street,** behind Bunning Field
▶ **South Street Park, on South Street,** near the Rancocas Creek
▶ **Tomlinson Park, on Main Street and Allen Avenue**

Now that you know all about the parks, you and your dog can go have a great time in historic Medford Village. You can window-shop for antiques, gifts, and more. There are brick sidewalks and tree-lined streets here, along with historic homes. Take your dog on a stroll around Medford, and stop by:

▶ **Kirby's Mill, Church and Fostertown Roads (275 Church Road).** A National Historic Site, this is the last commercial, water-powered mill in the state. The Medford Historical Society owns the mill complex, including a brick house built in 1785, a blacksmith shop, and a small barn, and the township owns the surrounding parkland, which you and your dog are welcome to enjoy. Bring your dog back for:

Kirby's Mill Apple Festival (October). Lots of apple cider and other apple products, pie, and ice cream. Also crafts, a Civil War encampment, and tours of the mill.

There are parades and festivals held in Medford throughout the year. You and your dog might especially want to come back for:

- ▶ **Historic Medford Village Festival of Art & Music (June).** Held along historic Main Street. Features an art show, eclectic music on three stages, and a picnic pavilion. Admission is free.
- ▶ **Halloween Parade (October).** Dress up your dog, dress up yourself, and go watch the fun.
- ▶ **Dickens Festival (Early December).** Held on a Friday evening on Main Street. Santa will be there, as well as singers and holiday celebrators of all kinds, both at stationary venues and strolling along with you. The festival features bell choirs, players, jugglers, bands, barbershop quartets, bagpipes, and a tree-lighting ceremony. You and your dog can also watch the Victorian horse-drawn carriage rides, which start next to the municipal building.

There's a really cool place where you and your dog can romp around a bit nearby:

- ▶ **Lewis W. Barton Arboretum and Nature Preserve at Medford Leas.** This site features 160 acres of landscaped grounds, meadows, woodland, and wetlands that you and your dog can explore together. There are mature woods, and the southwest branch of the Rancocas Creek borders on a section of the preserve, with a floodplain forest. The largest hickory tree in New Jersey is located here, as well as a pinetum including exotics, a rhododendron garden, and an herb garden. In fact, there are 40 small gardens designed by landscape architects or interns from the Morris Arboretum here. Open daily from 9:00 a.m. to dusk. Admission is free. Tour maps are available at the reception desk.

Marlton

Marlton has a little of everything to offer you and your dog, including several National Historic Sites. And there are events:

- ▶ **Granny's Yard & Attic Sale (Autumn).** Held in the rear parking lot of Wal-Mart, Route 70, and sponsored by the Evesham Historical Society. Admission is free. For information, call 856-983-0572.
- ▶ **Annual Olde Marlton Fall Festival (October).** Held on Main Street, and sponsored by the Evesham Township Historic Preservation Committee and the Women's League of Evesham. Admission is free. For information, call 856-985-7661.

And finally, there's a place for your dog to shop in Marlton:

- ▶ **Pet Valu, Evesham Plaza, 744 West Route 70, 856-810-9595**

Pemberton Borough

This small borough dates to 1752. Along Hanover and Elizabeth Streets, you and your dog can walk by lovely historic houses, including many Victorians, and a historic grist mill at 127 Hanover Street. The Pemberton National Historic District is bounded by Budd Avenue, Budd's Run, Egbert and Cedar Roads, the Rancocas Creek, and the New Jersey Central Power and Light Company.

What used to be an old blacksmith's shop is now Clark's Marina and Landing. You and your water dog can rent rowboats or canoes there and go as far as Browns Mills, 5 miles east of Pemberton, if you want to. (Both of you should wear life vests!)

There are Pemberton events that may be of interest to you and your dog, including:

- ▶ **Octoberfest (First Saturday in October)**
- ▶ **Homecoming Parade (November)**
- ▶ **Holiday House Decoration Contest (December)**
- ▶ **Holiday Appreciation Day (December).** Held at the municipal building. There is a tree-lighting ceremony with carols, and photos with Santa, who arrives on a fire truck.

While you and your dog are in Pemberton, stop at:

- ▶ **The Pineland Preservation Alliance, 114 Hanover Street.** You can get maps, fliers, and itineraries for hiking, canoeing, and camping in the Pinelands National Reserve from the alliance, as well as details on festivals held in the land preserve.

One final, great stop for you and your dog to make in Pemberton is a cultural one:

- ▶ **The Sculpture Garden, Burlington County College, County Route 530, 609-894-9311, ext. 7328.** You and your dog on-leash are welcome to peruse the sculpture and settings here.

Lebanon State Forest

Lebanon State Forest includes about 31,879 acres in the heart of the Pinelands. It is named for the 19th-century Lebanon Glass Works. There are picnicking and hiking facilities in Lebanon State Forest. And in the northern portion is:

- ▶ **Historic Whitesbog, Route 530 (mile marker 13), Browns Mills.** There are 3,000 acres of forests, ponds, bogs, cedar swamps, and fields here, open daily from dawn to dusk, as well as a historic village. Whitesbog Village was a company town, and the residential use continues. You can tour the site with your dog on-leash, as long as your canine companion is well-mannered and you bring supplies to clean up. The site used to contain the largest cranberry farm in New Jersey, and the first commercial high-bush blueberry was cultivated here. The village is a National Historic Site, and includes many original buildings. For more information, call 609-893-4646.

You can get guides to Whitesbog from the Whitesbog Preservation Trust, 120-13 Whitesbog Road, Browns Mills. You and your dog will have a great time in Historic Whitesbog, and you will both want to come back for the following terrific events:

Annual Whitesbog Blueberry Festival (June/July). Features food, crafts, folk music, Pinelands art, blueberries, and more. Admission is charged per car. Bring your dog on-leash to celebrate the village where the cultivated blueberry was born.

Dogs in the Bogs (October). In the past, this event has included retriever games, rescue and sled dog demonstrations, and an exhibition of the Pinelands hound dog. Keep an eye out for it in the fall: you can call 609-893-4646 or visit the village's Web site at www.whitesbog.org.

The Batona Trail

If you and your dog are up for some real exercise, head for the Batona Trail. The trail's 50 miles are marked with pink blazes, starting in Lebanon State Forest and traveling through Wharton State Forest, all the way to Bass River State Forest. Several roads cross the trail, so it can be reached by car at various points. It is a relatively easy hike. And you and your dog may even be able to see orchids growing naturally. There are trail maps, restrooms, water, and parking facilities available at park headquarters in both Lebanon State Forest and Wharton State Forest.

Wharton State Forest

At the other end of the Batona Trail you will find the largest state forest in New Jersey. There are a couple of spots within Wharton State Forest that you and your dog will want to visit:

▶ **Atsion Lake Recreation Area.** Located on Route 206 (10 miles south of Red Lion Circle, or $7^1/_2$ miles north of Route 30, above Hammonton). You and your dog are welcome to wander through, though not in the overnight areas, and there are parking fees. Other than that, there's boating, fishing, swimming in Atsion Lake, a nature trail, and a picnic area. And your dog and you may want to come back for:

Annual Atsion Flea Market (April). Bring your dog on-leash to browse through all the interesting items for sale.

On the other side of Route 206 is **Atsion Village**, a National Historic Site. You and your dog can wander around here as well and view a Greek Revival mansion built in 1826. Booklets on the history of this site, which was used for a bog iron furnace, a grist mill, three sawmills, a paper mill, and a peanut farm, are available at the Batsto Visitor Center (see page 122).

▶ **Historic Batsto Village.** Located 10 miles east of Hammonton, on County Road 542, this Pine Barrens village of 33 buildings includes the Batsto Mansion, a grist mill, a sawmill, a general store, workers' homes, and a post office. Sited along the Batona Trail, it is preserved as of 1766. You can simply walk the grounds with your dog and look at the buildings, or enjoy self-guided tours of the grounds and the **Batsto Pond Nature Trail,** a half-mile through the Pinelands. A food concession is open during the summer, and on weekends in May and September: there are picnic tables where you can eat with your dog. Pinelands crafts are demonstrated here during the summer. There is a parking fee on weekends and holidays from Memorial Day to Labor Day, but the village grounds are open daily from dawn to dusk. And you and your dog will want to come back for these cool events:

Earth Day (April). An annual event at which dogs on-leash are welcome. For more information, call 609-567-4559.

Art Show and Dog Show (September)

Batsto Country Living Fair (October). Features exhibits, crafts, live music, and food.

You and your dog can also explore the 9,449 acres of the **Batsto Natural Area.** There are two sections, along the Batsto and Mullica Rivers. This is a great place to explore the varied habitats of the Pine Barrens.

Hammonton

Although technically Hammonton is in Atlantic County, it is just down the road from Batsto Village, and there are a couple of reasons you and your dog might want to go there. First, there's a great festival:

▶ **Annual Red, White, and Blueberry Festival (June).** Sponsored by the Greater Hammonton Chamber of Commerce, the festival features music, entertainment, arts and crafts, blueberries, food, games, and a classic/antique car show. For more information, call 609-561-9080.

Second, there are a couple of places in Hammonton where you and your dog can go to get a Christmas tree in December:

▶ **Holly Ridge Tree Farm, 116 South Chew Road, 609-561-8575.** You can bring your well-mannered dog on-leash to get a tree, Tuesday through Sunday, from 9:00 a.m. to 5:00 p.m.

▶ **Petrongolo Evergreen Plantation, 7541 Weymouth Road, 609-567-0336.** Open daily from 9:00 a.m. to 5:00 p.m., they have restrooms, wrapping service, and a gift shop, as well as hayrides that even your dog can go on if no one else objects. They welcome dogs on-leash, and say that they seem to get more every year.

And on your way back (wherever "back" may be), if you happen to be passing through Gloucester County, there are a couple of places your dog may want to stop to go shopping:

▶ **Pet Valu, Winslow Plaza Shopping Center, 542 Berlin Cross Keys Road, Sicklerville, 856-629-3940.** You can bring your dog on-leash inside, and they have biscuits at the counter.

▶ **PETCO, 1730 Clements Bridge Road, Deptford, 856-384-9609.** You can, of course, bring your dog on-leash in here, and they have all the usual items for sale. They hold events such as grooming to benefit the Seeing Eye Dog Foundation, greyhound adoption, and obedience classes. What else? "Friendly, knowledgeable, helpful associates, clean, and a pleasant shopping experience," they say.

❖ POINTS NORTH IN NEW JERSEY

Bordentown

Bordentown City is a great, dog-friendly place on the Delaware River. It was settled in 1682 as Farnsworth Landing; Joseph Borden arrived in 1717, and by 1740 he had a line of stagecoaches and boats moving between Philadelphia and New York. In the late 1700s, Bordentown was home to Francis Hopkinson, Colonel Kirkbride, Colonel Hoagland, and Thomas Paine. Perhaps as a result of all that native patriotism, it was occupied by the Hessians in 1776, and was pillaged and burned by the British in 1778.

Today it is a wonderful place to explore, with a main street—Farnsworth Avenue—that is lined with bistros, places to pick up takeout food, art galleries, antique stores, and more. The window-shopping is terrific. So is the history—both residential and otherwise. And of course you will want to take your canine buddy for a stroll along the river.

You and your dog won't want to miss the community events:

▶ **Annual Sunset Stroll (April).** Meet the friendly merchants of Bordentown as you stroll the business district.

▶ **City Wide Yard Sale (June).** Sponsored by the Downtown Bordentown Association, the entire town puts out its bargains during this event. Browse items for sale along Farnsworth Avenue and in front of homes. Call 609-298-3334 for more information.

▶ **Inside/Outside Sidewalk Sale (July).** Sponsored by the Downtown Bordentown Association, the merchants of Bordentown offer bargains both inside and outside.

▶ **Annual Halloween Parade (October).** You and your dog can watch the floats, marching bands, and children in costume passing by.

▶ **Holiday Season (November/December).** There's caroling, entertainment, teas, and special events each weekend. Bordentown merchants dress up to make it a Victorian Christmas, and many serve refreshments.

There's at least one gallery in Bordentown where you can bring your dog on-leash inside:

▶ **Firehouse Gallery, 8 Walnut Street, 609-298-3742.** A great gallery in an 1886 firehouse where, according to owner Eric Gibbons, a very talented artist in his own right, "well-behaved and leashed dogs are welcome daily except at evening opening receptions. Patrons must pay for any artwork their dog may damage, though most work is at least three feet off the ground." Exhibits change monthly, and feature artists who work in all media.

Your dog may prefer a couple of other dog-friendly businesses you will come across in Bordentown:

▶ **Animal Kingdom Pet Store, 1800 Jacksonville-Jobstown Road, 609-265-1281.** You can bring your dog inside here, and they will offer a dog treat. I'm told you can also walk your dog through their 38-acre zoo. This is an interesting place.

▶ **Little Hearts, 137 Farnsworth Avenue, 609-298-5954.** This shop has a terrific selection of pet supplies and pet-related gift items. You can bring your dog with you as you browse around inside. For more information, call them, or visit their Web site at www.fnets.com/littlehearts.htm. They are very helpful, friendly folks.

Finally, you and your dog can stay overnight in Bordentown at:

▶ **Days Inn, 1073 U.S. Route 206, 609-298-6100.** This two-story facility with 131 rooms has exterior corridors. Your dog can stay here for no extra fee and with no restrictions, and they have grounds for walking and any necessary business your dog may have.

Frenchtown

Frenchtown is a lovely place. There are lots of interesting shops that make for fantastic window-shopping (and some of them might let you bring your dog inside). There's also some great architecture, including "New England–style" churches. For more information, visit the Frenchtown Web site at www.frenchtown.com.

To the right of the Frenchtown-Uhlerstown Bridge (Bridge Street) are hiking and biking trails along an old railroad right-of-way that you and your dog can enjoy. Come and visit with your dog any day, but the two of you might also want to come for these great events:

▶ **Frenchtown Freedom Festival (July 3–14).** Ten days of events, including entertainment, a community fun bike ride, a 5K run, "Cinema Under the Stars" behind Varieté (37 Bridge Street), a sidewalk art show, and fireworks.

▶ **Bastille Day Celebration (July).** The Arts & Commerce Council of Frenchtown sponsors street musicians, mimes, artists, and other street performers. There are also raffles and refreshments.

▶ **Annual Alexandria BalloonFest (August).** This event does not really take place in Frenchtown, but the balloons waft all over the area, so go to Frenchtown and hang out to do some balloon-spotting with your dog.

There are plenty of places in Frenchtown to get takeout food such as pizza and deli sandwiches. Or you and your dog can stop at:

▶ **Cornerstone Café, 12th and Harrison Streets, 908-996-2885.** This lovely café has a walk-up window in the spring, summer, and fall, and you can order something for yourself or your dog. They will accommodate your dog with a cup of water, or even a small dish of ice cream if you wish.

Then take your dog shopping:

▶ **Natural Instincts, 28 Bridge Street, 908-996-6304.** They will offer your dog a treat as you browse through their unique toys, treats, and accessories for pets. They are Frenchtown's "pampered pets" center, as they say. They also have nature-themed gifts for home and garden.

Finally, you and your dog can stay overnight together in Frenchtown at:

▶ **Frenchtown National Hotel, 31 Race Street, 908-996-4871.** This is an 1851 inn and restaurant. They will allow you to bring your dog if he or she is well-mannered and sociable enough to get along with the two dogs that live at the hotel. Call for more information.

Somerset

This is the home of the headquarters of the **Delaware & Raritan Canal State Park**, at 645 Canal Road. The park includes 3,785 acres centered along a canal tow-path. The park's 70 linear miles pass through lovely small towns such as Lambertville and Stockton. Along the way, there are 19th-century bridges, cobblestone spillways, bridgetender houses, locks, and hand-built stone culverts to see. You can canoe, jog, hike, bike, fish, or ride horses through the park. For information, call 732-873-3050.

Titusville

Titusville is a great town to wander in and explore with your dog. There are lovely homes and historic spots to admire, and the Delaware River to enjoy. The Delaware & Raritan Canal is right next door, along with:

▶ **Washington Crossing State Park, 355 Washington Crossing–Pennington Road (Route 546).** There are nearly 1,000 acres in this park, and you and your dog can picnic, hike, and tour here. There are historic structures such as the 18th-century Johnson Ferry House and the Nelson House, as well as 140 acres of natural area with plenty of trails. Don't forget to look for the double line of trees marking "Continental Lane," a preserved part of the road followed by the Continental Army on its march from the river toward Trenton after Washington's historic crossing of the Delaware. For more information on the park, call 609-737-2454. You and your dog may want to come back for these events:

   Days of the Past (September). Sponsored by the Delaware Valley Old Time Power & Equipment Association. Admission is charged.

   Making Strides Against Breast Cancer (October). Benefits the American Cancer Society. Show up with your dog on-leash for a 5-mile fundraising walk, with food and entertainment. You have to walk your dog anyway—might as well do it for a worthy cause.

There's a great place adjacent to Washington Crossing State Park where you and your dog can get a bite to eat together:

▶ **Fifty's Drive-In Restaurant, 1382 River Road, 609-737-0505.** Open from early April to Labor Day, seven days a week; Labor Day through mid-October, Saturday and Sunday only. You can get quality fast food and homemade ice cream here, and sit outside with your dog on-leash to eat. They will provide bowls of water for your dog, and they also have an outside faucet. "We are located in a great area for dog walkers—[you] can get to our restaurant by walking trails through the park."

Is it time to pick out a Christmas tree? Try:

▶ **Pleasant Valley Tree Farm, 47 Pleasant Valley Road, 609-730-1110.** Open Friday through Sunday from 9:00 a.m. to 4:00 p.m. They provide saws, and your dog on-leash can help you choose the perfect tree.

Stockton

Stockton contains about 200 homes. It started as Readings Ferry, then was called Howels Ferry, and finally was named Stockton in 1853. Just north of Stockton on Route 29, in the Delaware & Raritan Canal State Park, is the only pedestrian bridge crossing the river into Pennsylvania. You can take your dog to a lovely site:

▶ **Prallsville Mills, Route 29.** A 19th-century mill complex of grist and linseed oil mills, this is a really cool place to explore, with historic buildings and pretty views. We had a great picnic here with our dogs, sitting on a large rock. The Delaware & Raritan Canal State Park passes along here, so you can go for a long walk. There are sometimes **folk concerts, art shows, and other events** here, sponsored by the Delaware River Mill Society: if the events are outside, your dog on-leash can come. Events are planned annually, so keep an eye on the local newspapers, or call 609-397-3586.

Lambertville

This pretty town, connected by bridge to New Hope, Pennsylvania, was settled in 1705 on the banks of the Delaware River. It was known as Coryell's Ferry until 1814. There are lovely, historic homes in Victorian and Federal styles here, and on the main business streets you'll find galleries, shops, restaurants, and bistros. The Delaware & Raritan Canal State Park's towpath is available here to stroll or run along with your dog.

You and your dog will want to come back for Lambertville's premier event:

▶ **The Lambertville Shad Fest (April).** Held along Bridge and Union Streets, this is an all-day celebration of the Delaware River and the annual shad run. Includes a street fair with demonstrations, food, juried crafts, clowns, and music. The fest is free, and you can bring your dog on-leash to enjoy anything that takes place in a public space or along the street.

Are you and your dog browsers? Of antiques and collectibles, I mean. If so, you'll want to go here:

▶ **Golden Nugget Antique and Flea Market, 1850 River Road, 609-397-0811.** Open Wednesday, Saturday, and Sunday from 8:00 a.m. to 4:00 p.m., all year. There are about 250 outside tables, where it is okay to have your dog on-leash along as you browse. They say it is "one of the finest antique markets on the East Coast."

You and your dog on-leash can also spend some time at:

▶ **Holcombe-Jimison Farmstead.**   Located on the right just after the first exit off Route 202 after the toll bridge. There's a 1742 bank barn here, and various displays of farming tools. The farmstead is open Sundays, May through October, from 1:00 p.m. to 4:00 p.m. You can bring a picnic and eat it on the grounds. For more information, call 609-397-1810.

Delaware County

Delaware County is a mixed bag for dog owners. Some parts are extremely dog-friendly. Other parts aren't dog-friendly at all. The dog-friendly parts, however, are pretty incredible.

❖ NORTHERN DELAWARE COUNTY

Villanova (Western Main Line)

The Main Line is sort of a confusing place (there are actually those who believe it is that way on purpose). Quite a few Main Line "towns" extend over county lines, so that they could fit equally well in the Montgomery County section or in the Delaware County section of this book. Villanova is a good example. The centerpiece of Villanova, the university, is in Delaware County, so I'm putting Villanova as a whole right here. And why not make the university the first stop for you and your dog in Delaware County?

▶ **Villanova University and Arboretum Villanova, 800 Lancaster Avenue.** Open every day from dawn to dusk. Villanova was founded by the Augustinian Fathers, who purchased John Rudolph's Belle Air estate in 1841. There are 220 acres of rolling hills, with mature specimen trees scattered all over them. Come back in the spring, when tens of thousands of daffodils bloom on every part of the campus. You and your dog might also want to return for:

   Balloon Day (April). This is Villanova's spring carnival, held at the Connelly Center. For more information, call 610-519-7205.

When you have finished admiring the university, there are historic places that you and your dog can explore in other parts of the Villanova area. For instance, take a trip to the Harriton National Historic District, covering 1401 to 1415 Old Gulph Road. Find a place to park and take a walk, admiring the structures here.

Wayne/Radnor

Wayne is another western Main Line town, and more or less the active heart of Radnor Township. It's a nice historic area, with a great commercial district. There are wonderful shops with window displays to admire, and some shops may allow you to bring your dog inside. There are a few benches along the street where you and your dog can rest, and a nice park with a clock at the corner of Wayne Avenue.

If you and your dog are looking for a place to eat together, there are quite a few choices. **Bertucci's Brick Oven Pizzeria, 523 West Lancaster Avenue**, has benches out front where you can sit and enjoy some takeout Italian. **Spread Eagle Village, 503 West Lancaster Avenue**, has several options for takeout food, and a picnic table and other outdoor seating scattered around. Elsewhere there are more places for takeout and amenities:

- ▶ **Café Procopio, 1 West Avenue, 610-989-0541.** You can get coffee, tea, pastries, lunch, and ice cream here. They have two benches outside all year where you can sit with your dog, and they will provide water, ice, and doggy biscuits.
- ▶ **Dairy Queen, 138 North Wayne Avenue.** At this Dairy Queen Brazier there is a large area of benches where you and your dog can sit year-round. As for amenities: "Any dog owner can come in and get a dish of ice cream for their dog for free."
- ▶ **Station Café & Juice Bar, 135 North Wayne Avenue, 610-687-1931.** This is a coffee shop, juice bar, cybercafé, and "restaurant-to-be" in the historic Wayne Train Station, which is on the National Historic Register. There are great renovations in the works, including a brick terrace on the southeast side, which makes my ears perk up, along with my dogs'. As the café is now, you can bring your dog on-leash with you if you sit outside to eat, and there is outdoor seating whenever the temperature is over 50 degrees. The Station Café, in fact, is quite enthusiastic about dogs: "We love dogs, yes, yes, yes." They will provide your dog with a bowl of water ("Doggie Latte"), "interesting conversation," and "job placement (Seeing Eye dogs only)."

After you and your dog have had a bite to eat, stop by:

- ▶ **Finley House, 113 West Beech Tree Lane, 610-688-2668.** This is the home of the Radnor Historical Society. The oldest portion of the house was built about 1789. The grounds are always open, and dogs on-leash (as long as they are cleaned up after) are perfectly welcome to take a stroll and a sniff around. There's a large statue of a dog in front of the house that my dog Georgie was convinced was real but somehow paralyzed: she kept barking and barking at it, as if she were urging it to move, and looked at my husband and me as if we should help it. Besides Finley House itself, the grounds include a wagon house with a genuine Conestoga wagon inside.

Your dog will insist on coming back for the great events Wayne and Radnor Township hold, including:

- **Radnor Memorial Day Parade (May).** Bands, veterans, antique cars, fire engines, and Pals for Life animals march along Lancaster Avenue.
- **Wayne Sidewalk Sale (June).** Spread Eagle Village and downtown Wayne hold a three-day sidewalk sale. In the afternoons, you and your dog can enjoy entertainment, including strolling street performers, music, food, and more.
- **Radnor Summer Concerts (July and August).** Bring a blanket, a picnic, and your dog to enjoy such events as an Irish Music Festival, big band music, country/bluegrass sounds, Italian Night, and Scottish Night. Keep an eye on the local newspapers to find out about dates, times, and places.
- **"Dollars for Scholars" Main Line Run (September).** This event is part of Main Line Week, sponsored by the Main Line Chamber of Commerce. There's a 5K run or walk, as well as children's sprints, all of which raise money for college scholarships for area students. For information, call 610-687-6232.
- **Radnor Fall Festival (September).** Sponsored by the Wayne Business Association, the festival is held on the grounds of the Radnor Middle School, South Wayne Avenue. Admission is charged, but dogs on-leash are welcome and there's even an event just for them: the Top Dog Contests. When you've finished showing off your dog, the two of you can look at fire trucks, browse the local community organization tables, stop by the health fair or the strawberry festival, watch a karate show, and more.
- **Radnor Fire Company Auxiliary Flea Market and Craft Fair (October).** Your dog on-leash can browse the treasures on display right along with you.
- **Annual Radnor Run (October).** Sponsored by Wyeth-Ayerst, this run is over 20 years old and benefits the American Lung Association of Pennsylvania–Southeastern Region. You and your dog can watch runners follow a 5-mile course through the township. There is also a 1-mile fun run/walk. For more information, call 800-LUNG-USA.
- **Veterans Day Ceremony (November 11).** Held at the Radnor War Memorial, this is one of the most impressive Veterans Day ceremonies in the area.
- **The Santa Parade (First Saturday in December).** Sponsored by the Main Line Chamber of Commerce. After the parade, Santa sits on the porch of the Wayne Hotel, greeting kids, and there are clowns, balloons, candy canes, and cookies to be enjoyed.
- **Winter Holiday Celebration (December).** The Wayne Business Association sponsors the annual Wayne Tree Lighting at the Wayne Train Station: carolers, sleigh rides, fire engines, and musicians add to the festivities.

Do you and your dog have time for one more event? Then definitely go to:

- **One Sky, One World Kite Festival (September).** Held at the Cabrini College Athletic Field, 610 King of Prussia Road, Radnor. Besides lots of kites soaring aloft (hopefully!), you can see an animal safari show, a puppet show, and a magician and juggler, and browse among vendors, all with your dog on-leash. Bring your dog's kite, or, if you and your dog are one of the first 100 guests, you may receive a kite for free. For information, call 610-902-8255.

And there's another event in the area that you might want to know about:

- **Pals for Life Benefit (October).** Pals for Life provides companion animal visits to people who don't have other access to the kind of love a pet can give. The benefit party includes a pet photo contest, a silent auction, and more. For more information, call 610-687-1101.

Does your dog need to go shopping? There are a few choices:

▶ **Braxton's Animal Works, 620 West Lancaster Avenue, 610-688-0769.** Famous on the Main Line, and now new and improved and big, big, big. Believe it or not, Braxton's originally opened with an emphasis on birds. They still sell bird supplies, along with cat supplies and items for other small animals. But what you want to know about is the huge selection of dog items, from treats to flotation vests—you name it and Braxton's either has it or can get it for you. Bring your dog in and browse. The new two-story building is awesome.

▶ **PETCO, 132 East Lancaster Avenue, 610-341-0730**

▶ **Pet Valu, 555 East Lancaster Avenue, 610-254-9101**

Radnor Township has 20 parks, but only two permit dogs, so if your dog is hankering for grass, take him or her to:

▶ **Harford Park.** Located between Matsonford and Gulph Creek Roads, this is an open-space area with a fitness trail.

▶ **Emlen Tunnel Park.** At Garrett Avenue between Conestoga Road and Lancaster Avenue, the park has ballfields and picnic areas.

Usually there isn't any place in Wayne you can stay overnight with your dog. But during the Devon Horse Show and Country Fair (see page 146), you and your dog may be able to stay at:

▶ **Courtyard by Marriott, 762 West Lancaster Avenue, 610-687-6633.** Call them for more information.

(Haverford)

The area known as Haverford is another one that straddles both Delaware and Montgomery Counties. I've put it here because Haverford Township itself is in Delaware County. And I have some bad news for you. Dogs are not permitted in Haverford Township parks or on Haverford Township property.

Fortunately, within Haverford Township (mostly, anyway: part of it is in Lower Merion Township in Montgomery County) is Haverford College, a *very* dog-friendly spot, as well as other sites where dogs and their human companions can walk and run and have a good time. So don't despair! Take your dog to play at:

▶ **Haverford College, 370 West Lancaster Avenue.** Your dog on-leash is allowed everywhere here. Take your canine to run or walk along the nature trail that circles the campus. Watch the ducks on the duck pond. Romp across the open fields. And tour the campus, which not only has some remarkable buildings and sculpture, but is also an arboretum. The entire 216-acre campus of Haverford College was established as an arboretum in 1831, and designed in 1834. At the Physical Plant building you can pick up really wonderful arboretum brochures for self-guided tours of the Pinetum and center campus.

Haverford College puts on some good events that you and your dog might want to attend. Your dog will be especially interested in:

Celebration of Diversity (April). Held on Founders Green, this outdoor multicultural festival includes food, arts and crafts, and performances.

Annual Walk & Roll and Canine Carnival (June). A fundraising event for Independence Dogs, Inc., an organization that trains service dogs. Dogs that participate in the Walk & Roll receive a bandanna in exchange for the registration fee. After the Walk & Roll, you and your dog can spend the day enjoying the dog-oriented carnival, including agility events, flyball exhibitions (flyball is a four-dog relay race in which each dog retrieves a tennis ball and runs along a 51-foot course set with four hurdles—the racing dogs go *really* fast), obedience demonstrations, a rabies clinic (for a donation), dog-related vendors, dog-pulled wagon rides, demonstrations by a police K-9 division, search and rescue demonstrations, AKC Canine Good Citizen testing (for a donation), and more. Your dog will have a blast, and so will you. For more information, call 610-358-2723.

If your dog wants to pick up some supplies, you can go to:

▶ **PETCO, 532 West Lancaster Avenue, 610-527-9798.** Along with all the usual things you expect from PETCO, the store has a Halloween costume party in October, open to dogs and cats. There are bags of free goodies for all entrants, and prizes for the winners of contest categories including Most Original Costume, Costume That Best Suits Pet Personality, and Best Owner Involvement/Interaction.

Haverford Township puts on a couple of annual events at which you and your dog can have a great time:

▶ **Haverford Township Day (October).** Events start off with a 5K run, followed by a parade. There are also a variety of activities, craft vendors, a flea market, live music, a petting zoo, entertainment, and tons of fun along Darby Road and elsewhere in the township. Your dog on-leash is allowed everywhere but inside buildings.

▶ **Reindeer Romp 5K Fun Run and/or Walk (December).** Runners and walkers dress in holiday costume, which makes it especially fun for you and your dog to watch, and you might even be able to participate together. Brochures for the race, which benefits the American Cancer Society, are available from the Haverford Recreation Department. For more information, call 610-565-1009.

Pennfield/Penn Wynne

Pennfield is the Delaware County portion of an area that extends into Montgomery County (where it is called Penn Wynne). It is a nice neighborhood to walk around in, with some interesting homes to gaze at. Just don't take your dog to Powder Mill Valley Park along the Cobbs Creek: although it's a wonderful place, it's Haverford Township property, and dogs aren't allowed there.

There's an event in the area (actually on the Montgomery County side) that you and your dog might want to keep in mind:

▶ **Penn Wynne Fourth of July Parade and Carnival.** Lots of dogs march in this parade.

Havertown

Ah, Havertown. Since Haverford Township is not particularly dog-friendly, it's tough to find dog-friendly spots in Havertown. That includes places to grab a bite to eat with your dog. As a spokesperson for Carmine's Café (French Creole cuisine), 5 Brookline Boulevard, stated, "I would [allow people to sit outside with their dogs] if the township would allow it, but they won't even permit outside seating! I love dogs—I own two and I am obsessed with them!"

So, regular restaurants are sort of out of the question here. But you and your dog *can* go to:

▶ **Rita's Water Ice, 55 West Eagle Road.** Outdoor seating is available all season, so you can sit with your dog and enjoy what you've gotten from the walk-up window. The staff at Rita's has provided cups of water for dogs, and their policy is "All are welcome."

▶ **Baskin-Robbins, 1304 West Chester Pike.** Outdoor seating is available all year here, and you can sit outside with your dog. The staff will provide water, ice, or dog treats on request. Or you can get your dog a small bowl of ice cream.

Marple

Unlike Haverford Township, Marple Township allows dogs in all its parks, as long as they are on-leash. Try one of these:

▶ **Kent Park.** Located at the end of a driveway off Cedar Grove Road, there are 42 acres here that you and your dog can explore: there are nature trails, benches, and a stream called Trout Run. Bring a picnic and your dog and enjoy. The park is underused, so dog owners tend to let dogs off-leash to run and play in the creek. Legally, of course, dogs are required to be leashed.

▶ **Veterans Memorial Park, Lawrence Road.** Dogs are permitted here except in the active-play areas and on the walking/exercise trails. Restrooms are available here.

There's an even better place to visit, however, with some history mixed in:

▶ **Thomas Massey House, Lawrence and Springhouse Roads.** This National Historic Site includes one of the oldest English Quaker homes in Pennsylvania, and it is well worth a visit with your dog. Thomas Massey, an indentured servant who received 50 acres of ground from his ex-master and another 50 from William Penn, ultimately was able to purchase 300 acres of land in Marple in 1696. There was an existing log house on the property, to which Thomas Massey added a brick portion, and about 1730 his son replaced the log portion with a stone house and kitchen. Further changes were made in 1860. The house and one acre of ground were purchased by the township in 1964 and restored. You can't bring your dog into the house, of course, but you are welcome to stroll the grounds, which are always open, with your dog on-leash. There are also a couple of events that take place at the Thomas Massey site:

Harvest Festival (September). Colonial foods are available.
Frost Bite Run (November)

After you've finished enjoying some exercise with your dog, you can go shopping at:

▶ **PetsMart, 2940 Springfield Road, Broomall, 610-353-4446**

Newtown Square

This is a great historic area. The Newtown Square Historical Society is head-quartered at the **Paper Mill House Museum, Paper Mill and St. Davids Roads.** This is a par-ticularly interesting historic site, and includes a restored 19th-century mill worker's home and mill ruins, along with a bridge, a creek, and trails. Despite many attempts to contact the historical society regarding this site, I was unable to reach them for a definitive answer about dogs. All I can tell you is that there are no postings prohibiting dogs. It's well worth a visit, so stop by and take your dog for a walk on the grounds (if no one instructs you to the contrary).

❖ EASTERN DELAWARE COUNTY

Upper Darby

This is an interesting area with some stunningly beautiful homes tucked away in it. It's a great place to go for a walk with your dog and explore the pockets of unique homes. Drexel Park (roughly the area between School Lane and Garrett Road, and Argyle Road and Forrest Avenue), and the areas of Upper Darby across from Drexel Park, contain some truly remark-able houses.

When your dog has had enough of touring, head to:

▶ **The Swedish Log Cabin, 9 Creek Road.** Built during the area's New Sweden era, and pos-sibly the oldest log structure in North America. The grounds around the cabin are always open, and you are welcome to bring your dog for a walk along the creek and around the cabin. The cabin itself is open on weekend afternoons, and donations are appreciated. Regu-lar events are held at the cabin, including **Midsummer's Day Picnic (June), Crafts & Friendship Day (October),** and **Trim-the-Tree Party (December).** For more information, call 610-623-1650.

Lansdowne

In Lansdowne, there is also a lot to see. Tour the Lansdowne Park National Historic District, roughly bounded by West Greenwood, Owen, West Balti-more, Windermere, and West Stratford Avenues. While you're in the area, look for the following National Historic Sites:

▶ **Lansdowne Theatre, 29 Lansdowne Avenue**
▶ **Twentieth Century Club of Lansdowne, 84 South Lansdowne Avenue**

Essington

Essington, in Tinicum and near the John Heinz National Wildlife Refuge, has a very nice site that you and your dog may want to visit:

▶ **Governor Printz State Park, 2nd Street and Taylor Avenue.** Johan Printz, governor of New Sweden, the first European settlement in Pennsylvania (founded in 1643), chose Tinicum Island for his house, the Printzhof. The park is an archaeological site on which Governor Printz is honored with a statue. There's a wonderful view of the Delaware River, and a self-guided walking tour. It's free, and your dog on-leash is welcome to enjoy the park with you.

Across the Darby Creek from Tinicum is another site that you and your dog will want to see:

▶ **Morton Homestead, 100 Lincoln Avenue, Prospect Park.** A National Historic Site, this is the two-part log home of John Morgan, a signer of the Declaration of Independence and the great-grandson of Morton Mortenson, a New Sweden colonist. The homestead is typical of early Swedish log buildings. Dogs on-leash are permitted on the grounds, and it's free.

Swarthmore

Swarthmore Village is a great, dog-friendly area. You can have a good time simply strolling around and enjoying the window-shopping. Along South Chester Road, Dartmouth Avenue, and Park Avenue are a variety of shops where you can admire antiques, flowers, unusual gifts, clothes, and more. There are plenty of benches to sit on and take in the atmosphere. Or pick up some food at one of the local eateries and sit outside to enjoy it with your dog. Don't forget to admire the Swarthmore train station, the borough hall, and the library, as well as the post office, all of which are lovely. Then step over on two feet and four to see:

▶ **Swarthmore College, 500 College Avenue.** Established in 1864, the college has some really beautiful buildings, and the entire campus is an arboretum (see below). One thing you need to know as you consider taking a stroll around the campus with your dog is that they have something even better than benches to rest on: Adirondack chairs. You and your dog will love this place.

    The Scott Arboretum of Swarthmore College. Established in 1929 as a living memorial to Arthur Hoyt Scott, an 1895 alumnus, the arboretum covers the whole 300-plus-acre campus. There are over 3,000 kinds of plants in collections and distinct garden areas that are absolutely beautiful. You and your dog will enjoy all of the arboretum's features.

    Both of you are welcome to come back to the Scott Arboretum for these special events:

    Arbor Day Celebration (April). Free and open to the public.

Rose Garden Peak (June)
An Evening in the Arboretum (Summer). You can bring your dog to picnic on the grass of the arboretum's terraced amphitheater and listen to a concert, all for free.

And if your dog wants to go shopping, stop at nearby:

▶ **PETCO, 1307 Macdade Boulevard, Woodlyn, 610-833-9811.** Pet owners are encouraged to bring their dogs inside this store, and "we have a fine pet bar selection which holds many doggie treats." Dogs who come to shop will get treats either as they come in or as they leave. Twice a year, a photographer comes to the store to take pictures with pets, including casual poses and pictures with Santa Claus.

And if you are looking for a way to clean your dog without having to clean your bathroom (or your whole house!) afterward, try:

▶ **Bathe Your Pet, 904 East MacDade Boulevard, Ridley Park, 610-534-8180.** Everything you need to bathe and dry your dog is included in the fee at this self-service dog wash, and the raised tubs will save your back from strain. Dog treats and tub cleanup are also included, and you can wash your cat here as well.

Wallingford/Rose Valley

This beautiful, historic area contains some really wonderful landscape, and some great places to go with your dog. Head for these really cool, doggish places:

▶ **Thomas Leiper House and Park, 521 Avondale Road, Wallingford, 610-566-6365.** This is a National Historic Site owned by Nether Providence Township. The house was built in 1785, and there are four remaining outbuildings. Mr. Leiper had a milling and quarrying business around the Crum Creek, and provided housing for his workers in the area. There are many neat things to see here, and you and your dog on-leash are free to walk around. Leiper Park has tables and benches, so you can picnic beside the Crum Creek.

▶ **Leiper-Smedley Trail.** This is a paved, multi-use trail that links the Thomas Leiper House and Park to Smedley Park (see below). The trail is over 2 miles long, and allows walkers, joggers, and cyclists to enjoy the Crum Creek Valley. Along the trail, between Avondale Road and Rogers Lane, you and your dog can admire the ruins of the Italian Water Garden. Use caution where the trail crosses roads, keep your dog on-leash, and remember that the trail is closed from dusk to dawn and in inclement weather. Trail maps are available at the Leiper House and at the Nether Providence Township Building, 214 Sykes Lane, Wallingford.

▶ **Smedley Park** is at the northern end of the Leiper-Smedley trail. Smedley is a Delaware County park, with approximately 120 acres on both sides of the Crum Creek for you and your dog to enjoy. There are a variety of natural hiking trails, as well as picnic areas and athletic fields. The **Delaware County 4-H Club** meets here, in the historic Lewis Tenant house. Pet care is part of the 4-H curriculum, so if you have kids, you might want to call the Delaware County 4-H for more information, 610-690-2655.

There are a couple of other places in the area that you and your dog will very much enjoy. Start with:

▶ **Taylor Memorial Arboretum, 10 Ridley Drive, Wallingford, 610-876-2649.** Founded in 1931, this site has been managed by the Natural Lands Trust since 1986. There are 30 acres here to explore, located on a former mill site along the Ridley Creek. The arboretum is open daily from 9:00 a.m. to 4:00 p.m., and it is free. You and your dog on-leash are welcome to enjoy the property. Bring your dog back in October and November for the fall foliage.

One last lovely place in the area to take your dog is:

▶ **The Old Mill, Rose Valley Road.** This is a 1789 structure along the Ridley Creek. It is beautiful, and you and your dog on-leash can stroll the grounds and admire it. The site is definitely worth the trip.

❧ WESTERN DELAWARE COUNTY

Media

Founded in 1848, Media Borough has a nice, hometown feel. There are brick sidewalks and shade trees along the streets. Media's "Main Street" is State Street, which has a trolley that started running in 1913. State Street is also dotted with shops, restaurants, and parks. There is plenty of fast food, take-out food, coffee, and more along both State Street and East Baltimore Pike. There are benches along the streets, and on Jackson Street there's a pocket park with benches. And if that isn't enough, at State and West Streets is **Glen Providence Park**, Delaware County's first park, established in 1935. You and your dog on-leash are welcome in this or any other Media park, as long as no events are happening—the park events are too crowded, so the borough prefers that dogs not attend.

You and your dog may want to come back and enjoy the many street events held in Media, including:

▶ **Spring Super Sunday (March/April).** Music and food along State Street, sponsored by the Media Chamber of Commerce. Call 610-566-6755 for more information.
▶ **First Union Amateur Bike Challenge (May).** Starts at Front Street and Veterans Square.
▶ **Annual Antique, Classic, and Hot Rod Show (May).** Held along Orange Street to Edgmont Street.
▶ **Media Art Exhibition and Craft Fair (June).** Held along State Street.
▶ **Media Town Fair and Sidewalk Sale (June).** Held along State Street.
▶ **Media 5-Mile Run (June).** Starts at Old Borough Hall.
▶ **Fall Super Sunday (September).** Music and food along State Street.
▶ **Media Food and Crafts Festival (October).** Held along State Street. Restaurants and other vendors may have outdoor tables where you can sit with your dog. Check it out.
▶ **Media Halloween Parade (October).** Dress up your dog and find a good spot for watching.

▶ **Delaware County Veterans Day Parade (November).** This annual parade features bands, floats, veterans, and patriotic singing. This is the oldest parade in the tri-state area.

▶ **Santa Arrival and Festival of Lights (End of November).** Held along State and Jackson Streets.

Media is also the home of the **Delaware County SPCA, 555 Sandy Bank Road, 610-566-1370.** The Delco SPCA has some annual events that may interest you:

▶ **Wags 'n' Whiskers Luncheon–Fashion Show (Late April or early May).** This event includes raffles, a silent auction, door prizes, and more. Besides the human models and fashions, shelter animals selected for sociability and good nature are groomed, beribboned, and presented on the runway. This is a big fundraising event for the Delco SPCA, so if you can, make a point of going.

▶ **National Adoptathon at PetsMart (May).** The Delco SPCA has participated in the Adoptathon at the Broomall PetsMart store (see listing on page 134).

▶ **Open House/Blessing of the Animals (First Sunday in October).** Pets are blessed in honor of St. Francis of Assisi, the patron saint of animals.

▶ **Photos with Santa (December).** Your pup must be on-leash, but a professional animal photographer will take pictures with Santa for a small contribution to the SPCA's operating fund. Dogs will get a treat if they smile for the camera.

There's a great place to take your dog to play near Media:

▶ **Hildacy Farm, Natural Lands Trust, 1031 Palmers Mill Road.** There are 55 acres of rolling hills, woodlands, a pond, and the Crum Creek as well as two tributary streams, all of which you and your dog on-leash can enjoy on a 2-mile trail. A trail map is available at the Natural Lands Trust's office there. There are also 18th- and 19th-century structures to see: a farmhouse, a springhouse, and a barn. Picnicking and bicycling are prohibited.

(Rose Tree)

Just north of Media is Rose Tree. And there is an incredible place here for you and your dog to enjoy:

▶ **Rose Tree Park, East Rose Tree Road.** Located between Providence Road and—interestingly enough—Dogkennel Lane, Rose Tree Park has 120 acres of rolling hills, picnic areas, a nature trail, woodland, a gazebo, and a former steeplechase area. There are restrooms available. Historic buildings include the Rose Tree Tavern, the Hunt Club Building, and Leedom Farmhouse. The Rose Tree Tavern is a National Historic Site, built around 1739. About 1859, the tavern became affiliated with the Rose Tree Fox Hunting Club (that could be why there's a "Dogkennel Lane"). Your dog on-leash is welcome here, but I'm told that Providence Township has been cracking down on people who let their dogs off-leash, so be aware.

There are plenty of events held in Rose Tree Park that you and your dog will want to attend:

Ride Against Cancer (May). Horses and riders compete in this benefit for the American Cancer Society.

Delaware County Summer Festival (Mid-June to late August). Outdoor concerts take place throughout the summer, free of charge. Bring a blanket and your dog and enjoy the music from one of the four grass terraces surrounding the amphitheater. Also keep an eye out for other summer events in the park, such as fairs, kite-flying, and poetry reading.

Festival of Lights for Peace (December). A tree-lighting ceremony opens this annual festival. There is music, and the lights decorate 50 trees donated by area residents. Santa also arrives in person.

You can get food in the area at:

▶ **Boston Market, 1123 West Baltimore Pike.** You can pick up some food here and sit on the lawn outside to picnic with your dog. They will provide your dog with water and even scraps of food ("no chicken bones!").

Are you and your dog ready for some more active recreation? Head south to:

▶ **Wawa Preserve, Valley Road.** This is a Natural Lands Trust property of 70 acres. You and your dog on-leash can enjoy woodland and a meadow stream valley along a mile of the **Middletown Trail,** which passes through the property. Picnicking and bicycling are not permitted on Natural Lands Trust preserves.

Or, head north:

▶ **Ridley Creek State Park and National Historic Site, Routes 3 and 352, Edgmont.** This is a truly great park, open daily from 8:00 a.m. to sunset, with plenty of hiking trails (12 miles' worth, and the trails at the southern end connect with trails in Tyler Arboretum—see below), horseback riding, a paved bike trail, fishing along the Ridley Creek, and 15 picnic areas, on 2,600 acres. Our dogs love it. There are restrooms within the park. Also within the park is the Ridley Creek Historic District, containing a small, 18th-century village, Sycamore Mills: there's a miller's house, an office and library, and small millworkers' dwellings currently used as private residences. Also at the park is the Colonial Pennsylvania Plantation, a living history farm, but you cannot take your dog onto the plantation grounds.

▶ **Tyler Arboretum, 515 Painter Road.** The arboretum has 650 acres adjacent to Ridley Creek State Park. Its 20 miles of marked trails wind through 450 acres of natural field and forest. You and your dog on-leash can browse through the Painter Trees, several of which are state champions; the 85-acre pinetum; or the Native Woodland Walk, featuring native Delaware County trees. There are specialty gardens including a fragrance garden, a butterfly garden, and a bird garden. The arboretum is open daily from 8:00 a.m. to dusk. Admission is charged for non-members. (Note: There has been some talk of prohibiting dogs at the arboretum because of owner irresponsibility; please keep your dog on-leash and remember to clean up as necessary. Not that anyone reading this book needs a reminder, right?)

There are a couple of events at Tyler Arboretum that you and your dog may wish to attend:

Arbor Day Open House (April)

Pumpkin Day and Fall Festival (October). Admission is charged for this annual weekend event, but it's lots of fun. There are crafts, games, live music, and refreshments.

If all that arboretum touring has gotten your dog in a gardening mood, make a stop at:

▶ **Phillips Nurseries, 508 Smithbridge Road, Glen Mills, 610-459-1127.** You and your dog on-leash can browse through the nursery stock together.

🐾 SOUTHERN DELAWARE COUNTY

Upland

Chester Township was settled in 1644 by Swedes and Finns, and is one of the oldest settlements in the commonwealth. It was originally called Upland, and part of it still is. You and your dog will absolutely want to visit:

▶ **Caleb Pusey House & Landingford Plantation, 15 Race Street.** This is the restored 1693 home of William Penn's miller, and the only building still standing that was definitely visited by Penn. The house is built of handmade bricks, and stands on 27 of the original 150 acres that made up Landingford Plantation, adjacent to the mill site along the Chester Creek. You and your dog on-leash are welcome to stroll the grounds: there are even trails to enjoy. Admission is free, but donations are very welcome.

And there's another place where you and your dog can take a nice, long walk:

▶ **Upland Park, 6th Street.** Across the Chester Creek from Landingford Plantation, this 60-acre park includes wooded picnic groves, more woodland, and plenty of grass. There is also plenty of parking.

Marcus Hook

Marcus Hook is tiny and mostly industrial, but there are a couple of events that you and your dog will want to know about:

▶ **Summer Music Festival (June through July).** Free concerts are held at **Market Square Memorial Park, at Market Street and Delaware Avenue.** Your dog is welcome to enjoy the music with you. Call 610-485-1341 for the schedule.
▶ **Annual Marcus Hook Holiday Parade (November).** Marching bands, string ensembles, antique cars, fire companies, and civic and other local organizations participate. A festival of lights continues through the holiday season. The walkway, bordered by decorations and arches of pine and white lights, makes this display truly a wonderland.

While you and your dog are in the general area, you might want to take an exploratory tour around Lower Chichester, just north of Marcus Hook. Older row homes here create a quaint town community, and there are shops and eateries along Lower Chichester's "Main Street," Chichester Avenue. Check it out.

Bethel

Bethel Township is a very historic area, and one highlight you and your dog will want to take a long look at is:

▶ **Chelsea Village.** This is a small community at a five-point intersection in the northern tip of the township. Foulk (Route 261), Chelsea, Concord, and Valley Brook Roads come together where the village stands. First settled by English Quakers, there are remnants here of the village's 18th- and 19th-century past, including a blacksmith shop built in 1800 that operated until 1984. Portions of five historic homes still stand at the intersection itself, including the McCall-McKinley House and the McCall-Booth-Coleman House, which retain original details. The visual relationships between the buildings around the intersection make Chelsea a wonderful example of an early-19th-century crossroads village. Bring your dog back to Chelsea for the **Founders Day Festival (October 2).**

Concordville

Here's another pocket of history that you and your dog can take a gander at together. The Concordville National Historic District spreads along Concord Road and Baltimore Pike. And you can take your dog to a couple of terrific parks in the Concordville area:

▶ **Clayton County Park, on Route 322 between I-95 and Route 1.** With 170 acres, including a golf course, this is Delaware County's largest park, and includes shaded picnic groves and acres of woodland for you and your dog to explore. There is plenty of parking. There is also a nature trail that wanders through the park.

▶ **Newlin Grist Mill, Baltimore Pike and South Cheyney Road.** This was the site of a 1704 grist mill, and it is on the National Historic Register. There are both restored and re-created structures here to admire, including the miller's house (built in 1739), as well as the mill pond, nature trails, and picnic areas, on 150 acres of rolling countryside. Open from 8:00 a.m. to dusk. No admission is charged and your dog on-leash is very welcome to enjoy the grounds with you, but no wading in the mill race, streams, or ponds, okay? The park staff told me that dog shows are frequently held in the park by various kennel clubs. Your dog on-leash can even come to the special events held here: the **Craft Show & Sheepshearing Festival (June)** and the **Fall Festival (October).**

If you have a gardening dog, while you're in the area stop in at:

▶ **J. Franklin Styer Nurseries, U.S. Route 1, 610-459-2400.** Your dog on-leash can browse through the nursery stock with you.

Chadds Ford

The Chadds Ford area spreads into Chester County, but I'm going to do the whole thing here, if you don't mind. This is a beautiful area, one of my favorites in the whole world (not that I've seen the whole world, of course), and my dogs love it too. There are simply amazing places that you can visit with your dog here.

The Chadds Ford National Historic District is centered at the intersection of U.S. 1 and Route 100. Take your dog to check out:

▶ **The Barns-Brinton House, Route 1.** Managed by the Chadds Ford Historical Society, this National Historic Site was once a tavern owned by William Barns. There's a footpath that leads to the Chaddsford Winery next door (see below).

▶ **John Chads House, Route 100.** John Chads was a farmer and a ferryman, and Chadds Ford was named for him. The John Chads House is a bluestone building built circa 1725. It is a great example of an 18th-century Pennsylvania bank house, and is a National Historic Site managed by the Chadds Ford Historical Society.

▶ **The Chadds Ford Historical Society** itself **(610-388-7376, Route 100, ¹/₄ mile north of Route 1)** is housed in a building modeled after an 18th-century Pennsylvania bank barn, standing on the site of an old dairy barn. The façade is of local fieldstone. You can't take your dog into the building, but the two of you can walk around the grounds. And the society holds some outdoor fundraising events that you and your dog can enjoy (they do get a lot of kids at these events, so keep your dog leashed and well-behaved):

   Antique Car and Antiques Show (June). This event is held every two years, so check with the society to find out if it's being held the year you want to go. You and your dog can enjoy an open-air car show in the society's meadow, across from the John Chads House. Pre-1977 automobiles are featured, and there are also lots of antiques and collectibles for sale. There's music, and great food is available. Admission is charged.

   Chadds Ford Days (September). This annual event also takes place in the meadow opposite the John Chads House. You and your dog can enjoy colonial craft demonstrations, browse through books and prints, enjoy a Brandywine Valley art show, listen to old-fashioned music, get some great food, and buy crafts from over 70 traditional craftspersons. Admission is charged.

   The Great Pumpkin Carve (October). You and your dog can admire huge pumpkins, carved by artists, on the grounds of the Chadds Ford Historical Society. The wonderful jack-o-lanterns are lit and judged when night falls.

What other wonderful places can you take your dog to in Chadds Ford? Try one of these:

▶ **Brandywine River Museum, Routes 1 and 100.** You can't take your dog inside the museum, but the restored mill that houses it is a very neat building to look at from outside. And there are gardens on the grounds, as well as sculpture. While the Brandywine River Museum would rather not be inundated with dogs, you can tour the gardens discreetly. The Brandywine Creek is very pretty, and you and your dog can follow the **River Trail** all the way to the John Chads House meadow.

▶ **Chaddsford Winery, 632 Baltimore Pike, 610-388-6221, www.chaddsford.com.** Open daily from April to December, closed from January to March. You can't bring your dog here during their special events, but on ordinary visits, you and your dog are welcome to tour the grounds. There's a footpath lined by a worm fence that will take you to the Barns-Brinton House. The winery has some outdoor tables, and some outdoor tastings (in nice weather). Or you can bring a meal, buy a bottle of Chaddsford vintage wine, and picnic with your dog on the grounds.

▶ **Brandywine Battlefield Park, Route 1.** The site of Washington's effort to block British occupation of Philadelphia in September 1777—the biggest engagement of the American Revolution—this is a National Historic Site. The Benjamin Ring House and the Gideon Gilpin House, the houses occupied by General Washington and the Marquis de Lafayette, respectively, are included within the park. Both houses really let you go back in time to 1777. Dogs on-leash are permitted in the park whenever the park is open: Tuesday through Saturday from 9:00 a.m. to 5:00 p.m., and Sunday from noon to 5:00 p.m. Bring a picnic and a blanket, and relax on the beautiful grounds before or after a long walk around.

Dogs on-leash are also permitted during events at the park, although you should be aware that most events involve guns being fired, which may frighten dogs not used to the sound. On the other hand, you can probably keep your dog at a safe distance. So feel free to try:

George Washington's Birthday (February 22). Share birthday cake and watch young recruits get signed up for the Continental Army, as well as 18th-century camp life demonstrations. Admission is charged.

Revolutionary Times (September). Commemorates the Battle of Brandywine with a daylong event. Hundreds of reenactors in uniform demonstrate the British and Continental strategies. You and your dog can browse among sutlers and crafters demonstrating and selling their 18th-century goods, watch the entertainment for kids, and enjoy the great food that is available. There is some gunfire involved in this event, but the battlefield is large, so the sounds are mostly fairly distant. Admission is charged.

Is your dog in the mood for another trip to a winery? Here's another one to visit:

▶ **Smithbridge Winery, 159 Beaver Valley Road.** Tours and tastings are on weekends from noon to 5:00 p.m. They are very dog-friendly here and have fabulous and extensive grounds (they are next to the Woodlawn Trustees Wildlife Preserve, where dogs are not permitted, so be careful to stay on the winery grounds). The winery hosts barrel tastings, a harvest festival, and other events. Dogs can come to everything that's held outside. For more information, call the winery at 610-588-4703, or visit their Web site at www.smithbridge.com.

You and your dog can get a snack in Chadds Ford at:

▶ **Rita's Water Ice, 159 Wilmington–West Chester Pike.** Enjoy some ice cream or water ice in the outdoor seating area, available all season. They will provide a cup of water for your dog, and they say, "All are welcome."

You and your dog, if he or she is small, can stay overnight in Chadds Ford at:

▶ **Brandywine River Hotel, Route 1, 610-388-1200.** Your dog must weigh less than 20 pounds and must be crated while in the room, and they will charge your dog $20 per night. But there are grounds for walking, and the hotel is lovely.

One final thing you might want to know about Chadds Ford: this is the home of **Independence Dogs, Inc.**, the organization that holds the Canine Carnival at Haverford College. IDI raises, trains, and places assistance dogs with people who need them. Besides attending the carnival, you can help out the organization by purchasing IDI's annual calendar, which is ready for distribution in November of each year. You can preorder one at a very reasonable cost. Write to IDI at 146 State Line Road, Chadds Ford, PA 19317, call 610-358-2723, or visit IDI's Web site at www.independencedogs.org.

Chester County

Chester County is one of the most historic counties in the Greater Philadelphia area, and full of places that will make you want to stop the car, get out, and explore with your dog. From tiny historic districts to larger but still comfortable towns, Chester County has it all. And as if that weren't enough, Chester County is where some serious horse events go on. You and your dog can keep in mind this general rule: horses and dogs go together. In other words, dogs on-leash are usually more than welcome at horse events. If you go, you'll probably notice that the "horse's dog" is the Jack Russell terrier, but I'm told that Welsh corgis are gaining in popularity among equestrians.

🐾 CHESTER COUNTY OPEN SPACES

Your dog will think that Chester County is nothing but a big, doggish playground. There are several county parks with a total of over 3,500 acres for you and your dog to explore: **Hibernia County Park, Nottingham County Park, Springton Manor Farm County Park,** and **Warwick County Park**. The Chester County Department of Parks and Recreation frequently holds **"Evenings of Music"** in the parks during the summer: bring a lawn chair or blanket and a couple of snacks, and sit back with your dog to enjoy the music under wonderful Chester County stars. Check with the department for the concert schedule by calling 610-344-6415.

But county parks are only the beginning. There are excellent state parks, including **Marsh Creek State Park** and **French Creek State Park.** There are also two major hiking trails that run through Chester County:

▶ **The Horse-Shoe Hiking Trail.** You can pick up this trail in a variety of places: it passes through or near French Creek State Park and Warwick County Park, and the state game land in between the two, Saint Peters Village, Chester Springs, and the portion of Valley Forge National Historical Park that dips into Chester County.

▶ **The Mason-Dixon Hiking Trail.** This trail passes through Pennsbury Township and can take you all the way into Delaware—either the county or the state, depending on which way you head.

But wait, there's more! Try Struble Lake, or Chambers Lake, or Marsh Creek Lake. Not enough water for you and your dog? There are lots of creeks to walk along and dip your feet and paws in, from the French Creek, which runs from French Creek State Park through Phoenixville to the Schuylkill, to the Pickering Creek, which runs into a reservoir near Valley Forge and supplies water for Phoenixville. Then there's the Brandywine Creek: two-branched, 60 miles long, falling over 1,000 feet over its length, and the former home of about 130 mills. And how about the White Clay and Red Clay Creeks, which start in the southeastern corner of Chester County and run into the state of Delaware? The Big and Little Elk Creeks run from south-central Chester County into Maryland. The Octoraro Creek forms a large part of Chester County's western boundary. And the Chester Creek supplies water to West Chester.

Okay, your dog is now standing at the door, leash in mouth, frantically trying to indicate to you that it is time to go out and explore Chester County. So go do it!

🐾 FAR WESTERN MAIN LINE

Strafford

The first stop on the Main Line in Chester County is Strafford, and you and your dog may want to spend a little time looking around here. The Strafford Train Station was built around 1876, and is a Stick-style building with exposed timbering and ornate framing. There are many Colonial Revival homes clustered around the station: walk around and explore. If you follow Old Eagle School Road to Old Gulph Road, you and your dog will find **Strafford Park**, where your dog can do some sniffing and some business.

Also of interest in the general area is:

▶ **Peaches & Gable, Route 30 and Eagle Road, Lancaster County Farmers Market, 610-688-0057.** Open Wednesday, Friday, and Saturday from 7:00 a.m. to 4:00 p.m. You can't bring your dog inside here, but they have wonderful and unique gifts for pets and pet fanciers. They frequently have a booth at events like the Devon Horse Show (see page 146).

Devon

There's an extremely important place in Devon:

▶ **The Devon Horse Show Grounds, Route 30 (Lancaster Pike) and Dorset Road.** Your dog on-leash is permitted at every event held here. Call 610-688-2554 for information on what's happening, or visit the Web site at www.thedevonhorseshow.org, but tried-and-true events you and your dog won't want to miss include:

Devon Horse Show and Country Fair (May). This is one of the leading equestrian events in the country, and over 1,200 horses compete in two rings during this weeklong event. Besides the equestrian competitions, you and your dog can enjoy an antique carriage parade and the Carriage Pleasure Drive competition, and browse together among the open-front booths of the country fair, where vendors display everything from clothing to gifts. Reasonable general admission is charged, or you can check out the reserved seating options.

Classic at Devon (June). Call for the details, or keep an eye on the local newspapers.

American Gold Cup and Fall Festival (September). This is a very exciting, four-day equestrian event with some of the top horse-and-rider teams on the Grand Prix Show Jumping circuit competing for $150,000 in prize money. Besides the competition, you and your dog can browse the open-front booths of over 40 vendors offering clothing and gift items from the ordinary to the unusual. The Gold Cup competition benefits the New Bolton Center of the University of Pennsylvania's School of Veterinary Medicine as well as the Small Animal Hospital, and on Saturday (Family Day), you and your dog can head over to the "MASH" tent and watch vet students from Penn "curing" stuffed animals brought by young spectators. Your dog can also compete in the Celebrity Dog Show by dressing in costume, performing tricks, or simply being beautiful. A reasonable general admission is charged, or you can look into reserved seating options.

Dressage at Devon (Late September/early October). This is the premier event of its kind in North America, and combines world-class dressage competition with a complete breed horse show. In dressage, the horse and rider demonstrate the natural paces of the horse in harmony with the rider: it is quite beautiful. Along with the competition, you and your dog can enjoy special exhibitions for horse and non-horse people, or once again browse through open-front booths of over 50 vendors with equestrian products, art, antiques, clothing, and food for sale.

Berwyn

Berwyn is a village area that straddles township lines between Easttown and Tredyffrin. You and your dog can find some great history on the Easttown side of Berwyn (south of the railroad tracks). Take a walk and look for Victorian houses and commercial buildings.

While you're in the area, you and your dog can get some coffee and a bite to eat together at:

▶ **The Berwyn Coffee Company, 720 Lancaster Avenue, 610-640-4545.** Offering coffee, espresso, cappuccino, lunch, and fresh baked goods. They have outdoor seating year-round, and you and your dog can sit there together. They will provide your dog with water on request.

Your dog can pick up any needed supplies at:

▶ **Pet Valu, Swedesford Plaza, 436 West Swedesford Road, 610-296-8166**

And then the two of you can go for a great recreational walk in:

▶ **Sharp's/Canterbury Woods, Argyle Road and Byrd Drive, 610-525-7530.** This is Natural Lands Trust property, with 28 acres of meadows, woodland, and streams. There are $2^1/_2$ miles of well-maintained trails, including footbridges over the streams. Picnicking, bicycling, and swimming are prohibited in Natural Lands Trust preserves. Your dog must be on-leash, and be aware that some preserves have a hunting program in November and January: signs are posted when the preserves are closed.

You and your dog may want to come back to watch this:

▶ **Upper Main Line YMCA's New Year's Eve 5K Run.** Call 610-647-9622 for more information, and bring a canned good to donate.

Just north of Berwyn is a place where you and your dog might want to go shopping together:

▶ **The Shops of Chesterbrook, 500 Chesterbrook Boulevard, 610-644-8680.** Dogs on-leash are allowed in the courtyard, and you can get in some nice window-shopping. Some of the shops may even let you bring your dog inside. You can pick up some Italian, deli, Chinese, or other food from one of the center's eateries and enjoy it outside with your dog. And as a bonus, on summer Thursdays at lunchtime the shops sponsor outdoor concerts in the courtyard. Something else for you and your dog to enjoy!

Paoli

There's a very nice place in Paoli for you and your dog to visit:

▶ **Waynesborough, 2049 Waynesborough Road, 610-647-1779.** This lovely 1715 Georgian stone mansion was the home of General Anthony Wayne. You and your dog on-leash are welcome to walk around the grounds, which are always open, and you can bring your dog to some events. Waynesborough events include the **Family Halloween Festival (October)** and the **Greens, Holiday Plants, and Attic Treasures Sale (December).** Call for more information.

There's another Paoli event that may interest you and your dog:

▶ **Royer-Greaves School for the Blind Fall Festival.** Sponsored by the First National Bank of West Chester, the festival includes pony rides, games, food, entertainment, music, and a pet show. Call 610-644-1810 for more information.

Malvern

You and your dog can spend some wonderful mornings, afternoons, and evenings in Malvern Borough. It's a very dog-friendly (and pedestrian-friendly) place, about 1.2 square miles, and dates to Victorian times.

Along King Street, you and your dog can do some great window-shopping (and shopping, if the shops will let your dog come in), and there are places to get takeout food, and lots of benches to sit on and eat it. You can continue shopping along Warren Avenue: from antiques to clothes to gifts, Malvern has it all.

Malvern also has some very nice parks, and dogs on-leash are welcome in all of them, including:

▶ **Samuel & M. Elizabeth Burke Park, Warren Avenue and Roberts Lane.** Located one block from the municipal building, the park's 1.4 acres are used for festivals, concerts, and general recreation. There's a gazebo here and a landscaped area for you and your dog to enjoy. **Family movies** are shown here in the summer, and **summer concerts** are performed from the gazebo. Bring a blanket and your dog and enjoy a film or some music.

▶ **Theodore S. A. Rubino Memorial Park, Broad Street and Old Lincoln Highway.** This third-of-an-acre play area is fenced and available for picnicking.

▶ **Horace J. Quann Memorial Park, First and Warren Avenues.** This park has 1.6 acres of active-play areas and open space.

Bring your dog back to Malvern for the fabulous events that take place in the borough:

▶ **Malvern Memorial Day Parade and Celebration (May).** The oldest continuously held parade in the country, and over Memorial Day weekend, Malvern also celebrates Malvern Founders Days. During this three-day event, you can enjoy sidewalk sales and al fresco dining with your dog, browse through flea markets, and enjoy music, dancing, and entertainment (including a dog rescue show) at the gazebo in Burke Park. On Memorial Day, Revolutionary War reenactors perform, and, of course, there is the parade. You and your dog can see floats, military guards, and more.

▶ **Indoor/Outdoor Craft Festival (Early October).** Held at the Gallery at Cedar Hollow, 2447 Yellow Springs Road. You and your dog on-leash can browse through the outside tables of crafts and gifts. For information, call 610-640-ARTS.

▶ **Malvern Fall Fun Fest (October).** Malvern holds a sidewalk sale with refreshments, and there's a pumpkin-carving and scarecrow-making contest at the gazebo in Burke Park.

▶ **Malvern Halloween Parade (October).** All ages can participate—and so can dogs! This is the oldest Halloween parade in the country, I've been told. Participants in the doggy division must be leashed—the ones on four legs, anyway.

▶ **Malvern Trick or Treat (October 31).** Bring your dog out to watch as the merchants of Malvern give out treats (and some of them might have dog treats, too).

▶ **Malvern's Victorian Christmas (December).** Santa arrives on a fire engine and receives visitors at the gazebo in Burke Park. There is a tree-lighting ceremony and lots of caroling. Put on your dog's Santa hat and come out and enjoy the festivities. (Actually, we have an elf outfit for Georgie.)

▶ **Holiday Shopping in Historic Malvern (December).** Every Wednesday, merchants stay open until 7:30 p.m. Wandering carolers add to the ambience as you and your dog stroll the streets.

Within Malvern Borough, there is a wonderful place to take your dog:

▶ **Malvern Preparatory School, Warren Avenue and Paoli Pike.** This is a very pretty campus, with a pond, and you and your dog are welcome to ramble about the grounds. Adjacent to the school, and owned by it, is:

▶ **The Paoli Battlefield Site and Parade Grounds.** On the National Historic Register, and bounded by Warren and Monument Avenues and Sugartown Road, this was the site of the Paoli Massacre in September 1777.

Are you and your dog hungry? The two of you can try:

▶ **Historic General Warren Inne, West Old Lancaster Highway, 610-296-3637.** Owned by the Malvern Prep School and operated as a restaurant and bed and breakfast, the General Warren Inne offers fine dining with Continental cuisine. They have outdoor seating from May to October, and if you sit outside, your dog can sit with you. They will provide water for your dog on request.

Does your dog need to pick up some supplies? Stop by:

▶ **PETCO, 181 Lancaster Avenue, 610-644-9959.** You can bring your dog inside to browse the full line of dog and puppy supplies and the treat bar. They also have costume contests and photo events.

You and your dog can stay in Malvern at:

▶ **Summerfield Suites Hotel, 20 Morehall Road, 610-296-4343.** Your dog can stay here for a $150 nonrefundable fee. There are grounds where you can walk your dog.

There's one more thing in Malvern—one more really wonderful, dog-friendly site—that you and your dog need to know about:

▶ **Radnor Hunt, 826 Providence Road, 610-644-4439.** Radnor Hunt is one of the oldest recognized hunts in the country: foxhunting has been held here three days a week from September to March for the last 50 years. And in case you're worried, I've been told that the fox almost always gets away. It's the chase that's the fun part.

There are special events at Radnor Hunt that may interest you or your dog:

Racing for Open Space/Radnor Hunt Steeplechases (May). This event benefits the Brandywine Conservancy's regional environmental programs. There are theme picnics, music, a carriage parade, spectator contests, three stake races, and seven races in all. Dress yourself up, dress up your dog, and come on out. One caution: this is not an inexpensive event. But it is great fun, and you can cut down on the cost by ordering tickets in advance. For more information, call the Radnor Race Hotline at 610-647-4233, or visit www.radnor-races.org.

The Annual Bryn Mawr Hound Show (June). Foxhounds from across the U.S. and Canada come to be shown off. You cannot bring your dog (because of insurance concerns of the foxhound exhibitors, I'm told), but you can certainly *see* a lot of dogs.

Day in the Country (June). This event includes a barbecue, music, dancing, a horse-jumping exhibition, a hound parade, a Wild West show, and kids' activities. Admission is charged, but food and beverages are included.

Radnor Hunt Concours d'Elegance (September). Over 100 antique autos are displayed at Radnor Hunt. Admission is charged, but your dog on-leash is welcome. And don't miss the road rally, for which you needn't have a vintage car (though you do have to pay a fee) to participate. For more information, call the Radnor Hunt Club at 610-644-4439.

Radnor Three-Day Event (October). Benefiting Paoli Memorial Hospital's community services and support groups, this is also an equestrian qualifier for the Olympics, and one of the most elite equestrian events in the country. There are three days of competitions, as well as food, art, crafts, clothing, and antiques for sale on the grounds. You and your dog can watch dressage on Friday, speed and endurance on Saturday, and stadium jumping on Sunday. You can also enter the pet parade (there's an entry fee). General-admission tickets are available for each day, or you can get a pass for the whole event. Parking is included in the price of the tickets.

There are other events held throughout the year at the adjacent Radnor Hunt Pony Club, including hunter trials (where teams of two horses and riders compete for the fastest or ideal time on a course almost 6 miles long), numerous horse shows, pony shows, and gymkhanas (equestrian field days with exhibitions of horsemanship and pageantry). You and your dog can spectate for free. Call 610-644-4350 for more information.

Frazer

Just past Malvern, there are a couple of interesting businesses in Frazer that you and your dog may want to visit:

▶ **Dogomat, Frazer Village, Routes 30 and 352, 610-296-8006.** This do-it-yourself dog wash and canine café is the home of the Original Doggie Salad Bar, with 18 kinds of gourmet and healthy dog treats. It is closed Monday, but open Tuesday through Friday from noon to 6:00 p.m., and Saturday and Sunday from 9:00 a.m. to 5:00 p.m. There are bathing stations here with elevated tubs that your dog can walk right into, and all the tools and equipment you need to give your dog a good grooming without messing up your house. Dogomat staff members clean and disinfect the stations. You can choose among 11 shampoos and get a free spritz of doggy cologne for your pup. Two towels and a pet blow-dryer are included for your use. The Dogomat runs on a first-come, first-served basis, and isn't limited to dogs—you can bring your cat, monkey, ferret, or potbellied pig here as well.

Once your dog is all clean and spiffed up, you can head to:

▶ **Rita's Water Ice, 430 Lancaster Avenue.** Outdoor seating is available from March to September, and you and your dog on-leash are welcome to sit there and enjoy a snack together. "We will upon request provide water for the dogs. Some customers buy water ice or soft custard for their pet. A group of dog owners come to our store weekly following dog obedience school."

⁂ NORTHERN CHESTER COUNTY

Phoenixville

Phoenixville, founded in 1731, lies along the Schuylkill River. It was incorporated as a borough in 1849, when the principal industry was the Phoenix Iron

Works, the ore for which came from Chester Springs. Phoenixville has a nice, "small-town America" feel to it, and there is a historic commercial district along Bridge Street as well as some great old residences along Main and Starr Streets—the largest nationally registered historic district in Chester County.

At the intersection of Bridge and Main Streets is a pocket park with a wonderful mural, an interpretive sign, and benches where you and your dog can sit and contemplate the art, resting and enjoying the ambience. Then take a walk along Main Street, window-shop along Bridge Street, and go look at some of Phoenixville's 1,200 historic buildings. Finally, go romp in a park. **Reservoir Park, at the end of Franklin Street,** and **Reeves Park, between Starr and Main Streets and 2nd and 3rd Avenues,** are particularly nice.

You and your dog might want to come back for some events in Phoenixville, including:

▶ **Summer Concerts in Reeves Park.** Bring a blanket and your dog on-leash, and enjoy the music together. Call 610-933-3070 for more information.
▶ **The Phoenixville Fame Festival (June).** Features arts and crafts on Bridge Street. Call 610-640-ARTS for details.

If you and your dog are looking for more active recreation, head for the area around the Black Rock Bridge (listed on the National Historic Register), which carries Township Road 113 over the Schuylkill River to Mont Clare, just on the other side in Montgomery County. On the Phoenixville side of the river there is a trail network from Bridge Street to the Black Rock Dam, and on to Upper Schuylkill Valley Park in Montgomery County. (See "Mont Clare" for more information on the recreational opportunities presented there.)

Charlestown

Once called "Hardscrabble," Charlestown Village is one of those great spots in Chester County where you'll want to find a place to park and just walk around with your dog, immersing yourself in history. The Charlestown Village National Historic District includes portions of Charlestown Road, Church Road, and Pickering Road.

Once you've explored Charlestown, you might want to head to the **Horse-Shoe Hiking Trail** for some more active recreation. Pick up some food and water if you haven't brought any with you, and go hiking with your dog. You can pick up the trail along State Road (follow Pickering Dam Road from Charlestown Road).

Kimberton

This is another small Chester County gem. The Kimberton National Historic District encompasses both sides of Hare's Hill Road, between Prizer and Coldstream Roads. The Kennedy Covered Bridge crosses the French Creek north of Kimberton, and was built in 1856 with portals to add to its architectural interest. Although it burned in 1986, Chester County restored it two years later. Also in the Kimberton area are Rapp's Dam Covered Bridge, built in 1866 and repaired in 1996, and Sheedar-Hall Covered Bridge, built in 1850 and restored in 1996. You and your dog can have a great time just strolling around here. And then come back in December to get a Christmas tree:

▶ **Yeager's Cut-Your-Own Tree Farm, Western Road, 610-933-7379.** Your dog on-leash can help you select a white pine, Norway spruce, blue spruce, Fraser fir, or Douglas fir tree.

Chester Springs

This is the site of **Historic Yellow Springs**, an 18th-century health resort that is great to tour on foot, and that also has some terrific, dog-friendly events.

The village grounds and gardens are open all year. Admission is free, but donations are always appreciated. There are hiking trails in the area among trees that are centuries old. You can simply explore, but there are private residences and property here, so it might be better to get the self-guided walking tour brochure available from Historic Yellow Springs, Inc., on Art School Road, 610-827-7414.

If you and your dog are hungry after touring the village, stop by:

▶ **America Bar & Grill, 499 East Uwchlan Avenue, 610-280-0800.** Both fine and casual dining are available here. They provide a selection of contemporary American dishes, have a full-service bar, are cigar-friendly, and offer a fine selection of wines as well as 19 beers on tap. If you sit outside, your dog can sit with you, as long as your dog is on-leash and well-behaved (of course). There is outdoor seating from spring to fall, as long as the weather is temperate.

Once you've gotten to know Yellow Springs, or even if you haven't yet, your dog will want to take you to the marvelous events held in the village. All outdoor events are dog-friendly (just don't take your dog into any buildings that may also be part of the events), including:

▶ **Sundaes on Sundays (June to August).** Musical performances, puppetry, dancing, ice cream sundaes (of course), and more. Admission is free for families.
▶ **Annual Yellow Springs Craft Festival (June).** There are plenty of fine-quality traditional and contemporary American crafts at this juried show. Besides the crafters' field, there is live music, a food festival grove, and more. Admission is charged to the crafters' field, but parking is free. Last year we saw lots of dogs come to enjoy the craft festival and listen to the music. For more information, call 610-827-7414.
▶ **Day at the Spa (September).** You and your dog on-leash can enjoy a parade, antique cars, bands, a picnic, and more.
▶ **Antique Show (October).** This is more than just an antique show. On Saturday, a great fall tradition takes place: the Pickering Hunt "rides to hounds." The Pickering Hunt's pack is called the Penn Mary Del hounds. There's a traditional stirrup cup of port, sherry, or cider, and spectators are given a map to the Horse-Shoe Trail, where the riders pass. So come for

breakfast, raise a toast, and follow the hunt in your car. Admission is charged. On Sunday, the antique show is held inside, where your dog cannot go—but you and your dog *can* come back to see antique and classic automobiles in the Lincoln Building Grove.

▶ **Halloween Haunting (October).** You can take your dog on-leash on a walking tour along the "Trail of Tears," and to enjoy Halloween-style refreshments. Ghosts, goblins, and other things that go bump in the night will abound in this historic village. I don't think I would go *without* my dog.

And come back out to Chester Springs when it's time to get a tree for the holidays:

▶ **Chester Springs Tree Farm, 1263 Elbow Lane, 610-827-7003.** Your dog can help you select a tree on Sundays from 10:00 a.m. to 4:00 p.m.

▶ **Windridge Farm, Bartlett Lane, 610-469-9299.** You and your dog can choose and cut your tree together, or pick up a wreath, greens, holly, or a live balled tree. You can't take your dog on the weekend hayrides, though.

Ludwig's Corner

This is the site of the **Ludwig's Corner Horse Show Grounds**, located on Route 100 just north of Route 401. You and your dog can attend horse shows here, including:

▶ **The Labor Day Horse Show and Country Fair (September).** See hunters, jumpers, and carriages, a vaulting team exhibition, casting and fly-tying demonstrations, skydivers, and antique cars, and shop among vendors under a big tent. Great food will be available as well. Call 610-458-3344 for more information.

▶ **The Annual Pickering Pony Show (September).** Proceeds benefit the French and Pickering Creek Trust and the Lionville Fire Company.

There are other events held at Ludwig's Corner that you and your dog may want to come back for. One is:

▶ **Antiques Fair (June).** Features outside antiques and an Americana market. Admission is charged. Call 610-469-9296 for details.

Birchrunville

The Birchrunville National Historic District is located at the intersection of Flowing Springs Road and Schoolhouse Lane. This is another small historic area you and your dog may want to check out. The Birchrunville General Store, at the corner of Hollow and Flowing Springs Roads, is a National Historic Site. There's a covered bridge nearby, and 30 historic homes listed on the National Register.

And if you like it enough, come back for:

▶ **Fourth of July Parade.** An old-fashioned parade through the village, including horseback riders with flags, antique cars, floats, and farm tractors.

St. Peters Village

Yet another fun pocket of history to explore. Founded in the mid-1800s, and from the late 1960s to the early 1970s a haven for artisans and hippies, St. Peters has a nice, historic main street along the eastern edge of the French Creek, lined with 30 businesses and Victorian residences in pastel colors. There are some unique commercial enterprises here, from the Koller Artist Collective (which has a garden shop outside offering gift items such as tinware, wreaths, planters, and more) to the antique pinball arcade and a fudge shop. Be aware that during the week and in every season but summer, the shops are mostly closed. But come on summer weekends, and you and your dog will have a nice time.

Once you've explored St. Peters Village, you can take your dog hiking. Take the fudge you bought and head out on the trails that pass through the 12,000 acres of public land surrounding the village (Warwick County Park and French Creek State Park; see pages 155–156). At the end of the village (which is about 300 feet long), there's an ice cream stand (okay, pack away the fudge and get some ice cream) and a parking lot with a bridge leading out of it into the woods.

Or you and your dog can go to nearby:

▶ **Welkinweir, 1368 Prizer Road, 610-469-4900.** This is the headquarters of the Green Valleys Association, and you can bring your dog on-leash here, as long as you clean up. Welkinweir was purchased as a declining farm, and reestablished as a wonderful natural area surrounding a house, a springhouse, and gardens. There are 162 acres here for you and your dog to explore. The site is gorgeous.

Elverson

The Borough of Elverson began as the site of iron ore mines in the early 1700s. In the era of stagecoaches, a Reading–Kimberton route ran through the village, then called Blue Rock after the granite outcroppings in the area. In 1899, the village became Elverson.

Elverson experienced several phases of growth, and the Elverson National Historic District, bounded by Main, Chestnut, and Hall Streets and Park Avenue, reflects the borough's past as a 19th-century rural commercial center. You and your dog will have a great time walking around here, and there are neighborhood parks, should you need them. Or you could head to one of these wonderful places:

▶ **West Nantmeal Recreation Area, Route 82.** There's a picnic pavilion here, and you and your dog on-leash are welcome to attend the **outdoor concerts** held here. Admission is charged for the concerts.
▶ **Hopewell Furnace National Historic Site, 2 Mark Bird Lane, 610-582-8773.** You can bring your dog on-leash to this restored iron plantation and have a grand time. Hopewell Furnace produced cast and molded iron products from 1771 to 1883, using area iron ore,

charcoal from area hardwood forests, and limestone. There are living history programs during the summer, and self-guided walking tours year-round. The site includes 848 acres, including lots of woodland. Hiking trails on the site join up with trails at adjacent French Creek State Park (see below). Parking, restrooms, and a walking tour brochure are available at the visitors center. Hopewell Furnace is open from 9:00 a.m. to 5:00 p.m. every day except Thanksgiving, December 25, and January 1. Entrance fees are charged.

You and your dog might want to come back for some of the events at Hopewell Furnace:

March for Parks (April). Help clear the hiking trails and march along with Scouts.

Sheep Shearing (May). Watch traditional and modern methods of shearing sheep. (If your dog has a special or unfriendly interest in sheep, you should skip this one.)

Establishment Day (August 2). Celebrating the National Park Service's stewardship of the Hopewell Furnace site. Enjoy craft and metal casting demonstrations, and the lighting of wood to make charcoal.

National Parks Day (August 25). Celebrating the 1916 founding of the National Park Service, Hopewell Furnace is open free of charge.

Two Revolutions (September). Hopewell Furnace witnessed the American Revolution as well as the Industrial Revolution. Take your dog to see the encampment of the 4th Continental Light Dragoons. Admission is charged. Call 610-582-8773 for details.

Apple Harvest Day (September). Crafters, rangers, and volunteers demonstrate 1830s lifestyles and harvest activities.

Iron Plantation Christmas (December). An 1830s Christmas is shown throughout the historic village with vignettes.

Other recreation opportunities nearby include:

▶ **Struble Lake, between Elverson and Honeybrook along Morgantown Road**. Parking, picnic areas, and restrooms are available at this 146-acre site. Canoeing and small boat sailing are permitted on the lake. Bring a picnic and hang out, or go out on the water if you have a water dog. (Make sure you both have life vests on.)

▶ **French Creek State Park, 843 Park Road, 610-582-9680.** This park includes approximately 7,339 acres, and has two lakes: 63-acre Hopewell Lake and 21-acre Scott's Run Lake. There are also about 30 miles of well-marked hiking trails with trailhead parking: this is really a human and canine hikers' paradise. You can choose among a variety of trail types and lengths: Boone Trail, a 6-mile loop trail that takes about four hours to walk; Turtle Trail, which circles the western portion of the French Creek for 3.6 miles, and takes about two and a half hours to walk; Lenape Trail, $5^1/_2$ miles and three and a half hours to walk; Six Penny Trail, 3 miles and two hours to walk; Mill Creek Trail, 6 miles and four hours to walk; Buzzards Trail, 3 miles and two and a half hours to walk; Raccoon Trail, 1.7 miles and one hour to walk; and 8 miles of the Horse-Shoe Trail, which will take about four hours to walk. You and your dog will want to come back and try each and every one of these trails.

There's also a self-guided orienteering course that you can do with your dog: pick up the map (and a compass if you want) at the visitors center. Be aware that hunting is permitted in sections of French Creek State Park. These areas are clearly marked, and during hunting season you will want to make a practice of avoiding them (unless you and your dog are hunters, of course).

▶ **Crow's Nest Preserve, 201 Piersol Road.** There is parking available near a restored barn. This is a Natural Lands Trust property, and your dog on-leash is welcome here. There are 600 acres, restrooms, and 2 miles of trails that connect up to French Creek State Park and the Hopewell Furnace National Historic Site. Woodland, streams, meadows, and diabase outcroppings make this an interesting area to explore. Crow's Nest Preserve is also included in the North Warwick Historic and Archaeological District: many Native American artifacts have been found here, and the remains of pits used to burn wood for charcoal for the area's iron forges can still be seen. Picnicking, bicycling, and swimming are prohibited in Natural Lands Trust preserves. Be aware that some preserves have a hunting program in November and January: signs are posted when the preserves are closed.

▶ **Warwick County Park, 4 miles west of Route 100 off Route 23, Knauertown.** The French Creek and the Horse-Shoe Trail (which connects Valley Forge with the Appalachian Trail) both pass through this 455-acre park. There are miles of multi-use trails. The woodlands here once provided timber for charcoal used in the local iron industry. And there are marsh areas to explore as well. There are picnic pavilions where you and your dog can enjoy a meal together.

You and your dog might want to tour a vineyard here:

▶ **French Creek Ridge Vineyards, 200 Grove Road, Elverson, 610-286-7754.** Call for hours and information on what's going on here. There are very nice grounds here that you and your dog can explore. There is a resident dog.

🐾 CENTRAL CHESTER COUNTY

Lionville

Lionville is one of those explorable small pockets of history in Chester County that you and your dog may enjoy. The Lionville National Historic District runs along PA Route 100 and South Village Avenue. Historic buildings include the Edith P. Moore Lionville Schoolhouse (1859) and the Uwchlan Meeting House (1756).

Your dog on-leash can do some shopping at:

▶ **Pickering Valley Feed & Farm, Route 113 and Gordon Drive, 610-363-8810 or 610-696-6169.** Open from 8:00 a.m. every day but Sunday. This is a family-run business offering supplies and food for animals ranging from fish to horses—or, as they say, "We carry everything your pet may need . . . from an elephant to a mouse!" They will also help you solve any problems you may be having with your pet. And they will provide water to your dog on request, and offer free samples of products.

Exton/West Whiteland Township

The Exton and West Whiteland Township area is large and loose, but there are some clusters of nationally registered historic addresses. Be prepared for some real exploring—maybe by foot, maybe by car. As long as you're prepared (water and rest stops being especially important), either way you choose to travel, you and your dog will enjoy looking for the area's many historic sites.

If your dog would like to do some shopping, you can go to:

▶ **PetsMart, 1010 East Lancaster Avenue, 610-518-0250**
▶ **Pet Valu, 121 West Lincoln Highway, 610-280-7430**

And you and your dog can stay overnight in the area at:

▶ **Comfort Inn, 5 North Pottstown Pike, 610-524-8811.** There are no restrictions, but your dog is charged a small fee per night (one person told me $5, another told me $10). There are grounds for your dog to take care of business.
▶ **Hampton Inn, North Route 100 and Route 113, 610-363-5555.** There is no extra charge here, and no restrictions. They have grounds for walking your dog.
▶ **Holiday Inn Express, 120 North Pottstown Pike, 610-524-9000.** Dogs are charged $5 per day, but there are no restrictions and there are grounds for walking your dog. While here, keep an eye out for:
 Concerts in Miller Park (Summer). Miller Park is next to the Holiday Inn Express. Bring a blanket and a picnic and enjoy the music. There's a special concert followed by fireworks for the Fourth of July. And they also have events like Family Night, which includes a variety show. Call 610-524-9000 for information and a schedule.

Downingtown

Downingtown is Chester County's oldest town. You can get information on a walking tour of Historic Downingtown by calling 610-269-7619. The town features one of the oldest remaining dwellings in the county:

▶ **The Downingtown Log House, 15 East Lancaster Avenue.** Built in 1700 on the banks of the Brandywine, it is a National Historic Site and part of the East Lancaster Avenue National Historic District, which forms an irregular pattern along East Lancaster Avenue, with a total of 20 historic structures. Historic buildings along East Lancaster are well marked, so you can take a walk with your dog to view them (and they are mostly on the north side of the road, so you don't have to worry about crossing the street).

Then take your dog for a stroll along the streets of Downingtown's commercial area to admire the Italianate stores built after the arrival of the railroad in the mid-1800s. There are places to pick up food here, including:

▶ **Elizabethan Tea Shop, 128 East Lancaster Avenue, 610-873-2366.** This shop offers traditional English foods such as ploughman's lunch, Cornish pasties, and afternoon or high tea sandwiches with a wide selection of teas. They have two benches in a small courtyard where you can sit with your dog on-leash year-round. If you ask, they will give your dog water or ice.
▶ **Rita's Water Ice, 84 West Lancaster Avenue.** You can sit outside with your dog from March to October. They have had customers buy water ice and custard for their dogs.

There are some events in Downingtown that you might want to come out to watch with your dog, including:

▶ **Memorial Day Commemoration (May).** There's a parade on Pennsylvania Avenue that ends up in Kerr Park. There are marching bands and more, which is great for getting dogs used to loud noises—they may never like the drums, but at least they'll learn to remain calm. Unfortunately, you can't take your dog into Kerr Park for the rest of the festivities, but look for other street events during the year, where your dog on-leash will be welcome.

There are some major parks nearby that are very dog-friendly. Try:

▶ **Springton Manor Farm County Park, 860 Springton Road, Glenmoore, 610-942-2450.** Five miles west of Downingtown, this county park is open daily from 8:00 a.m. to dusk. There are 300 acres here, with picnic areas and a demonstration farm. Originally, this land was part of a William Penn manor, and has been used for agriculture since the 18th century. There's an interpretive nature trail that ends at a pond, and Springton Manor itself has Victorian gardens, a gazebo, and a terrace to be admired from a distance with your dog (though if you go closer, they may not shoo you away). There are also events held here that may interest you and your dog:

    Sheep & Wool Day (April). You can see sheep shearing, weaving and spinning, and sheep herding by border collies. Admission is free.

    Family Day (September). Watch farm-related activities and games, and browse through the craft vendors.

▶ **The Struble Trail.** With access and parking in Kardon Park along Norwood Road, this is a county facility that runs along the eastern branch of the Brandywine Creek, beginning in Downingtown. Currently, it is 5 miles out and back. Between dawn and dusk, you can hike and picnic along the trail with your dog: horses, snowmobiles, and vehicles are prohibited on the trail. It is 10 feet wide, and paved with gravel. Ultimately it will be 16 miles long. Call Springton Manor Farm County Park at 610-942-2450 for more information.

And if you and your dog *really* want to recreate, you need to go to:

▶ **Marsh Creek State Park, 675 Park Road, 610-458-5119.** This is a treasure of a park that you and your dog will love. There are restrooms, a food concession, picnic areas, and equestrian and hiking trails, all in the rolling hills of central Chester County. The park has 1,705 acres, including 535-acre Marsh Creek Lake. You can rent paddle boats, canoes, and windsurfers, and take your dog out on the water, but remember to wear those life vests! Boating on Marsh Creek Lake is limited to sailboats and boats using electric motors.

    The 6 miles of hiking trails here will take you and your dog to see the Larkins Covered Bridge, built in 1881 and relocated to the park in 1972: this is a National Historic Register site. There are also about 6 miles of bridle trails, and hunting in some areas, with hunting dog training permitted during hunting season. (Be careful with your dog at those times. Be sure to avoid the hunting areas. Since one of our dogs resembles a medium-sized black bear, we have a red doggy backpack for her to wear that we hope will differentiate her.) You can also go birding and do winter sports in Marsh Creek State Park.

    The Marsh Creek Sailing Club holds regular races and regattas on Marsh Creek Lake from April to October, mostly on Sundays, with the occasional Saturday event thrown in. The club welcomes both novice and experienced sailors, ages 16 to 65. For directions and information, visit the club's Web site at members.aol.com/SailMCSC. If your dog knows how to sail (with a doggy life vest), check this club out. If not, just go and watch. Spectating lakeside at a sailing race is a great way to spend a beautiful afternoon.

Finally, you and your dog can come back to the Downingtown area when it's time to get a holiday tree:

▶ **Tricolor Tree Farm, 1480 Hall Road, between West Chester and Downingtown, 610-269-1034.** Your dog can help you make your selection from more than 30,000 Douglas fir, blue spruce, Norway spruce, and white pine trees.

(Coatesville)

Coatesville is located in the midst of the Chester Valley, along the Brandy-wine River, on the site of what used to be a Native American village. It started out as a trading center for fur trappers: a marker on Oak Street recognizes Peter Bazillion, a fur trader and merchant. In 1787, Moses Coates purchased the land that now forms the center of town, and in 1810, the Brandywine Iron Works and Nail Factory began, the predecessor of Lukens, Inc.

You and your dog will enjoy a walking tour of the Lukens Historic District. The Graystone Society's Historic House Museums, 76 South First Avenue, 610-384-9282, can provide you with walking tour literature. The Graystone Society also holds some events, such as 1999's July Victorian Ice Cream Festival, which featured games, music, and an arts and crafts show. Proceeds go toward the restoration of Graystone Mansion. Contact the society for more information on events in which you and your dog might be interested.

In the Coatesville area, you'll find Speakman's Bridge, built in 1881 and rebuilt in 1996; and two bridges open to foot traffic only (whether biped or quadruped) in Laurel Lands, owned by the Brandywine Conservancy, reached by a 1-mile trail open Wednesday through Sunday from 9:00 a.m. to 5:00 p.m.

There are places to pick up takeout food in Coatesville, and the downtown **Dairy Queen** has a separate table area where you and your dog can sit together. You can also get a snack at:

▶ **Rita's Water Ice, 1809 East Lincoln Highway.** They have outdoor seating where you and your dog on-leash can sit from March to October and enjoy your food.

If you and your dog want to get some exercise that isn't on pavement, head to nearby:

▶ **Hibernia Mansion and Hibernia County Park, 1 Park Road, Wagontown, 610-384-0290 (mansion), 610-383-3812 (park).** Hibernia Mansion is a former ironmaster's house, and technically your dog is not permitted on the grounds. However, I'm told people do still walk their dogs there, and the staff doesn't kick them off. Dogs *are* permitted in the adjoining park, so people probably get confused.

At 800 acres, Hibernia is Chester County's largest park. There are $2^1/_2$ miles of paved hiking and biking paths, and 8 miles of multipurpose trails, as well as open areas and woodlands. Hibernia Mansion sits on the hillside overlooking the park, and there are five 18th-century cottages. Hibernia Park also contains Chambers Lake, 90 acres of water available for nonmotorized boating.

You and your dog can come back to Hibernia for events such as:

Easter Egg Hunt (March/April). You and your dog can watch kids hunting for colored eggs.

Old Fiddlers' Picnic (August). This is a wonderful event sponsored by the Chester County Board of Commissioners, through the recreation department, in league with the Chester County Old Fiddlers' Association. Not only do musicians perform on the stage, they perform throughout the woodlands of Fiddler's Field. All musicians are encouraged to bring fiddles, banjos, guitars, and dulcimers. The picnic also includes square dancing, some waltzes and polkas, and country western line dancing. A reasonable admission is charged per car.

🐾 SOUTHERN CHESTER COUNTY

West Chester Borough

West Chester—the "Athens" of Pennsylvania—is a dog-friendly bonanza. Two districts in West Chester are on the National Historic Register: the West Chester Downtown Historic District, bounded by Biddle, Matlack, Barnard, and New Streets; and the West Chester State College Quadrangle Historic District, bounded by South High and South Church Streets and College and Rosedale Avenues. New Street has some truly beautiful structures on it. West Chester is a wonderful place to explore on foot and paw, and simply a great place to spend some time.

Downtown West Chester is lovely, and while Market Street has no outdoor seating, Gay Street has benches at several places midstreet. You can get deli and other takeout food and sit outside enjoying the town with your dog. Or the two of you can eat at:

▶ **Penn's Table Restaurant, 100 West Gay Street, 610-696-0677.** This is a luncheonette-style restaurant with home-cooked food. They also serve dinner on Thursday and Friday. Outdoor seating is available whenever the weather permits, and if you sit outside, your dog can sit with you. They happily provide bowls of water, ice, or doggy treats for your dog. "As owners of two yellow Labradors, we know how much a part of the family dogs are. We enjoy seeing people being able to spend time with their dogs at our restaurant."

▶ **Rita's Water Ice, 323 East Gay Street.** Outdoor seating is available all season: you and your dog can sit and enjoy ice cream or water ice together, and Rita's will provide cups of water for your dog. "All are welcome."

West Chester has a lot of neighborhood parks, open from dawn to dusk, should your dog have a need to use one:

▶ **Everhart Park, at West Miner Street and South Bradford Avenue**
▶ **Rustin Park, at South Walnut Street and East Rosedale Avenue**

- Nield Street Park, at South New and West Nield Streets
- Green Field Park, at South Franklin Street
- Mosteller Park, at South Penn Street and Joseph Alley
- Memorial Park, between West Washington and Biddle Streets
- Fugett Park, at East Chestnut and North Penn Streets
- Marshall Square, at North Matlack and East Marshall Streets
- Market Street Park, at West Market and South Everhart Streets
- Hoopes Park, at Hoopes Park Lane and West Ashbridge Street
- You and your dog can also explore **West Chester University** if you want to: dogs are okay on the campus as long as they are leashed and you clean up. It's an interesting campus, and if you are into college campuses (like my husband is), you'll want to check it out. And come back for:

    Renaissance Faire (April). Held at the Quad on High Street. Features music, dancing, and other free entertainment. Stop by and see what fun is happening! Call 610-436-2266 for information.

West Chester is the home base of the **Chester County SPCA, 1212 Phoenixville Pike, 610-692-6113, ext. 215, www.ccspca.org.** The Chester County SPCA provides pet adoption programs, emergency ambulance service, investigations into animal cruelty, educational programs, and pet visitation programs. Annual fundraising events for the CCSPCA include:

- **Annual "Walk for Paws" and Spring Music Festival (May).** Held at the Myrick Nature Center, Route 842 in West Chester. You can either pay a registration fee or get sponsors for the walk, which benefits the SPCA's programs and services. Bring your dog and walk for a good, doggish (and cattish) cause. After the walk, the SPCA will feature a beer garden, with food and a free musical performance.
- **Annual "Forget Me Not" Garden Party (June).** This event is held at a private home in Chadds Ford. Many guests bring their companion animals, some of whom may have been adopted from the Chester County SPCA. This fundraising event includes a horse and carriage parade, animal demonstrations (such as herding, a flyball relay race, musical freestyle obedience, and search and rescue dogs—Newfs!), live music, displays of rare dog and cat breeds, a full bar, a champagne bar, and food provided by area caterers and restaurants. Reservations are required to attend, and yes, it will cost you some money.
- **Annual Benefit Horse Show (September).** Held at the Radnor Hunt Pony Club, so your dog can come. This is the SPCA's oldest fundraising event, and it includes two rings, with 16 divisions and classes for kids and adults. This event funds the SPCA's cruelty investigations. There is an entry fee for riders. The show is free to spectators, but food and drink, raffle tickets, and gift items are available for purchase, so you can help out even if you don't ride.
- **Annual Dilworthtown Wine Festival (October).** Held outside at the Dilworthtown Inn, 1390 Old Wilmington Pike, West Chester. You can't bring your dog, but you can enjoy over 100 selections of fine wine along with gourmet food, live music, a silent auction, and specialty booths. Admission is charged since it is a fundraising event: tickets are available at the door or can be reserved, and major credit cards are accepted.

    In December, look for the CCSPCA's Companion Animals of Chester County Calendar. It is available for purchase and features collages of pictures submitted by area pet owners and art by kids, as well as practical pet tips. You can order the calendar from the CCSPCA, or get it at the **CCSPCA gift shop** in the **Frazer Shopping Center, 480 Lancaster Avenue, Malvern, 610-251-5006.** The shop carries quality gifts for both people and animals.

What else can you and your dog do in the West Chester area? You can go to:

▶ **Myrick Conservation Center, Route 842.** It is a nice place to visit, and **summer concerts** are held here, all free. For information, call 610-793-1090.

▶ **Oakbourne Mansion in Oakbourne Park, 1014 South Concord Road.** The historic mansion is lovely, and the park is great: you and your dog on-leash can have a wonderful time here (outside only, of course). You can also come back for events sponsored by the West Chester Department of Recreation, such as:

Spring Craft Festival. Everything from folk art to pottery, and food, is available during the festival. Admission is charged. Call 610-696-9949 for details.

Summer Series Concerts. Westtown Township's free series begins in July. Bring a blanket and your dog to Oakbourne Park and enjoy. Call 610-436-9010 for more information.

Fall Craft Festival (October). The festival features over 100 artisans offering folk art, furniture, dolls, jewelry, antiques, collectibles, and more. Specialty foods are also available, and merchandise is restocked daily. For more information, call 610-647-6228.

There are plenty of other West Chester events that you and your dog will want to come back for, including:

▶ **Kite Day (May).** Held at the East Bradford Township Building, this annual event features stunt kite flying, homemade kites, sack races, and food. Bring your dog on-leash and watch the beauty of the kites moving in the wind. For information, call 610-436-9010.

▶ **Annual Arts Extravaganza (Memorial Day weekend).** Held at 100 North Bradford Avenue. Sponsored by the Chester County Art Association, the event features outdoor "clothesline" exhibits and displays.

▶ **Super Sunday in Downtown West Chester (June).** Enjoy crafts, food, antiques, antique cars, games, music, and entertainment along Gay Street. Call 610-436-9010 for details.

▶ **Turk's Head Music Festival (July).** Includes music, crafts, food, and activities in Everhart Park at West Miner Street and South Bradford Avenue. For information, call 610-436-9010. (West Chester was originally called "Turk's Head," after a local tavern.)

▶ **Family Fun Day (September).** Held at the East Bradford Township Building. Call 610-436-9010 for details.

▶ **West Chester Halloween Parade (October).** Starts at Market and Darlington Streets. For more information, call 610-436-9010.

▶ **Old-Fashioned Christmas (First week of December).** Includes a parade, carolers, seasonal music, a tree-lighting ceremony at High and Market Streets, entertainment, and more. For further information, call the Greater West Chester Chamber of Commerce, 610-696-4046 or 610-696-9110, or visit their Web site at www.gwcc.org.

What else can you do in West Chester? If your dog is into gardening, take him or her to:

▶ **Bradford Nursery, 1121 Downingtown Pike, 610-269-7771.** You and your dog on-leash can browse the nursery stock together.

▶ **Montgomery Nurseries, 1531 Telegraph Road, 610-436-4511.** They have a dog on the premises, but otherwise you and your dog are free to wander around together to select trees and shrubs.

When you've finished meeting your dog's gardening needs, go enjoy:

▶ **Stroud Preserve (formerly Georgia Farm), 454 North Creek Road, 610-696-6187.** The preserve has 485 acres (including Harney Preserve), with parking available along Creek Road, across from the main entrance. There are 15 miles of trails, and a trail map is available. This is Natural Lands Trust land, so your dog can admire the rolling hills, stream valleys, meadows, and ponds with you, as well as the main house and barn, which are on the National Historic Register. Picnicking, bicycling, and swimming are prohibited in Natural Lands Trust preserves. Your dog must be on-leash, and be aware that some preserves have a hunting program in November and January: signs are posted when the preserves are closed.

Finally, you and your dog can stay overnight in West Chester at:

▶ **Abbey Green Motor Lodge, 1036 Wilmington Pike, 610-692-3310.** They have grounds and a field nearby for walking your dog.

Marshallton

Marshallton is a mostly untouched historic village and a National Historic District. Find a place to park, and take your dog on a walking tour, strolling down Strasburg Road, Marshallton's "Main Street." The village starts on Strasburg Road (Route 162) at an 1810 bed and breakfast. Next door is the 1891 stone Marshallton United Methodist Church. Next to that is the Marshalton Inn, a National Historic Site, the original structure dating to 1793. Across the way is the Four Dogs Tavern. At the end of the village is the Spaulding gas station, which includes a sandwich shop and grocery. The Brandywine Conservancy holds 100 acres to the west of the village, 250 acres to the east, and 130 acres to the south.

☙ DEEP SOUTHERN CHESTER COUNTY

Although they are a bit farther away, there are some excellent doggish spots here that simply have to be pointed out.

Pennsbury

There's a great event in Pennsbury that you and your dog will want to attend:

▶ **Pennsbury Land Trust Balloon Festival (September).** Held at **Pennsbury Municipal Park,** behind the municipal building on Baltimore Pike. For more information, call 610-388-7323.

Kennett Square

Kennett Square ("The Mushroom Capital of the World") has amazing community spirit, and more history than you might expect. In 1810, it was a village of about eight structures, including five made of logs. By 1853, there were enough citizens to petition to form a borough. Kennett Square was a station along the Underground Railroad, with many of its most prominent citizens involved. It has an outstanding collection of 19th- and early-20th-century buildings. You and your dog can stroll tree-lined streets and admire architectural styles ranging from Federal to Italianate to Queen Anne Revival.

You can grab a bite to eat with your dog in Kennett Square at:

> ▶ **Harrington's Coffee Company, 127 East State Street, 610-444-9992.** You can get coffee, espresso, morning pastries, and light lunches here. Outdoor seating is available from April to October, weather permitting, and you can sit there with your dog on-leash. They will provide bowls of water or ice for your dog on request.

Kennett Square's diverse community puts on some great events that you and your dog will want to come back for. The biggest one is:

> ▶ **The Mushroom Festival (September).** Held along State Street, the festival features lots of great arts and crafts, fire truck displays, rides for kids, mushroom judging, mushroom cooking lessons and contests, an exhibit on how mushrooms are cultivated, eight bands playing on two bandstands, and more—and your dog on-leash can enjoy the whole thing with you. On Saturday there is a parade with floats, bands, and other features. After the parade there's a swing and blues concert in Anson B. Nixon Park (admission is charged).

You and your dog may also want to try:

> ▶ **Kennett Square Sidewalk Sale Day (June).** Includes live entertainment, food, and bargains. Browse the tables with your dog.
> ▶ **Anson B. Nixon Park, on North Walnut Street, just off State Street,** is a great place to hang out with your dog. The park is open from 7:00 a.m. to sunset, and you and your dog on-leash are welcome to explore the 83 acres of meadows, woodlands, and the east branch of the Red Clay Creek, as well as two ponds. There are all kinds of features that you and your dog will enjoy on an everyday basis, but you will also want to come back for events such as:
> > **Kennett Mile Run (May)**
> > **Community Tree Ribbon Display and Unity Day (Memorial Day weekend).** Includes the Parade of Nations at noon, and an international day of crafts, music, and exotic foods. You and your dog can enjoy classical music, country music, and Western African drumming bands. There are pony rides, dog-training demonstrations, and a petting zoo.
> > **Concerts at Anson B. Nixon Park (Summer).** From June to September, bring a blanket or lawn chair and come to hear big band, bluegrass, and other music. Admission is charged.
> > **Community Talent Show (July)**
> > **Family Fun Day (July).** Clowns, entertainment, and more.
> > **Community Carnival (September)**

Halloween Hayride and Bonfire (October). Come and enjoy the evening festivities.
Christmas Opening Night (November). Dedication of community holiday tree.

There are two more events in or around Kennett Square to keep an eye out for:

▶ **Kennett Square Lions Club Annual Mardi Gras Masquerade Ball (February/March).** Benefits Canine Partners for Life, a group that purchases or rescues dogs to train and place with the physically disabled as service dogs. Only CPL dogs can attend, but it sure is a worthy cause and a lot of fun. For information, call 610-869-4902 or e-mail info@k94life.org.

▶ **Annual Duck Race (June).** Starts on the east branch of the Red Clay Creek in **Kennett Firehouse Picnic Park.** Proceeds benefit the Kennett Senior Center. For a small contribution, you can "adopt" a rubber duck. This is a very fun event.

In December, you and your dog can get a Christmas tree together at:

▶ **Pond View Tree Farm, 115 Corman Drive, 610-444-6046.** You can bring your dog to help you choose among balsam fir, Douglas fir, Fraser fir, white pine, and white spruce trees. The folks here told me that insurance statistics for choose-and-cut tree farms list dog bites as the number-one category of claims over the last 10 years, so please keep your dog on-leash and well controlled so you can continue to Christmas tree—hunt together.

Willowdale

▶ The feature you and your dog want to know about here is the **Willowdale Steeplechase**, located at Routes 82 and 926 (101 East Street Road), where your dog on-leash is welcome at all events. For more information, visit www.willowdale.org, or call 610-444-1582. Events include:

The Willowdale Steeplechase Point-to-Point (March)

The Willowdale Steeplechase (May). You can reserve tickets in advance, as well as tailgating parking spaces. The event benefits the Stroud Water Research Center. A 12-foot water jump, brush hurdles, and other obstacles challenge the horses, and between horse races there are Jack Russell terrier races and an antique carriage parade to enjoy. There are vendor and food tents as well. It's a great event.

Brandywine Carriage Driving Show (June). One of the top pleasure-driving shows in the U.S. Turnout, and reinsmanship, timed obstacles, cross-country, and a Concours d'Elegance are featured. Carriages and sleighs are exhibited throughout the day. Equestrian-related boutiques and food vendors are also present. The event benefits the New Bolton Center.

The Willowdale Gold Cup (September). Features amateur steeplechase races, Jack Russell terrier races, activities, and shopping.

The Willowdale Steeplechase (October). A benefit for Chester County Hospital, this event includes six steeplechase races, pony races, terrier races, a petting zoo, an antique car show, vendors, and food.

Unionville

There's an area of history here that you might want to explore with your dog: the Unionville Village National Historic District, along PA Routes 162

and 82. But let's face it, you and your dog are in Chester County horse country. So take your dog to see:

▶ **The Laurels Combined Driving Event (September).** The National Combined Driving Pony
Championships, the United States World Singles Driving Championships Selection Trials, and the
World Four-in-Hand Driving Championships Selection Trials all happen here, along with the
first leg of the Jaguar Triple Crown of Combined Driving, Hunt's Harness Laurels Team Challenge,
and the Bellcrown Carriages Preliminary Pony Triple Challenge. The event benefits the Brandywine Conservancy, the Cheshire Hunt Conservancy, and the Large Animal Protection Society. For
more information, call 610-486-6484, or visit the event online at www.laurelscde.com.

▶ **The Pennsylvania Hunt Cup (October).** The course is on Newark Road, a half-mile north
of Route 926 in Unionville. Races include a pony race, the Arthur O. Choate Jr. Memorial
Trophy race, the Pennsylvania Hunt Cup itself, and the Athenian Idol. You and your dog
should feel free to tailgate before the races. Besides the races, there's a carriage parade and
"Canine Puissance" (dog jumping). This event benefits the Magee Rehabilitation Center. General admission per person is charged. For information, call 610-869-0557.

Avondale

You can get a bite to eat here with your dog at:

▶ **Hartefeld National Golf Course, 1 Hartefeld Road, 610-268-8800.** This is a full-service
bar, restaurant, banquet facility, and golf course. Patrons who sit outside can bring dogs
on-leash, and outdoor seating is available from May to September. They will provide your
dog with ice, water, or bones on request. "Pooper-scoopers are a MUST!"

Or you can take a picnic to one of the greatest events for a dog and its owner
(did you forget you were in horse country?):

▶ **Brandywine Polo Club.** Many of the games benefit charities and civic groups, and they
are extremely fun to watch. The first Chukkar Cup happens on Memorial Day weekend, and
there are games every Sunday, holidays included, from then until the last Chukkar Cup on
the first weekend in October. Tailgating is encouraged. So is bringing your dog on-leash.
Bring a picnic, tailgate, and go out at halftime to help stomp divots! If the field is wet, the
game will be called off, so confirm before you go by calling 610-268-8692. There's a small
general admission per person.

Landenberg

Landenberg is in New Garden Township, and is a historic village with a
hotel, a store, and the Wool House, the only structure remaining from the
Landenberg Woolen Mills. The bridge over the east branch of the White
Clay Creek takes Landenberg Road into the village. The Landenberg Bridge
itself is on the National Register of Historic Places because of its engineering
significance (it is a Pratt pony truss bridge, unusual for the area, with a can-
tilevered sidewalk). Unfortunately, the bridge is endangered, up for possible replacement by PennDOT.

You and your dog may want to come to Landenberg in December to get a Christmas tree at:

▶ **Schmidt's Christmas Tree Farm, 1741 Flint Hill Road, 610-274-8560.** Opens the day after Thanksgiving. Your dog can help you pick out a Fraser fir, Douglas fir, spruce, or pine on weekdays from noon to 5:00 p.m., and Saturday and Sunday from 8:00 a.m. to 5:00 p.m. You can also come to the farm in October for pumpkin season: dogs on-leash are allowed in the field.

❧ A FEW LAST RECREATION SPOTS

▶ **The White Clay Creek Preserve, Route 896.** Located 11 miles south of the Forrestville exit of Route 1, the White Clay Creek State Park of Delaware adjoins Chester County's preserve. The preserve's 1,253 acres are open for day use from 8:00 a.m. to sunset. The White Clay Creek Valley is the preserve's core, and you'll see people fishing for trout in the creek. A 3^1/$_2$-mile hiking trail ties to trails in the Delaware-side park, and there is a bridle path of 8 miles. Part of the preserve used to be a Lenni Lenape settlement called Opasiskunk, likely inhabited from the early archaic period to the mid-1700s. For more information, visit www.dcnr.state.pa.us/stateparks/parks/wclay.htm, e-mail whiteclay@dcnr.state.pa.us, or call 610-274-2900.

▶ **Chrome Barrens, Media Road, Oxford, 610-834-1323 or 610-932-6111.** This is a rare serpentine barrens, including prairie, savanna, and woodland areas. It is a beautiful and unique area, with rare plants and habitats, and you and your dog on-leash are free to explore it. There are birds and wildflowers in spring, butterflies in late summer, and colorful foliage in fall.

▶ **Nottingham County Park, County Park Road, Nottingham, 610-932-2589.** Located 6 miles south of Oxford, off Route 1, Nottingham has an outcropping of serpentine stone over one square mile in size, one of the largest on the East Coast. There is a self-guiding trail with eight stations interpreting the unique ecosystem of which the outcropping is a crucial part, and there are 8 miles of trails for hiking, biking, and horseback riding. Bring a picnic and your dog to admire the special beauty of this park. And you and your dog might want to come back for:

Freedom Fest (July). Enjoy an evening concert as well as fireworks. As always with events like this, you may want to take your dog home before the fireworks start, unless he or she is fireworks-jaded.

Industrial Heritage Day (August). Chromite and feldspar, used to produce paint, textiles, porcelain, and false teeth, were extracted from sites within Nottingham County Park in the 1800s and 1900s. Chromite mine and feldspar quarry sites can be toured during this event. More dog-friendly are historical displays and exhibits, a turn-of-the-century Italian immigrant workers' camp next to the Black Run Creek, a play, musical entertainment, folk songs, food vendors, and picnic opportunities. This is a free event—bring blankets or lawn chairs, and enjoy!

Instead of just leaving you here, let me mention a couple of events that happen everywhere, which you and your dog may want to keep in mind:

▶ **Annual Take Your Dog to Work Day (June).** This is a great idea, inaugurated in 1999 and sponsored by Pet Sitters International. Some companies and offices actually allow employees to bring their dogs to work every day. If yours isn't one of them, ask your employer if you can bring your best friend in for the day. Dogs work wonders for office morale, and thus for productivity. However, be considerate of officemates or coworkers who may be allergic to dogs. For more information, visit www.petsit.com/tydtwd1.asp.

▶ **National Night Out (August).** Many communities and neighborhoods have started to hold activities and celebrations, including parades, on National Night Out. Bring your dog and take advantage of the opportunity to meet your neighbors. There are about 30 neighborhood gatherings in Philadelphia alone, and many, many more throughout the Greater Philadelphia area. Watch your local papers to find out what's going on near you. You can find out if your community is a registered participant by visiting www.nno.org/nno.html.

APPENDIX A
Clubs, Shows, and Shelters

🐾 CLUBS AND SHOWS

There are lots of different clubs you and your dog may be interested in joining. There are activity-based clubs, training clubs, all-breed kennel clubs, and breed-specific clubs if you're an aficionado of one particular breed (like the breed your dog happens to be!).

All-Breed Kennel Clubs

All-breed kennel clubs usually put on annual shows and matches, which can be great fun for a dog lover to attend. American Kennel Club–approved shows technically do not allow spectator dogs, so the odds are your dog can't go with you to a kennel club show. However, lots of great vendors of dog-related supplies, treats, and gifts come to sell their wares at the shows, so you can always pick up a present for your dog as consolation for leaving him or her at home. If you are interested in attending a show, the best place to find one is at www.infodog.com.

Be aware when contacting kennel clubs that the person who receives your letter is usually a club member at his or her home address—there is no official "club headquarters" and club members aren't paid for their time, so please be patient. In some cases, contact information may have changed, but the person your letter reaches should be able to direct it to the new official club spokesperson. Area all-breed kennel clubs include:

Pennsylvania

▶ **Bryn Mawr Kennel Club, 334 Crum Creek Lane, Newtown Square, PA 19073.** The Bryn Mawr Kennel Club holds an annual show in June at the Ludwig's Corner Horse Show Grounds in Chester County.

▶ **Bucks County Kennel Club, 524 Upper Stump Road, Chalfont, PA 18914.** The club holds its annual show in May in Tinicum Park.

▶ **Chester Valley Kennel Club, 2301 Eagle Farm Road, Chester Springs, PA 19425.** This club holds a point show in May, on the 19th or 20th Saturday of the year, with a match show the day before. The public is invited to both shows (there's a fee for the match show). The shows are held at the Ludwig's Corner Horse Show Grounds.

▶ **Delaware County Kennel Club, 254 Auburn Road, Landenburg, PA 19350, www.geo cities.com/Petsburgh/Zoo/7141.** The club holds a point show at the Ludwig's Corner Horse Show Grounds in June and an AKC-sanctioned match in Newlin Mill Park in September. Classes in show handling and pet therapy are offered.

▶ **Devon Dog Show Association, 1264 Prizer Road, Pottstown, PA 19465.** Their annual show is held in October at the Ludwig's Corner Horse Show Grounds.

▶ **Greater Philadelphia Dog Fanciers Association, 28 Brookside Road, Erdenheim, PA 19038, members.aol.com/GPDFA/GPDFA.html.** Show handling and obedience classes are offered, and the club's annual show is held in June at the Temple University Ambler campus.

▶ **Hatboro Dog Club, 21 Creek Road, Chalfont, PA 18914.** The Hatboro Dog Club holds its annual show in October. The location varies.

▶ **Huntingdon Valley Kennel Club, P.O. Box 1214, Glenside, PA 19038.** The club's annual show is held at Temple University's Ambler campus in June.

▶ **Montgomery County Kennel Club, 604 South Washington Square, Apt. 2811, Philadelphia, PA 19106.** This club hosts the Montgomery County Terrier Show, one of the country's most prestigious of such shows. The club's annual match is held at the Temple Ambler campus in October.

▶ **Perkiomen Valley Kennel Club, 2091 Hendricks Station Road, Harleysville, PA 19438.** The club's show is held in August. The location varies.

▶ **Valley Forge Kennel Club, 2598 Washington Drive, Gilbertsville, PA 19525.** This club's annual breed and obedience match is held in September at the Kimberton Fairgrounds on Route 113, with free admission and parking. The Valley Forge club is also a great example of what a kennel club can be. They have both AKC-registered and "pet-quality-only" dogs as members. They hold meetings at Suburban General Hospital along Route 202 in Norristown, and they are a very active club. They make a point of going to area community days, like Lower Providence Funday and the Lansdale Mardi Gras Celebration, where the club sets up educational booths. Club members go out and clean up local parks to make up for the irresponsible dog owners out there. The club also sponsors new-puppy ownership seminars at a local veterinary hospital, offers obedience classes from September to June, and is involved in a therapy-dog program.

New Jersey

▶ **Burlington County Kennel Club, 1818 Route 70, Southampton, NJ 08088.** This club's annual show has been held at the Burlington County Institute of Technology, in June.

▶ **Camden County Kennel Club, 18 Honeysuckle Drive, Port Deposit, MD 21904.** This club's annual show is held at the South Jersey Expo Center in Pennsauken, in February.

Training Clubs

There are a lot of ways to get training for your dog—by individual trainers (either at your home or their place), at training schools, and even through classes offered by pet supply stores. Another source of training is an AKC-associated training club: club members are seriously into training and obedience work, and can draw on incredible experience to train you and your dog. My inexpert guess is that somewhere between 50 percent and 90 percent of dog training really consists of training owners to be the alpha "dogs" in their packs, and teaching them how to communicate in a way that dogs can understand. Most training clubs offer training beyond the basics, so you can keep going as far as you and your dog want to—Georgie had a blast showing off her competence at the club she attended. You and your dog may even decide you want to pursue obedience competition.

Area training clubs include:

Pennsylvania

▶ **Lower Bucks Dog Training Club, 39 Conifer Road, Levittown, PA 19057**
▶ **Philadelphia Dog Training Club, 4019 Crescent Avenue, Lafayette Hill, PA 19444, members.aol.com/jdicanio/phildog.html.** Classes include puppy kindergarten and basic obedience, and there are novice, open, and utility classes.

New Jersey

▶ **Lower Camden County Dog Training Club, 141 Broadway, Runnemede, NJ 08078**

Other Clubs

Interested in training your dog to do something besides basic (or even advanced) obedience? How about agility? Carting? Frisbee? Musical freestyle? Water rescue? Search and rescue? Animal-assisted therapy? Flyball? Backpacking (they make doggy backpacks—Georgie has one!)? Tracking? Schutzhund? Weight pulling? If any of these sound interesting and fun for you and your dog, and you would like to find out more about them, ask a local kennel club how to get started, contact a breed-specific club about activities that are the best for your breed of dog, or, if you have a computer and Internet access, just type an activity into your search engine and see all the amazing sites that pop up. Local kennel clubs should be able to direct you to breed-specific clubs as well.

❖ SHELTERS

There are different kinds of shelters, the best ones, of course, being "no-kill" shelters. No-kill shelters provide care for homeless animals, including any necessary medical attention, until someone is kind enough to adopt them. Rather than euthanize, some shelters try to foster animals out when space gets tight, with varying degrees of success. Of course, some shelters just don't have the resources to do much more than keep an animal for a week or two, and then they have some very tough decisions to make. All-breed as well as breed-specific rescue groups all over the country focus on rescuing animals from shelters and placing them in good homes, which is of some help. (In fact, if you or someone you know is ever in the position of having to give up a pet, rescue groups are an excellent way to go as an avenue for very careful and caring placement.)

Maybe you adopted your dog from a shelter—if you did, BRAVO! Even if you didn't, however, there are plenty of ways to help the homeless animals temporarily cared for by shelters. You can volunteer at a shelter, take homeless animals into foster care when space is short, donate money, or donate goods: food, toys, bedding—anything you use with your own dog (or cat or other small animal) can be used by shelters. Give a shelter a call, and see how you can help—your dog will be very proud of you.

Area no-kill shelters include:

▶ **Animal Adoption Center, 501 North Berlin Road, Lindenwold, NJ, 856-435-9116.** This shelter was established in 1991. You can check out their Web site at www.animal adoption.com.

▶ **Francisvale Home for Smaller Animals, Upper Gulph and Arden Roads, Radnor, PA, 610-688-1018.** There's an annual December buffet dinner event held at the Willows that benefits Francisvale—keep it in mind. Besides the buffet itself, there is music, a gift boutique, and visits from friends from the shelter.

▶ **Hope for the Animals, P.O. Box 877, Morrisville, PA 19067, 215-945-6204**

▶ **Northampton-Boro Animal Shelter, 1401 Laubach Avenue, Northampton, PA, 610-262-7387.** This shelter has been helping animals for over 10 years.

Other area shelters include:

Pennsylvania

▶ **Animal Rescue and Referral, P.O. Box 16, Richboro, PA 18954, www.voicenet/com/~marklz/ARR.html (or access the site from www.sas.upenn.edu/~sdoyle/pets.html).** For general information or adoption information, call 215-322-9251. For placing dogs or to be a publicity volunteer, call 215-741-1291. Fundraising volunteers should call 215-757-0495.

▶ **Montgomery County SPCA, 19 East Ridge Pike, Conshohocken, 610-825-0111**

▶ **Morris Animal Refuge, 1242 Lombard Street, Philadelphia, 215-735-3256, www.libertynet.org/morris**

▶ **Philadelphia County SPCA, 350 East Erie Avenue, Philadelphia, 215-426-6300**

▶ **Women's Humane Society, 3839 Richlieu Road, Bensalem, 215-750-3100**

New Jersey

▶ Animal Placement, 206 Lippincott Avenue, Riverton, 856-829-7332
▶ Animal Welfare Association, 509 Centennial Boulevard, Voorhees, 856-424-2288
▶ Burlington County Animal Shelter, 15 Pioneer Boulevard, Westhampton, 609-265-6073
▶ Camden County Animal Shelter & Adoption Center, 125 Barnsboro-Salina Road, Blackwood, 856-401-1300
▶ Save Our Small Dogs, 18 Downing Street, Cherry Hill, hometown.aol.com/sosdogs, sosdogs.petfinder.org, or SOSDOGS@aol.com
▶ Voorhees Animal Orphanage, 419 Cooper Road, Voorhees, 856-627-9111, access Web site through www.gsd-rescue.com/available/shelters.html
▶ West Jersey Animal Shelter, 1 Pennsauken Creek, Pennsauken, 856-486-2180, www.petfinder.org/shelters/NJ75.html

😾 DISASTER RESCUE FOR ANIMALS

There are a number of organizations that have set up programs to provide disaster relief for animals. Trained volunteers rescue, provide medical treatment for, and shelter animals during natural and man-made disasters including floods, fires, tornadoes, oil spills, earthquakes, and hurricanes. These organizations can always use donations, or you may even want to join them and play a more active part. National organizations include:

▶ **The American Humane Association, 63 Inverness Drive East, Englewood, CO 80112, 800-227-4645, www.amerhumane.org/disaster.** The association fights both child and animal abuse, and in the animal side of its operations has set up a Regional Response Program to provide disaster relief for animals, with animal professionals acting as volunteers. The association's relief efforts date to 1916, when they served the horses, mules, dogs, and pigeons used in World War I.
▶ **American Veterinary Medical Foundation, 1931 North Meachem Road, Suite 100, Schaumburg, IL 60173, 800-248-2862, www.avma.org/avmf.** The AVMF has a program for animal disaster relief that uses participating veterinarians for emergency preparedness and recovery efforts. Donations to the AVMF's Disaster Relief Emergency Fund are always needed. Currently there are four teams operating, one of which is VMAT-2, which covers Pennsylvania as well as Maryland, Virginia, and Delaware.
▶ **United Animal Nations' EARS (Emergency Animal Rescue Service), 5892A South Land Park Drive, P.O. Box 188890, Sacramento, CA 95818, 916-429-2457, www.uan.org/programs/ears.** EARS' stated mission is to assist pets, farm animals, and even wildlife during disasters. They work with animal welfare groups and veterinarians to rescue and provide shelter and medical treatment for animals until they can be re-placed with their human guardians, or adopted if necessary. EARS can always use donations and volunteers. The organization presents workshops to make volunteering easier.

Finally, in the local area:

▶ **Paoli Vetcare Companion Animal Hospital, 1476 Lancaster Avenue, Paoli, PA, 610-644-5360, www.paolivetcare.baweb.com.** Paoli Vetcare has joined PetNet, a Pennsylvania SPCA program that offers emergency boarding of pets for women trying to leave an abusive domestic situation. Women's shelters notify the PSPCA when PetNet services are needed, and the PSPCA transports the pets from the women's shelter to the PSPCA for up to seven days. After that, the pet is taken to a satellite facility for up to 35 days—all free of charge and completely confidential. This is an important program, and if you and your dog would like to help, donations can be sent to the PSPCA at the Philadelphia County branch, 350 East Erie Avenue, Philadelphia, PA 19134. The Pennsylvania SPCA can be reached at Mansfield Road, Wellsboro, PA 16901, 507-724-3687.

▶ **Evesham Veterinary Clinic, 800 Route 73 South, Marlton, NJ, 609-983-9440, www.southjerseypets.com/vet.** The New Jersey Veterinary Medical Association has formed an Animal Emergency Preparedness and Response Committee (AEPARC) for the state, creating a state disaster plan for the rescue of animals, and the Evesham Veterinary Clinic has set up a county plan for Camden County. They need volunteers, foster homes, and food and other donations. Give them a call and see how you can help.

APPENDIX B

Special Services You and Your Dog Might Need or Enjoy

Because the popularity of dogs just seems to keep on growing these days, there are many special services available to you and your dog. Some are fun, some are more practical, but the range of services out there will probably surprise you.

🐾 DOGGY PORTRAITS

This is a great way to immortalize the beautiful creature you have the privilege of sharing your life with. There are both photographers and artists who will do a portrait of your dog. Artists are a little more difficult to find: keep an eye out for them at arts and crafts shows. Or try:

▶ Michael A. Kuyper, artist, 401 Edgewood Avenue, Horsham, PA, 215-441-0780

You might also want to know about:

▶ Pet Drawings, 125 Bortondale Road, Media, PA, 215-477-6797, www.petdrawings.com. They don't do personal portraits of your dog, but artist Soren Christiansen has created 11" x 14" portraits of the top 50 AKC breeds (and is working on more), which are reproduced on high-quality, acid-free, three-ply Strathmore paper. The cool part is that if you buy a portrait, the proceeds benefit shelters and rescue efforts: the particular organization you want to help can be specified on the order form.

Pennsylvania Pet Photographers

▶ Briar Photography, 138 East Gay Street, West Chester, 610-692-2880
▶ Clearview Studio, 623 Ridge Pike, Lafayette Hill, 215-828-8899

- Custom Photography Studios, 20 Waterloo Avenue, Berwyn, 610-640-1331
- Gordon & Lowy Photography, 246 Haverford Avenue, Floor 2, Narberth, 610-664-1475, www.lowyphoto.com
- John H. Ansley, 219 Lancaster Avenue, Devon, 610-688-2398
- John Kellar Photography Studio, 1184 Route 113, Skippack, 215-489-0500
- Lindelle Photography & Video, 1920 County Line Road, Justa Farm Shopping Center, Huntingdon Valley, 215-364-2234; 724 Old York Road, Jenkintown, 215-572-8900
- Mills-Callan Photography and Video, 200 Wistar Road, Fairless Hills, 215-949-3819
- Pam Hesler & Associates, 1217 West Chester Pike, West Chester, 610-692-2740
- Paul Facenda Photography, 43 Bishop Hollow Road, Newtown Square, 610-356-5382
- Photo Express, 3515 West Chester Pike, Newtown Square, 610-356-5269
- Photo Pro, 501 Baltimore Pike, Stoney Creek Center, Springfield, 610-543-1100, dwp.bigplanet.com/photopro
- Steve's Photo Center, 1745 South Easton Road, Doylestown, 215-343-2339
- Webber Studio, 1105 Brinton Bridge Road, West Chester, 610-793-3952

New Jersey Pet Photographers

- Bleiman Photography, 248 South Church Street, Moorestown, 856-235-8905
- Krassan & Kovnat Photography, 1900 Greentree Road, Cherry Hill, 856-424-6555

🐾 DOG PARTIES

Plenty of people are celebrating their dogs' birthdays and other achievements these days. Where can you throw your pooch a soirée? Try:

- **Gloria's Pet-A-Rama, 6368 Germantown Avenue, Philadelphia, PA, 215-438-0204.** Along with vacation boarding, pet sitting, and doggy day care, Gloria's offers birthday and theme parties for your dog and his or her friends. Give them two weeks' notice, and they will show your pup a great time.
- **Three Dog Bakery, 113 Kings Highway East, Haddonfield, NJ, 856-857-1770, njthreedog@ aol.com.** The bakery not only makes birthday cakes so you can throw your own bash for your dog, they'll also do the whole thing for you, at their place or yours. Party packages range from a simple cake and party hats to a several-course meal, doggy games and prizes, and more.

🐾 PET CEMETERIES, CREMATORIES, AND SUPPLIES

This isn't something we like to think about. But it's nice to have a plan for when the inevitable happens—a chosen way to celebrate your dog one final time. Many veterinary hospitals offer pet funeral–related services, but there are other options.

Pennsylvania

- Brandywine Pet Cremation Co., 899 Fernhill Road, West Chester, 610-692-1965

▶ Brickhaven Pet Caskets and Urns, 610 New Rodgers Road, Bristol, 215-785-1766
▶ Dear Pet Memorial Park, Richlieu Road, Bensalem, 215-355-3140
▶ Farview Pet Cemetery, 1587 Farmington Avenue, Pottstown, 610-323-2451
▶ Francisvale Home for Smaller Animals, Upper Gulph and Arden Roads, Radnor, 610-688-1018
▶ Great Valley Pet Cemetery, 124 Phoenixville Pike, Frazer, 610-647-3330
▶ New Britain Pet Cemetery, 238 Almshouse Road, New Britain, 215-340-1790
▶ Parkview Pet Cemetery (Whitemarsh Memorial Park—Wayside Chapel), 1169 Limekiln Pike, Ambler, 215-646-1294
▶ Paws to Heaven Pet Crematory, 5301 Tacony Street, Philadelphia, 215-744-4400
▶ Pet Cremation Service, 2621 Philmont Avenue, Huntingdon Valley, 215-947-9970
▶ Pet Memorial Services, 319 Westtown Road, West Chester, 610-430-7978
▶ Pet Rest Park (White Chapel Gardens Memorial Park), 140 West Street Road, Langhorne, 215-357-8463
▶ Pets Are People Too, 2449 Golf Road, Philadelphia, 215-871-7682. Services include burial, cremation, pet removal, transfer to final disposition, urns, caskets, embalming, refrigeration, taxidermy referral, limousine service.
▶ Philadelphia Pet Funeral Services, 5126 Roosevelt Boulevard, Philadelphia, 215-533-1225
▶ Portrait Urns by Twila R. Herot, 2000 Three Mile Run Road, Perkasie, 215-453-0432, www.whiteshepherd.com/urns/urnindex.htm
▶ Tri-County Pet Cemetery, 44 Swamp Pike, Royersford, 610-495-3010

New Jersey

▶ PetFriends, P.O. Box 131, Moorestown, NJ 08057, 800-404-PETS. A pet grief hotline.
▶ Pet Friends for Pet Loss Grief, Merchantville, 856-667-1717
▶ Pet Lawn Memorial Park, State Route 73, Berlin, 856-767-1564
▶ Pet Lawn Memorial Park, Merchantville, 856-663-1508

❖ PET WASTE REMOVAL

Yes, there really are people who will clean up after your dog for you—they'll come as often as you like and de-poopify your yard.

Pennsylvania

▶ Doggie Bags, 1465 Makefield Road, Morrisville, 215-736-9255. They also provide pet-sitting services, daily exercise, gift baskets, and pet portraits.
▶ Four Paws Scooper Service, P.O. Box 1461, Blue Bell, PA 19422, 610-275-4235, Ddixon@seic.com

New Jersey

▶ Messy Paws, 211 Prospect Avenue, Audubon, 856-546-3974
▶ Major Doody's Dog Waste Removal Service, 908-672-8059, www.majordoody.com,

mastogen@aol.com. They provide bonded and insured service in all New Jersey counties, twice a week, weekly, or biweekly.

PET TRANSPORTATION SERVICES

Pennsylvania

▶ **Best Friends Express, Lansdowne, 610-284-9969; Philadelphia, 215-969-9003**
▶ **Main Line Pet Limousine, 610-525-5851**
▶ **Pets Come First, Southampton, 215-942-7846**

DOGGY DAY CARE AND CANINE RESORTS

This is a growing phenomenon for working and traveling doggy parents. Below are day care and boarding places that go far beyond your run-of-the-mill kennel.

Pennsylvania

▶ **A Better Way, 258 Auburn Road, Landenberg, 610-274-0553.** Boarding and pet sitting with a training twist, provided by Susan Strickland, the obedience instructor for the Philadelphia Dog Training Club. I've seen her in action: there is no dog she can't handle, and dogs love her.
▶ **A Home Away from Home Kennel, 428 Brownsburg Road, Newtown, 215-598-3951.** The kennel is located at Keystone Veterinary Hospital. Your dog can not only get loving vet-supervised care here, he or she can enjoy outside exercise—including swimming!
▶ **All Breeds Kennels, 4115 East Swamp Road, Doylestown, 215-348-7605.** This is a small kennel catering (literally) to people whose dogs normally enjoy home-cooked meals: they will cook your dog's food during his or her stay. They also operate a mobile grooming van.
▶ **Amber Beech Kennels, 1040 Taylorsville Road, Washington Crossing, 215-493-2201.** Along with large, individual indoor/outdoor runs, they have separate kennels for small dogs, and will provide pickup and delivery service.
▶ **Animal Country Resort, 92 Level Road, Collegeville, 610-489-2424, www.animal countryresort.baweb.com.** Features include day care and boarding, a fitness center with treadmill walks, hiking, and Yappy Hour, complete with doggy ice cream and birthday surprises.
▶ **Animal Inn of Richboro, 700 2nd Street Pike, Richboro, 215-364-2088.** Besides offering climate-controlled boarding, they will bathe and groom your dog if you so desire, and dogs can enjoy indoor/outdoor exercise runs during their stay.
▶ **Animal Resorts, 301 Jefferis Road, Downingtown, 610-942-0388, www.animalresorts .com.** This facility is sited on 16 acres that include indoor/outdoor kennels, a grooming shop, a training area (indoors and out), fenced land, nature trails, an agility field, and a creek with a waterfall and pond. Boarding includes an indoor, heated, sunny room with an outdoor patio area. Playtime, laundry service, supervised play with other dogs, hiking and swimming, and even massages are available for your dog to enjoy. Animal Resorts also offers doggy day care.

▶ **Barks N Purrs Plus, Broomall, 610-353-1846.** This bonded and insured company provides either boarding or in-home sitting. They offer progress notes on your dog's daily routine, 24-hour emergency family service, and a pet fitness program. The company is a member of Pet Sitters International.

▶ **Beech Hill Kennels, 2626 Murray Avenue, Bensalem, 215-639-5789.** They offer large, individual indoor and outdoor runs, heat and air conditioning, pickup and delivery, a walking service, and even personalized diets.

▶ **Bow Wow Boutique, 132 Hansen Access Road, King of Prussia, 610-265-3646.** They provide doggy day care and long-term boarding in a climate-controlled facility. Your dog can enjoy indoor and outdoor runs, playtime, and quality care, including administration of necessary medications. Grooming is also available.

▶ **Buttonwood Animal Inne, 30 Meng Road, Schwenksville, 610-287-6251.** They offer country boarding in a climate-controlled environment, with individual indoor/outdoor runs. Grooming is available.

▶ **C M Kennel, 106 West Lancaster Pike, Malvern, 610-644-6918.** This is a clean, comfortable, climate-controlled facility, with large indoor/outdoor exercise runs and stereo entertainment. Your dog can stay daily or weekly, and grooming is available.

▶ **Club Canine, Chambley & Co., 621 South 21st Street, Philadelphia, 215-545-6730.** Fun, safe day care for your dog, with supervised play, nap time, and brushing. Chambley & Co. also provides daily dog-walking services.

▶ **Club Le Pooch and the Feline Penthouse, at the Old Marple Veterinary Hospital, 820 West Springfield Road, Springfield, 610-328-1300.** This is a climate-controlled facility with individual, outdoor exercise runs, as well as an enclosed $^1/_{10}$-acre play yard.

▶ **Contented Pets Sitter Service by Marcia Pilotti, Berwyn, 610-647-1283 or 610-644-3661.** This service provides doggy day care and boarding in a private home, where your dog can enjoy personalized care, and pool privileges in the summer. In-home daily visits are available.

▶ **Country Kennel & Pet Resort, 1375 Yellow Springs Road, Paoli, 610-648-0917.** This kennel is family-owned and -operated, with recently renovated, state-of-the-art facilities. Your dog can enjoy indoor/outdoor runs, central air conditioning, and an exercise and play yard, all on the 32-acre, fenced Great Scott Horse Farm.

▶ **Doggie World Daycare, 858–862 North 3rd Street, Philadelphia, 215-238-7200.** They are open daily for day care and boarding. Facilities include an 8,000-square-foot, fenced dog park for supervised play. Pickup and delivery service is available.

▶ **Eagle Kennel, 931 Pottstown Pike (Route 100), Chester Springs, 610-458-5900, www.eaglekennel.com.** Lots of amenities are offered, including extra-large indoor/outdoor runs, a large, grassy play area with supervised playtime, central air conditioning and heat, a security system, individualized meals, treats, and medication—and classical music playing throughout the kennel, along with a big-screen TV! Grooming service is also available.

▶ **Elkins Park Boarding Kennels, 315 Township Line Road, Elkins Park, 215-379-2747.** This newly renovated facility includes 24-hour surveillance of the animals, outdoor exercise facilities, and both a groomer and a vet on the premises.

▶ **4 Legged Kids, 1215 East Lancaster Avenue, Bryn Mawr, 610-527-0540.** They offer doggy day care, Monday through Friday, with lots of play opportunities, and your dog can be groomed if you want. Rumor has it they may begin doing doggy birthday parties soon. They also offer overnight doggy camp through the summer (May 1 to September 30). You can pack up your dog's food, toys, and other belongings to keep in a personal storage space, and your dog can enjoy camping out at night and playing during the day.

▶ **George's All Breeds Groom and Board, Willow Grove, 215-947-7605.** This is a climate-controlled boarding facility with 100 kennels, outdoor areas and runs, and a play yard.

▶ **Holiday House Pet Resort, 380 North Shady Retreat Road, Doylestown, 215-345-6960.** This facility offers climate-controlled boarding in the country, with suites of various sizes, all with adjoining patios. A daily report card lets you know how your dog did during his or her stay. There are fenced areas with views, where the staff will throw a Frisbee for your dog and give him or her a hug. They provide quality food or will serve food you bring from home. Your dog can also enjoy a therapeutic bath and be brushed. Pickup and delivery service is available.

▶ **Kennel of Frazer, 25 Davis Avenue, Malvern, 610-296-8330.** This facility doesn't use dog-runs: instead, they have a fenced yard, including a low-level agility course. "Luxury packages" are available.

▶ **Laurel Lane Farm, 412 Swamp Road, Newtown, 215-968-2500.** They offer full-service boarding with indoor/outdoor runs, and grooming is available.

▶ **Mackensen Kennels, 1085 Reading Avenue, Yardley, 215-493-2717.** This facility has been in operation for 100 years. They have indoor/outdoor runs and a dog-related retail store. Grooming is available.

▶ **Molly's Run Country Kennels, 2205 Wentz Church Road, Lansdale, 610-584-6515.** Providing doggy day care as well as boarding, in climate-controlled runs, Molly's Run Country Kennels will offer your dog walking, swimming, hiking—and barbecues.

▶ **Noah's Pet Farm & Motel, 1661 South Hanover Street, Pottstown, 610-323-2206.** This is a climate-controlled facility offering spacious, indoor rooms with connecting covered outdoor runs. A personalized play area is available.

▶ **Pets Are Inn, 299 West Main Street, Lansdale, 215-412-7387, www.petsareinn.com.** And now for something completely different: "No kennels, no cages, no strangers in your home," the advertisement said. It was like a riddle—but the solution is great. Pets Are Inn is an alternative to both kennels and in-home sitting: they will place your beloved dog in a carefully screened host family's home, where he or she can enjoy constant personal attention—petting, playing, walking, a comfortable place to sleep, and food the way your pet wants it. You send along your dog's toys, blankets, and treats, and a note with extra information, including any medication instructions. The idea is to maintain your dog's routine as closely as possible. Pets Are Inn serves Bucks and Montgomery Counties, and all areas along the Blue Route (Interstate 476).

▶ **R and B Dog Service, Levittown, 215-547-7687.** This is a variety of services in one: do-it-yourself dog-wash facilities, grooming with playtime in a yard, and dog-walking, dog-sitting, boarding, and yard waste removal services. If it is dog-related, chances are R and B does it.

▶ **Sanmann Kennels Limited, 1825 Diamond Street, Sellersville, 215-257-7375.** They offer indoor/outdoor runs, walks, and community playtime. Grooming and training are available.

▶ **Steward's Pet Resort, 3914 Pyle Road, Chadds Ford, 610-459-1534.** This is a Best Friends Pet Resort & Salon (see page 181 for a Best Friends in New Jersey), and that means a somewhat luxurious place for your best friend to stay. Spacious doggy suites offer lamb-skin bedding and "daily maid service." Daily playtimes, from passive to active, can be scheduled. They offer state-of-the-art grooming services, training, and treats after meals, and will keep medical, personality, and special-needs records on your canine.

- **Town & Country Kennels, 393 Langhorne Avenue, Langhorne, 215-752-3661.** These state-of-the-art facilities feature modern, solar, climate-controlled kennels. The staff will provide pickup and delivery service anywhere in Philadelphia and the suburbs, as well as make flight arrangements and provide ground transportation if you are having your dog travel after you. During his or her stay, your dog can enjoy at least twice-daily walks with 10 to 15 minutes of exercise, oversized dog-runs, twice-daily feedings (or any other arrangement you request), IAMS or Science Diet food (or food you bring from home), and playtime activities tailored to your dog. They have an in-house vet.
- **Windruff Kennels, Coventryville Road, Pottstown, 610-469-6430.** This climate-controlled facility provides your dog with an indoor/outdoor run, walks, and playtime in a 1-acre fenced area. Grooming is also available.
- **Wonmanog Kennels, 108 Union Road, Coatesville, 610-384-6365.** This is a modern facility in a quiet country setting, with large, fenced exercise areas.

New Jersey

- **Barking Hills Country Club, 765 Frenchtown Road, Milford, 908-996-9911, www.barking hills.com.** About 1.5 miles from Frenchtown is a place so amazing it just has to be included here. Your dog can't stay overnight here. Neither can you. But there are hotels nearby where you both can stay, and during the day, you can spend some vacation time at Barking Hills. The club encompasses 7 acres of fields, woods, and streams, with a 4-plus-acre, fenced open space surrounded by another 6-foot-high, double-gated fence for safety. In this setting, you and your dog can try all kinds of activities for the sheer fun of it—and you may find you like something so much you both want to pursue it in competition. Agility, flyball, carting, lure coursing, tracking, herding, and even tunneling (for earth dogs like my Meg) are some of the things you and your dog may sample. Or get in some extra obedience training, or even training for pet-assisted therapy. It's a great place—check it out!
- **Best Friends Pet Resort & Salon, 585 Route 73 North, West Berlin, 609-719-0888.** See full description under Steward's Pet Resort, in Chadds Ford, Pennsylvania, on page 180.
- **Breezewood Kennels, 216 Hartford Road, Medford, 609-654-2140.** This kennel features indoor/outdoor runs and an exercise program. Grooming is also available.
- **Clif Wyck Farms Boarding Kennels, Kenilworth Road (off Route 73), Marlton, 856-983-3050.** This climate-controlled facility features a quiet, country setting, indoor/outdoor runs, personal attention, and an owner who lives on the premises. An exercise program is available, as are day care and grooming.
- **Country Kennel, 2750 Egg Harbor Road, Lindenwold, 856-784-4559.** They offer large, indoor/outdoor dog-runs, a playtime program, doggy pool parties, and a treat cart at bedtime. The owners live on the premises.
- **Lakeside Kennel & Cattery, 341 Route 73, Voorhees, 856-424-1768.** Offering climate-controlled day care and boarding, they feature a 1.5-acre, fenced exercise area. Grooming is available.
- **Pet Country Club, 1040 State Route 12, Frenchtown, 908-996-7200.** You can board your dog here and know that walks and 20-minute play dates will be part of his or her stay. The club provides pickup and delivery service within a reasonable distance, and grooming is available. They also have an extraordinary training center, providing training and socialization for overly aggressive dogs that have been given one last chance to become good citizens. I like that a lot.

IN-HOME PET SITTERS

An alternative to boarding your dog, or a way to make sure there are no accidents while you are at work, pet sitters are proliferating, and most are very professional. Pet sitters may offer daily visits or overnight stays, will feed, water, and administer any required medication to your dog, and may even collect mail, water plants, and turn lights on and off for security while you're away on a trip. Many leave a daily log of your dog's activities and moods while you are gone. It's a great way to avoid pestering your relatives, friends, and neighbors, while providing your dog with the security of routine in the comfort of his or her own home.

Pennsylvania

- **Animal Care Services, 2404 Spruce Street, Philadelphia, 215-772-9247.** Insured and bonded, they provide in-home pet sitting and daily dog exercise 365 days a year.
- **Animal Instincts Pet & House Sitting Services, 224 Gravel Pike, Perkiomenville, 610-489-1034.** Specializing in aggressive dogs, they will also sit for sheep and horses.
- **Around Town Pet Services, 4th and Vine Streets, Philadelphia, 215-922-6798.** They provide pet-walking services.
- **Brandywine Pet Pals, Chadds Ford, 610-358-0811, www.brandywinepetpals.com.** In-home sitting services include feeding, watering, walking, and playing with your dog, either while you are on vacation, or as a break while you're at work. They will collect mail and perform other house-sitting services during your vacations. The company is insured, bonded, and a member of both the National Association of Professional Pet Sitters (NAPPS) and Pet Sitters International (PSI). It serves a 10-mile radius around Chadds Ford.
- **Bucks County Pet Services, 183 South Woodbine Avenue, Langhorne, 215-757-8440.** In-home pet care—in your home or theirs. They are bonded and insured, and offer daily dog walking.
- **Canine to Equine Pet Sitters, 10 Amy Lane, Malvern, 610-251-2159.** Bonded and insured, and a member of NAPPS, they offer at-home TLC while owners are on vacation, traveling, or at work, seven days a week, year-round. During daily visits, they will feed, water, exercise, and play with your dog, as well as administer medications. Daily midday walks and housewatching services are also available.
- **Charlene's Pet Sitting Service, Norristown, 610-489-3880.** Daily in-home visits include feeding and companionship. Dog-walking and pet taxi services are available. Fully insured and bonded.
- **Creature Comforts of West Philadelphia, 215-729-6889, fattitude.frogspace.net/cs .html.** They provide dog-sitting and house-sitting services, including feeding, walking, administering medicine, collecting mail, watering plants, and turning lights on and off for security.
- **Creature Comforts Petcare, 3441 Ainslie Street, Philadelphia, 215-438-2769.** They offer dog walking, quality-time pet sitting, and personalized care.
- **Critter Companions, 677 Farnum Road, Media, 610-565-2781, www.crittercompanions .com.** A member of NAPPS, and bonded and insured. They provide daily dog walking, and in-home pet sitting including an unlimited number of visits per day, fresh food and water,

yard clean-up, and administration of medication. They will also collect mail, water plants, and turn lights on and off for security. They even have a resident artist who can draw or paint a portrait of your dog.

▶ **Critter Sitter, Morrisville, 215-428-0154, www.veternet.com/CritterSitter.html.** Calls are monitored 24 hours a day. A member of PSI, Critter Sitter will provide fresh water and bedding for your dog, feed him or her (including accommodating special dietary needs), walk or run and play with your dog, administer medication, and do some basic grooming. House-sitting services are provided as well. Areas served include Langhorne, Morrisville, Newtown, Yardley, and Washington Crossing.

▶ **Dog Gone It, 720 Hamilton Road, Bryn Mawr, 610-517-3886.** They offer complete in-home pet care, and a pet waste removal service.

▶ **Family Pet Sitting Services, 443 Old Elm Street, Conshohocken, 610-834-1891.** They will make personal visits to your home to walk, feed, exercise, and play with your dog. Bonded and insured.

▶ **For Pets Sake, Audubon, 610-666-6624.** They provide pet sitting in your home; daily visits include feeding, walking, companionship, and TLC. Bonded and insured.

▶ **Happy at Home, Exton, 610-363-5212; Phoenixville, 610-933-9255.** They provide daily visits, loving pet care, overnight care, and exercise. Insured and bonded.

▶ **Happy Tails Pet Sitting, Warrington, 215-491-1155.** They offer at-home pet sitting, dog walking, home care, administration of medications, and overnight sleepovers.

▶ **Home Alone Pets, Glenolden, 610-586-3950.** An insured member of NAPPS offering daily walks and complete in-home care.

▶ **Home and Pet Watch, 225 Fox Road, Media, 610-566-4558.** A member of PSI, bonded and insured, they provide feeding, watering, walking, overnight house sitting, health care maintenance, home care, and more.

▶ **Home Sitting Services of Main Line, Bryn Mawr, 610-525-6114.** They offer at-home pet-sitting and pet-tending services, 24 hours a day, seven days a week. Bonded and insured.

▶ **In Demand, Bala Cynwyd, 215-878-6108.** An insured and bonded member of NAPPS, they offer in-home care, and can be paged for last-minute needs.

▶ **Irish Sitter, 1797 Janney Lane, Morrisville, 215-493-7459.** Offering in-home pet sitting, they will also water plants, and more. Bonded and insured.

▶ **Lee's Pampered Pets, 111 Freedom Valley Circle, Coatesville, 610-383-6211.** Lee's offers at-home pet sitting.

▶ **LOV IN Care, 402 Rosewood Avenue, Trevose, 215-355-9023.** They provide in-home sitting and customized pet care. Bonded and insured.

▶ **Love 'M & Leave 'M Home, 610-541-0294, www.geocities.com/Petsburgh/Park/1488.** A member of PSI, serving Delaware, Chester, and Montgomery Counties. They offer daily care, will make veterinary appointments for you, will care for pets with special needs, and provide overnight stays on request. House-sitting services are also available.

▶ **Mary Ellen's Pet Sitting, 2316 Belmont Avenue, Ardmore, 610-642-6244.** They provide in-home pet care, daily walks, and care while owners are away. Bonded and insured.

▶ **My Buddy Pet Sitting, Southampton, 215-942-0780, www.mybuddy.baweb.com.** Personalized in-home care provided by a bonded and insured member of PSI. Feeding, exercising, and administration of medications will all be taken care of. House-sitting services are also provided while you're away. And they'll write a daily log detailing how your dog's day was.

- **No Furry Worries, Bryn Mawr, 610-526-2767.** A bonded and insured member of NAPPS providing at-home care while owners are working or traveling.
- **Noah's Bark In-Home Pet Care, Newtown Square, 610-356-0159.** A bonded and insured member of NAPPS and PSI, available on short notice. They will visit your home as many times a day as you want, and will walk, feed, and play with your dog and provide any necessary special care. They offer a daily walking service and transportation to regular vet appointments or grooming. They will also water plants and collect mail if owners are away.
- **Pet Nanny, Philadelphia, 215-868-5278, www.petnanny.net.** They offer daily exercise and feedings, and personalized care.
- **Pet Sitters Unlimited, Wayne, 610-935-2577, www.petsittersunlimited.net.** At-home care by licensed veterinary nurse Kim Champy, offering puppy care while you work, or in-home care while you vacation. Kim also offers midday walks if you work long hours. Pet Sitters is available 365 days a year, checks for messages often, and has pagers for emergencies. Serving most of the upper Main Line, Pet Sitters specializes in the care of pets with medical conditions.
- **Precious Pet Professional Pet Sitting Service, 514 North Pennsylvania Avenue, Morrisville, 215-736-9558.** Service provided by a veterinary technician who specializes in dogs with medical needs, serving Bucks County.
- **Priceless Pets, 4412 Longshore Avenue, Philadelphia, 215-624-2461.** Provides midday walks or at-home pet sitting during your vacation. They will also water plants and turn lights on and off.
- **TLC Pet Sitting, Haverford, 610-649-2321.** Bonded and insured, they offer in-home care and daily dog walking.
- **Wags to Whiskers, Malvern, 610-644-5816.** They offer in-home care, and will respond to an emergency pager. Insured and bonded.

New Jersey

- **Creature Comforts Pet Sitting, 526 Hanover Avenue, Cherry Hill, 856-661-0078**
- **Little Critters Pet Sitting Service, Hammonton, 856-768-4004.** A member of Pet Sitters International.
- **Pals for Pets, 121 West Park Avenue, Haddonfield, 856-428-0221**
- **Pet Patrol, 125 Lotus Avenue, Voorhees, 856-216-9636**
- **Pet Sitting by K-9 Masters, Merchantville, 856-665-0215**
- **Pet Sitting by Sue, 276 Kingwood Station Barbeto Road, Frenchtown, 908-996-2731**
- **Rusty's Pet Sitting Service, 12 Pine Avenue, Bordentown, 609-291-9551**
- **S&R Pet Sitting Service, Moorestown, 856-234-8887.** All at-home services are provided.

❖ MOBILE GROOMERS

Another growing phenomenon is the mobile grooming van—instead of your having to take your dog to the groomer, the groomer will come to your dog. Providers of this service include:

▶ **Cleo's Salon on Wheels, 529 Stanbridge Street, Norristown, PA, 610-272-8886.** A fully equipped van for stress-free grooming comes to your house; evening and weekend appointments are available. Owner Jennifer Farnum used to be a veterinary technician.

▶ **Curbside K-9 & Feline Mobile Grooming, Morrisville, PA, 215-295-8658.** Boasts a state-of-the-art, climate-controlled grooming van.

▶ **Going to the Dogs, Glenside, PA, 215-887-3647**

▶ **Going to the Dogs, 87 Katie Drive, Langhorne, PA, 215-579-7078.** Provides grooming service from a fully equipped van.

▶ **Grooming Express, 12 Kenmore Road, Yardley, PA, 215-295-7297.** A state-of-the-art, mobile pet salon. They use natural products and no tranquilizers.

▶ **Lucky Dogs Mobile Grooming, 4836 Danielle Drive, Buckingham, PA, 215-794-0322**

▶ **Pooch Caboose Mobile Dog Grooming, Southampton, PA, 215-364-4433**

▶ **Ty-D-Paws Express, Collingswood, NJ, 856-854-4771.** Offers mobile pet grooming in a self-contained grooming van.

▶ **Waggin' Tails, MacDade Boulevard, Darby, PA, 610-461-6878.** Offers at-home grooming, rather than mobile grooming, for people and dogs who for one reason or another cannot go out to a groomer.

APPENDIX C

Pet-Oriented Businesses

Agway Collegeville Yard-Garden-Pet Place
Animal Kingdom Pet Store
Bathe Your Pet
Bow Wow
Braxton's Animal Works
Bristol Feed & Grain Company
Bryn Mawr Feed & Seed Company
Chester County SPCA Gift Shop
City Critters
Creatures Feeds & Needs
Dr. Marc's Animal Crackers
Dogomat
Happy Hound, The
Lansdale Feed & Pet Supply
Lick Your Chops
Little Hearts
Natural Instincts
Paws & Claws Pet Shoppe
Peaches & Gable
Pet Diner (multiple locations)
Pet Fantasy
Pet Valu (multiple locations)
PETCO (multiple locations)
PetsMart (multiple locations)
Pickering Valley Feed & Farm
Rittenhouse Square Pet Supply
Three Dog Bakery
Velvet Paws

Eateries

Albrecht's Gourmet Market
America Bar & Grill
Back Porch Café
Baskin-Robbins

Bean Café
Beau Monde
Bertucci's Brick Oven Pizzeria
Berwyn Coffee Company
Blue Ox Brauhaus Restaurant
Borders Café
Boston Market
Broadway Deli & Café
Bruno's Restaurant
Bucks County Coffee Company
Café Procopio
Cafette
C'est La Vie
Charcoal Steaks N' Things
Chloe's Water Ice & Ice Cream
Continental Restaurant & Martini Bar
Cornerstone Café
Cresheim Cottage Café
Dairy Queen (multiple locations)
Devon Seafood Grill
Dock Street Brasserie
Elizabethan Tea Shop
Fairmount Bagel Institute
Fifty's Drive-In Restaurant
Fill A Bagel
Food Source by Clemens
Fork
Freddy Hill Farms
Gallery Café
Garden Gate Café
General Lafayette Inn & Brewery
General Warren Inne
Geno's
Giuseppe's Pizza and Family Restaurant
Harrington's Coffee Company
Hartefeld National Golf Course

Havana
Irish Bread Shoppe
Jamaican Jerk Hut
Juice & Java
La Patisserie Francaise
Landing Restaurant
Langhorne Coffee House
Le Bus Main Street
Lucy's Hat Shop Restaurant and Lounge
Mace's Crossing
Main Street Bakery Café
Main-LY Desserts
Mal's American Diner
Manhattan Bagel
Marmont
McDonald's (multiple locations)
Millennium Coffee
MontSerrat American Bistro
Mother Bruce's Café
Night Kitchen
Paradise Found
Pat's King of Steaks
Peacock on the Parkway
Penn's Table Restaurant
Petrucci's Dairy Barn
Philadelphia Fish & Co.
Philadelphia Java Company
Point, The
Renzulli's
Rhino Café
Rita's Water Ice (multiple locations)
Robin's Nest Bakery & Café
Rouge
Spice Smuggler, The
Spring Mill Café
Square Bar, The
Starbucks (multiple locations)
Station Café, The
Station Café & Juice Bar
Stellar Coffee
Ted's Lakeside Deli
Trax Café
Two Sisters Ala Mode
UMMM Ice Cream Parlor
Valley Green Inn
Walter's Swiss Pastries
White Dog Café
Wildflowers Restaurant and Garden
    Café
xando Coffee & Bar (multiple locations)
Zagara's

Lodgings

Aaron Burr House
Abbey Green Motor Lodge
Best Western Center City Hotel
Best Western Inn (multiple locations)
Brandywine River Hotel
Clarion Suites
Comfort Inn (multiple locations)
Courtyard by Marriott
Crowne Plaza Philadelphia
Days Inn (multiple locations)
Four Seasons Hotel
Frenchtown National Hotel
Haddonfield Inn
Hampton Inn (multiple locations)
Hilton at Cherry Hill
Holiday Inn (multiple locations)
Holiday Inn Express
Homestead Village
Inn at Plymouth Meeting
Korman Suites (multiple locations)
Marriott, Center City
Marriott, Philadelphia Airport
Motel 6 (multiple locations)
New Hope Motel in the Woods
Park Hyatt Philadelphia at the Bellevue
Radisson Hotel
Ramada Inn, Airport
Red Roof Inn (multiple locations)
Residence Inn by Marriott (multiple
    locations)
Rittenhouse Hotel
Summerfield Suites Hotel (multiple
    locations)
Ten-Eleven Clinton
Track & Turf Motel
Umpleby House
Warwick Hotel
Wedgwood House

Miscellaneous Shopping

Active Acres
A.G.A. Farms
Boswell's Cut-Your-Own Christmas Tree
    Farm (2 locations)
Bradford Nursery
Bryan's Farm
Chester Springs Tree Farm
Coventree Farm
D'Angelo Bros.

Dilworth Lawn Ornaments
Firehouse Gallery
Golden Nugget Antique and Flea Market
Grist Mill Craftsmen's Village & Market
Hilltown Garden & Flea Market
Holly Ridge Tree Farm
J. Franklin Styer Nurseries
Kulpsville Antique and Flea Market
Kutz Christmas Tree Farm
Laurel Hill Gardens
Lucca's Christmas Tree Farm
Mapes 5 & 10
Montgomery Nurseries
Narberth Video
Peddler's Village
Penn's Purchase Factory Outlet Stores
Petrongolo Evergreen Plantation
Phillips Nurseries
Pleasant Valley Tree Farm
Pond View Tree Farm
Rancocas Woods Village of Shops
Rogers Road Stand and Garden Center
Schmidt's Christmas Tree Farm
Shops of Chesterbrook
Smith & Hawken (multiple locations)
Spread Eagle Village
Suburban Square
Tricolor Tree Farm
Tuckamony Christmas Tree Farm
Westlake Tree Farm
Windridge Farm
Yard Co.
Yeager's Cut-Your-Own Tree Farm

Trails   (many parks also contain trails)

Batona Trail
Batsto Pond Nature Trail
Brandywine River Trail
Creek Road Trail
Delaware & Raritan Canal State Park
    Towpath
Delaware Canal State Park Towpath
Green Ribbon Preserve Trail
Horse-Shoe Hiking Trail
Leiper-Smedley Trail
Mason-Dixon Hiking Trail
Middletown Trail
Pennypack Creek Trail
Pennypack Parkway
River Walk Trail
Schuylkill River Trail
Struble Trail

Sites

American College
American Swedish Historical Museum
Antique Row
Arch Street United Methodist Church
Atsion Village
Azalea Garden
Barns-Brinton House
Bartram's Gardens
Betsy Ross House
Boathouse Row
Bonnie's Bridge
Brandywine River Museum
Bristol Lagoon
Bryn Mawr College
Buckingham Valley Vineyards and
    Winery
Bucks County Horse Park
Caleb Pusey House & Landingford
    Plantation
Chaddsford Winery
Chelsea Village
Clifton House
Cliveden
Delaware Canal Locktender's House
Deshler-Morris House
Devon Horse Show Grounds
Downingtown Log House
Drexel University
Edgar Allan Poe National Historic Site
Elfreth's Alley
Fairmount Water Works
Finley House
Fonthill
Fort Mifflin
Founders Garden
Franklin Court
Freedoms Foundation at Valley Forge
French Creek Ridge Vineyards
Gatehouse at Colestown Cemetery
Gloria Dei (Old Swedes') Church
Griffith Morgan Homestead
Growden Mansion
Grumblethorpe
Hamilton Walk
Harriton House
Haverford College
Hibernia Mansion
Highlands, The
Historic Batsto Village
Historic Fallsington
Historic Whitesbog Village

Historic Yellow Springs
Holcombe-Jimison Farmstead
Hollywood
Hope Lodge
Hopewell Furnace National Historic
   Site
Horticulture Center
Independence Square
Jenkins Homestead
John Chads House
John F. Kennedy Plaza
John Woolman House
Kirby's Mill
Lansdowne Theatre
Locust Walk
Loudon Mansion
Ludwig's Corner Horse Show Grounds
Malvern Preparatory School
Mather Mill
Mennonite Heritage Center
Mercer Museum
Merion Tribute House
Moravian Tile Works
Morton Homestead
Mummers Museum
New Hope Winery
Oakbourne Mansion
Old Mill, The
Old Schoolhouse, The
Old Veterinary Hospital, The
Paoli Battlefield Site and Parade Grounds
Paper Mill House Museum
Peace Valley Winery
Pearl S. Buck House
Pen Ryn Mansion on the Delaware
Penn's Landing
Pennypacker Mills
Peter Wentz Farmstead
Piers 3 and 5
Pomona Hall
Pottsgrove Manor
Prallsville Mills
Quadrangle, The
Radnor Hunt
Reading Terminal Headhouse
Rittenhouse Town
Rosemont College
Rushland Ridge Vineyards Winery
St. Joseph's University
Samuel Coles House
Sansom Common
Sansom Row

Sculpture Garden at Burlington County
   College
Shady Brook Farm
Smith Walk
Smithbridge Winery
Sunrise Mill
Swarthmore College
Swedish Log Cabin
Temple University (Philadelphia and
   Ambler campuses)
Thomas Massey House
Twentieth Century Club of Lansdowne
University of Pennsylvania
Ursinus College
Villanova University
Washington Square
Waynesborough
Welkinweir
West Chester University
Willowdale Steeplechase

Parks/Recreation Spaces

Andorra Natural Area
Anson B. Nixon Park
Arboretum Villanova
Ashland Park
Atsion Lake Recreation Area
Austin Memorial Park
Awbury Arboretum
Barclay Farmstead
Barness Park (Warminster)
Barness Park (Warrington)
Bass River State Forest
Batsto Natural Area
Benjamin Rush State Park
Berlin County Park
Bicentennial Park
Black Ditch County Park
Black Rock Road Site
Blanche Levy Park
Blooming Glen Playground
Bob Bende Park
Bob Meyer Memorial Park
Bob White Park
Borough Park (Dublin)
Bradford Dam Park
Brandywine Battlefield Park
Bristol Marsh
Burholme Park
Burpee Park
Canal View Park
Carpenter Park

Carpenter Woods
Center City Dog Park
Central Park
Central Perkiomen Valley County Park
Challenge Grove County Park
Chapman Park
Chickenfoot Park
Chrome Barrens
Churchville County Park
Cianfrani Park
Clark Park
Clayton County Park
Cobbs Creek Park
Colwell Park
Community Center Park
Community Fields Park
Cooper River Dog Run
Cooper River Park
Core Creek County Park
Coventry Park
Cranberry Hall Park
Croft Farm
Crow's Nest Preserve
Curtis Arboretum
Cynwyd Station Park
Dark Hollow County Park
Deep Meadow Park
Delaware & Raritan Canal State Park
Delaware Canal State Park
Delaware River Access Area
Dr. Ulysses S. Wiggins Waterfront Park
Dodge Preserve
Dog Park (Orianna Hill Park)
Dudley Grange
Eagleville Park
East Plymouth Valley Park
East Rockhill Township Park
Eaton Park
Eco Valley Nature Park
Eden Hall (Fluehr) Park
Edward Hicks Parry Bird Sanctuary
Elmwood Park
Emlen Tunnel Park
Evansburg State Park
Everhart Park
Executive Estates Park
Fairmount Park
Falls of the Delaware County Park
Falls Riverfront Park
Fallsington County Park
Farnham Park

Fitler Square
Fonthill
Fort Washington State Park
Franklin Delano Roosevelt Park
Freedom Park
French Creek State Park
Front & Chestnut Dog Park
Frosty Hollow County Park
Fugett Park
General Wayne Park
George A. Perley Bird Sanctuary
Glen Foerd
Glen Providence Park
Gorgas Park
Goshenhoppen Park
Governor Printz State Park
Graeme Park
Green Acres Park
Green Field Park
Green Lane Park
Grove Park
Grundy Park
Guinea Lane Park
Gwynedd Wildlife Preserve
Gypsy Woods/Gulph Mills Preserve
Haddon Lake Park
Hal H. Clark County Park
Hampton Chase Park
Hansell Park
Harford Park
Harriet Wetherill Park
Henry Lane Park
Henry Schmieder Arboretum of Delaware
    Valley College
Hibernia County Park
Hidden Pond Park
Hideaway Hills Park
High School Park
Hildacy Farm
Hillside Park
Hilltown Civic Park
Holicong Park
Hoopes Park
Hopewell Furnace National Historic Site
Hopkins Pond County Park
Horace J. Quann Memorial Park
Hunting Park
Igoe Porter Wellings Park
Independence National Historical Park
Ivy Woods
Jarret Road Park

John F. Kennedy Park
John Heinz National Wildlife Refuge
Kelly Park
Kemper Park
Kenealy Nature Park
Kennett Firehouse Picnic Park
Kent Park
Knight Park
Kohler Park
Krupp Memorial Park
Lake Lenape Park
Lansdale Park
Laurel Acres Park
Lebanon State Forest
Lewis W. Barton Arboretum and Nature
 Preserve at Medford Leas
Liberty Lands
Log College Park
Lorimer County Park
Lower Nike Park
Lower Perkiomen Valley County Park
Magill's Hill Park
Maple Park
Maria Barnaby Greenwald County Park
Market Square Memorial Park
Market Street Park
Marsh Creek State Park
Marshall Square
McKaig Nature Education Center
Medford Park
Meetinghouse Road Park
Memorial Fountain and Park (Bristol
 Borough)
Memorial Park (Hatboro)
Memorial Park (Langhorne)
Memorial Park (Lansdale)
Memorial Park (Pottstown)
Memorial Park (West Chester)
Menlo Park
Merchantville Mile
Merion Square Road Site
Mill Creek Valley Park
Miller Park
Moland House Park
Mondauk Manor Park
Mosteller Park
Mount Pleasant Park
Munro Park
Myrick Conservation Center
Natural Lands Trust 1
Natural Lands Trust 2

Neshaminy State Park
New Britain Covered Bridge Park
New Camden Park
Newlin Grist Mill
Newton Lake Park
Nield Street Park
Nockamixon State Park
Norristown Farm County Park
Nottingham County Park
Oakbourne Park
Oxford Valley County Park
Palomino Park
Parkview Road Park
Pastorius Park
Pat Livezey Park
Peace Valley County Park
Pencoyd Park
Pennsbury Municipal Park
Pennypack Creek Park
Pennypacker County Park
Pinelands National Reserve
Playwicki County Park
Plymouth Hills Park
Plymouth Meeting Park
Prahl's Island
Queen Anne County Park
Ralph Morgan Park
Ralph Stover State Park
Rancocas State Park
Reeves Park
Reservoir Park
Ridley Creek State Park and National
 Historic Site
Rittenhouse Square
Riverbend Environmental Education
 Center
Riverfront Park (Norristown)
Riverfront Park (Pottstown)
Robinson Park
Rock Lane Park
Rolling Hill Park
Rose Tree Park
Ruck/Pennypack Preserve
Rustin Park
Samuel & M. Elizabeth Burke Park
Sandwood Park
Sauerman Park
Saunders Woods
Schuylkill Canal Recreation Area
Schuylkill River Boat House Park
Scott Arboretum of Swarthmore College

Sharp's/Canterbury Woods
Shortridge Memorial Park
Silver Lake County Park and Nature
    Center (Bristol Township)
Silver Lake Park (Clementon)
Smedley Park
Smithville Mansion Courtyards
South Street Park
Springton Manor Farm County Park
Spurline Park
Stone Hills
Stover-Myers Mill County Park
Strafford Park
Strawbridge Lake Park
Stroud Preserve
Struble Lake
Sweetbriar Park
Tacony Creek Park
Tamanend Park
Taylor Memorial Arboretum
Theodore S. A. Rubino Memorial Park
Thomas Leiper House and Park
Three Mile Run Road
Tinicum County Park
Tohickon Valley County Park
Tomlinson Park
Tookany Creek Park
Turk Parks I and II
Tyler Arboretum
Tyler State Park
Upland Park
Upper Merion Community Center Park
Upper Merion Township Building Park
Upper Schuylkill Valley County Park
Valley Forge National Historical Park
Valley Glen Park
Veterans Memorial Park (Doylestown)
Veterans Memorial Park (Marple)
Volpi Common
Walker Park
Wallworth County Park
War Memorial Field
Warminster Recreation Center
Warwick County Park
Washington Crossing Historic Park
Washington Crossing State Park
Washington Square
Wawa Preserve
Welcome Park
Wellwood Park

West Mill Creek Park
West Nantmeal Recreation Area
Wharton State Forest
White Clay Creek Preserve
Whitesbog
Williamson Park
Williamson Road Site
Willow Knoll Park
Wissahickon Creek Green Ribbon Preserve
Woodmont

Special Dog-Oriented Events

ALPO Canine Frisbee Disc Championships
ALPO Frisbee Disc Competitions Philadel-
    phia Community Finals
Annual Dog Days of Summer (Ambler
    Borough)
Annual Dog Walk at Cooper River Park
    (Pennsauken)
Annual DogWalk (Upper Merion
    Township)
Annual Puppy Promenade (Warminster)
Annual Walk & Roll and Canine Carnival
    (Haverford)
Ardmore Dog Show
"Bark-a-thon" at the Horticulture Center
    (West Fairmount Park)
Bastille Day at Cuvée Notredame (Fair-
    mount)
Bastille Day Dog Walk (City Hall/Broad
    Street)
Canine Companions for Independence,
    CCI Awareness Day
Canine Companions for Independence
    Snoopy's Dog Fest and Canine Educa-
    tion Fair
Clark Park Bark in the Park (West
    Philadelphia)
Dog Day Afternoon (Mount Holly)
Dog Days of Summer Dog Show (Hatboro)
Dog Lover's Holiday Bazaar (Northeast
    Philadelphia)
Dogs in the Bogs (Lebanon State Forest)
Houndoween (Northern Liberties)
Pet Parade (Kulpsville)
Pets on Parade (Cherry Hill)
Philadelphia Area Champions Dog
    Walk-a-thon
Philadelphia Dog Show
"Pooches & Polo" (Revere)

INDEX

OF RELATED INTEREST

Animal Patients: 50 Years in the Life of an Animal Doctor
Edward J. Scanlon, V.M.D.

Scanlon practiced along Philadelphia's Main Line for decades, often treating the pets of some of the area's most prominent families.

224 pages • $14.95

Philadelphia with Children, 4th Edition
Elizabeth S. Gephart

"A wonderful idea. Parents always ask me for advice on area things to do and places to go with the family. Now I refer them to this great guide."
—Kathy O'Connell, Host of "Kid's Corner," WXPN-FM

276 pages • illustrated • $14.95

The Philadelphia Inquirer's *Guide to Historic Philadelphia*
Edward Colimore

This is an indispensable guide for visitors to Philadelphia, for residents who want to know more about their city's past, and for anyone who has an interest in the history of one of our country's oldest and greatest cities.

224 pages • photographs and maps • $14.95

If you cannot find a copy of these books at your local bookstore, they can be ordered directly from the publisher at:

CAMINO BOOKS, INC.
P.O. Box 59026
Philadelphia, PA 19102

_____ *Philly Dogs Have More Fun* $14.95   _____ *Animal Patients* $14.95

_____ *Philadelphia with Children* $14.95   _____ Philadelphia Inquirer's *Guide* $14.95

Name_____

Address_____

City/State/Zip _____

All orders must be prepaid. Please add $5.95 for postage & handling for the first book, and $1.00 for each additional book.

www.caminobooks.com

58-9